The Injustice of Property

GEOGRAPHIES OF JUSTICE AND SOCIAL TRANSFORMATION

SERIES EDITORS

Mathew Coleman, *Ohio State University*
Ishan Ashutosh, *Indiana University Bloomington*

FOUNDING EDITOR

Nik Heynen, *University of Georgia*

ADVISORY BOARD

Deborah Cowen, *University of Toronto*
Zeynep Gambetti, *Boğaziçi University*
Geoff Mann, *Simon Fraser University*
James McCarthy, *Clark University*
Beverley Mullings, *Queen's University*
Harvey Neo, *Singapore University of Technology and Design*
Geraldine Pratt, *University of British Columbia*
Ananya Roy, *University of California, Los Angeles*
Michael Watts, *University of California, Berkeley*
Ruth Wilson Gilmore, *CUNY Graduate Center*
Jamie Winders, *Syracuse University*
Melissa W. Wright, *Pennsylvania State University*
Brenda S. A. Yeoh, *National University of Singapore*

The Injustice of Property
HOMELESS ENCAMPMENTS AND
THE LIMITS OF LIBERALISM

STEPHEN PRZYBYLINSKI

THE UNIVERSITY OF GEORGIA PRESS
Athens

© 2025 by the University of Georgia Press
Athens, Georgia 30602
www.ugapress.org
All rights reserved
Set in 10.5/13.5 Minion 3 by Mary McKeon

Most University of Georgia Press titles are
available from popular e-book vendors.

Printed digitally

EU Authorized Representative
Easy Access System Europe—Mustamäe tee 50, 10621 Tallinn, Estonia,
gpsr.requests@easproject.com

Library of Congress Cataloging-in-Publication Data
Names: Przybylinski, Stephen, 1986– author
Title: The injustice of property : homeless encampments and the limits of liberalism
 / Stephen Przybylinski.
Description: Athens : The University of Georgia Press, [2025] | Series: Geographies of justice
 and social transformation | Includes bibliographical references and index.
Identifiers:
LCCN 2024061773 | ISBN 9780820366401 hardback | ISBN 9780820373645 paperback |
 ISBN 9780820373652 epub
Subjects: LCSH: Homeless camps—Oregon—Portland | Homeless camps—Government
 policy—Oregon—Portland | Homelessness—Oregon—Portland
Classification: LCC HV4506.P6 P79 2025 | DDC 363.509795/49—dc23/eng/20250403
LC record available at https://lccn.loc.gov/2024061773

CONTENTS

List of Illustrations   vii

Preface   ix

Introduction. Liberalism, Property, and Homelessness in Portland   1

CHAPTER 1. Connecting the Evolution of Propertied Citizenship in American Liberalism with Homelessness   18

CHAPTER 2. Developing Portland's Homeless Encampment Model   41

CHAPTER 3. The Challenge of Collectively Managed Property   68

CHAPTER 4. Locating Responsibility for the Injustices of Liberal Property   89

Conclusion. Responding to Injustice   124

Acknowledgments   139

Notes   143

References   153

Index   163

ILLUSTRATIONS

FIGURE 1. Location of sanctioned self-managed encampments and nonprofit managed villages in Portland   43
FIGURE 2. Dignity Village   44
FIGURE 3. Right 2 Dream Too men's overnight guest tent   45
FIGURE 4. Hazelnut Grove   46
FIGURE 5. The original location of Kenton Women's Village   46
FIGURE 6. A "no camping" sign at Hazelnut Grove   70
FIGURE 7. The home of a Hazelnut Grove resident   76
FIGURE 8. The commons space at Hazelnut Grove   82

PREFACE

The seeds for this book were sown in March 2013. Once, while I was sitting at Townsend's Tea House (RIP) in Portland, Oregon, where I was a graduate student, I overheard the people sitting next to me talking about a tent city in downtown Portland. The discussion inspired me to interrupt them and ask, "Are you talking about the encampment downtown called Right to Dream Too (R2DT)?" "Yes," one of them said. "Do you know it?" I said I did. Indeed, like many urban geographers in training, I walked the city regularly, not just to get from point A to B but as a means of observing and "reading" the landscape simply to make sense of it. I had walked by R2DT many times and had also seen it featured regularly in the news and weeklies. Almost always the story would center on the tension between R2DT and city government and on the politics of the encampment's emplacement. I remember being amazed at how a tent city could even be located where it was, given what I knew then about the policing of houselessness in American cities.[1] I also remember feeling impressed and inspired that it had managed to continue operating as long as it had. The person I talked to that day turned out to be Trillium, one of R2DT's board members and most determined and dedicated supporters. Trillium invited me to stop by R2DT to meet the members and learn about how the space was organized. A few weeks later I showed up, and it was that first experience that propelled me to keep coming back to this and other encampments in the city over the following decade.

When I left Portland to pursue further graduate training in 2015, I continued to work with R2DT and other encampments around the city during a longer spate of fieldwork from 2017 to 2018. The basis of the research for this book was laid then, but my focus on houselessness has since broadened. When I began my fieldwork, I was interested in understanding how self-managed encampments like R2DT function, how the city's government understood the role of these encampments, and how unhoused communities simultaneously enact and are denied rights of citizenship within a broader policy landscape hostile to houselessness generally. Inspired by the ongoing "right to the city" discourse at that time, I too saw these encampments in that light: as a direct response (a claiming of a right to, and an insistence upon a place within, the city) against social marginalization resulting from the abstract logics of liberal capitalism. And while the encampments and villages that dot Portland's landscape today surely do represent that in different ways, I have come to see the encampments more specifically as a struggle over and against property.

It might seem evident that the commodification and privatization of housing in the United States, and the consequent lack of affordable housing that pushes people into houselessness, is at its core a struggle over property. In many ways, this is how I understood property when I began this research. But I could not shake the notion that unhoused people in the encampments in which I was working were not simply victims of a highly iniquitous housing market in the abstract, and that they were not unhoused just because the rent was "too damn high." That is a big part of it, of course. But the more time I spent in Portland, talking and working with unhoused members and guests at the city's many encampments, speaking with housed neighbors in opposition and in support of these communities, attending neighborhood organizations' meetings about encampments, and speaking with city staff working directly with the encampments, the more I began to see the structuring logics that make up the "relations" of property. In short, I came to understand that I was seeing how the many different social relations, political contestations, and legal restrictions that collectively make property what it "is" take place.

Through these many interactions, I started seeing property not only as an abstract commodity but also as a (contested) process always in the making, albeit one that is highly structured and maintained by and for the benefit of some over others. I have therefore come to see property as the dominant material relation affecting unhoused people, one mediating how well unhoused people are able to seek stability for themselves. At the same time, unhoused peoples' disadvantaged relationship with property is also dependent upon the housed public's positive relationship with property. Whether through one's ability to simply access by renting or owning and being able to determine property's uses in ways that unhoused people cannot, the rights and consequent relations of property control how unhoused people access and use property themselves. Because we are all placed within relations of property and thus uneven relations of power, all the interactions big and small that structure what property is, how it can be used, and who is allowed access and control over it matter immensely for shaping how unhoused people will become housing-stable. More to the point, and one of the primary ideas I hope readers will take away from this book, is that we cannot see the production and maintenance of houselessness without understanding property, nor can we understand the production and maintenance of property without seeing how it necessitates houselessness. To understand and attempt to mitigate houselessness as a condition, our conversations need to begin with disentangling how property enables this condition.

Though this is a book about houselessness in Portland, it is also a book about how property and houselessness are structured in liberal states and shaped through liberal ideology more broadly. The lessons from Portland are informed by, and may likewise inform, the circumstances of other places similarly seeking to address houselessness in more just and dignified ways. Of course, the specificity of Portland does matter too. In and outside the United States, Portland's reputation often precedes itself. Tired musings abound that depict Portland as a place where young, environmentally conscious hipsters spend their time biking to coffee shops, restaurants, and microbreweries, as one television show portrayed it. This coincides with the narrative that, at least historically, the city and state made progressive or forward-thinking planning and policy decisions surrounding land use and sustainable redevelopment, plans that have been championed by many. To what extent, if at all, such adulation of Portland recognizes how elements of these histories shaped the production and maintenance of houselessness and property in the city today is all but invisible. For few seem to be asking, who benefits from the construction of this "progressive" Portland? And who has been left behind, displaced, and even erased from the urban landscape in pursuit of this liberal-progressive "utopia?"[2]

Answers to these questions force us to reconcile with property's role in relationship to the city's and state's history of white supremacy. By this I mean the initial constitutional banning of people of color from the city and state, and once "allowed in," from owning property there (see introduction). And equally ominously, the legacies and continued inequities of racial differentiation that produce and maintain the city as white-dominant space remain ever present in property relations, however unintentionally. To the extent that white interests have literally and socially shaped the development of the city, so too then does the racialized set of relations surrounding property extend to the conditions of being unhoused in the city. And to the extent that we can see the problems of houselessness through relations of property, so too can we see how race is reified and differentiated through property's making.

One goal of the book is to thoroughly socialize property by expanding upon the idea that property is not simply a commodity affording its owners power; rather, relational processes that maintain the normative conditions of property are subject-*making*. By this I mean that property inserts itself as a powerful medium through which social differentiation is made and remade. While many relations of property seem innocent enough, it is precisely this logic—that property has no effect on others beyond the circumstances of its owners—that needs to be better understood. As I argue, it is precisely the fact that property ownership necessarily pulls all of us into everyday relations with one another, relations which can lead to more significant struggles, that means we cannot hope to mitigate houselessness without understanding housed peoples' relationship with property as well. For it is the "propertied citizens," the owners of property (homeowners, governments, corporations) that have historically controlled how and in what ways property matters to liberal society, and thus *who* matters to it as well.

What follows from this proprietarian logic of liberalism is that to unmake the deleterious and unjust relations of property, we need to unmake certain social relations with, and valuations of, property that have long been central to liberalism. My argument is less that unhoused people lack rights of citizenship due to unequal access to property (though this is absolutely true at times) than the fact that the prioritization of property over personal rights negates the authority presumably protected by personal rights for people who are precariously housed. This book, therefore, is not directly about why people become "homeless" per se as much as it is a sustained argument about what the circumstances of houselessness allow us to see about the political function of property in liberalism.

◻ ◻ ◻

The fieldwork for this book began during a research stay in Portland from fall 2017 until late summer 2018, with return trips taking place in summer 2019 and summer 2023. The book draws from a variety of sources to detail its stories and inform its arguments. These include formal interviews with unhoused people residing in self-managed encampments throughout the city; formal interviews with housed residents of two neighborhood organizations in which self-managed encampments are located; and formal interviews with government staff working on houseless policies from the City of Portland, the city-county collaborative institution known as the Joint Office of Homeless Services, and Clackamas County (neighboring Portland's Multnomah County). It also draws from my observations and informal conversations at encampment sites. Throughout my 2017–2018 fieldwork, I regularly attended the weekly or biweekly meetings of three encampments, Right 2 Dream Too (R2DT), Hazelnut Grove (HG), and Dignity Village (DV), where I listened to and learned about the myriad issues and everyday concerns of the residents there. In addition to observing community meetings, I regularly volunteered at two encampments, R2DT and HG. These opportunities were meaningful, but not only because they allowed me to give back to those who were so gracious to invite me into their world as a researcher: these experiences also painted a much broader picture about the circumstances of houselessness than one could ever get through formal interviews. I met and had conversations with hundreds of guests residing in these encampments, stories that helped me see the world beyond the encampments alone. Above all, my work with and in these encampments helped me to establish a sense of trust with the residents, some of whom I formally interviewed and others I only briefly came to know. I can only hope that my assistance there made a positive difference for the residents, who, whether or not they engaged with the formal aspect of this research process, were simply using these resources to survive.

My conversations and observations in the city's encampments certainly helped me gain a better understanding of others' lived experiences than I could gather from formal interviews with residents alone. But my research interests in understanding the relationality of property required that I speak with others outside of the encampments about how they understood and reacted to the development of these spaces. To better understand how neighbors of the encampments related to these spaces, I attended meetings of neighborhood associations that were "struggling" with a given encampment's existence in their neighborhood, or that were planning to accommodate a new self-managed encampment. These meetings helped me understand how neighborhood-level governance addresses and attempts to manage what was then a relatively new issue for neighborhood groups in Portland: the integration of self-managed encampments into neighborhood spaces. These meetings not only helped me connect with residents who I would later meet for formal interviews, they also led to many informal discussions about houselessness and citizens' perspectives on city governance concerning these issues more broadly. Finally, in a series of meetings that I had not anticipated prior to being in the field, residents at HG asked me if I would join them in their meetings with the Joint Office of Homeless Services throughout 2018. The purpose of those meetings was to find a suitable relocation site for HG, which it now has, in the form of St. John's Village in North Portland. I naively assumed that during those meetings, I would observe city/county staff being hostile to HG residents, dictating how the encampment should restructure itself and relocate. Instead, I found these government staffers to be thoughtful and genuinely concerned with what HG residents had to say about their desires and concerns (whether all HG residents were happy with the outcome of HG's relocation I cannot say with certainty). It was these types of events and communications, with the housed public, neighborhood organizations, and government employees, that animated more broadly why and how property was so central to the issue of houselessness in Portland. My return trips in 2019 and 2023 largely followed the same patterns, allowing me to see how the encampments were faring, what was new, and how the city's own policies were changing in a crucial period for houseless governance.

It is important to express that however "complete" and accurate that I know the following stories to be, they are necessarily partial, filtered through my observations, but not lived experience, of houselessness. How I went about this research and what I observed in Portland, what aspects of peoples' experiences they decided to share with me, and ultimately how I present these insights naturally reflects my position as a privileged researcher who has benefited from the very circumstances of property that this book critiques. Indeed, it seems impossible to reconcile how the potential benefits of writing a book about property, race, class, and political power—the very benefits inherited to me as a white "propertied citizen"—are often not forthcoming, and remain a struggle, for so many oppressed individuals and groups whose stories permeate the book. As I was a white person researching in "the whitest city in America," my racial identity likely enabled my ability to conduct research about property and houselessness in ways that seemed largely to go unquestioned by most of the white people I spoke with and interviewed, many of whom seemed more than happy to speak with me about what they saw as being the problem with houselessness and unhoused people. My racial and gender identity differently affected what my participants shared with me during this research, however, whether that be with residents of encampments, leaders of movements from historically marginalized backgrounds, city officials, or leaders of neighborhood organizations. Similarly, my class position was made ever apparent when I worked within the encampments, where I had the privilege of being able to return to an apartment at the end of the day after working with people who sometimes had not lived indoors for years. These differences, whether prominent or insignificant, are in one way or another reinforced during the research process, in which there is an unavoidable "taking" from those "being researched" by the researcher, such as when people who have been and remain victims of oppression share their stories and gain little if anything in return. So too then is there a duty incumbent on those researching to attempt to avoid potential injury to those giving their time and stories. While I hope that the energy I spent helping those most in need during my fieldwork was received as some form of reciprocation for their time and insights, I cannot be assured that it was. Above all then, I hope that these privileges afforded to me have been usefully parlayed to effect the positive changes that I and others I spoke with wish to see, not only in Portland but more broadly in a world intimately defined by property, power, and privilege.

□ □ □

In June 2024, the U.S. Supreme Court decided *Grants Pass v. Johnson*, a case that challenged the Ninth Circuit Court of Appeals' decision in the 2018 case *Martin v. Boise*, which found it unconstitutional to criminalize unhoused people sleeping in public spaces when there was otherwise no shelter for them to use. Reversing the decision in *Martin v. Boise*, the court ruled that it is not unconstitutional to ban unhoused people from sleeping outside in public spaces, even when there is no shelter available. While there is much to be concerned about regarding the likely increase in severity of policing and criminalization of the unhoused as a result of the SCOTUS decision, one may more broadly read the ruling as being about how unhoused people are forced to precariously exist within relations of property without even bringing property to the fore. At the same time, the City of Portland has begun a new phase of houseless governance that only began to take shape as this book was being finalized. As the number of unhoused people has continued to grow in Portland, the city has implemented a daytime camping ban and has initiated a plan to open six mass encampment sites throughout the city that will hold up to 250 persons per site; as of this writing, the first mass encampment has been open for one year. Because I did not have enough time to analyze these new developments, they are not incorporated into the book.

Unfortunately, the timely issues that I did not have the opportunity to incorporate herein are not so much new actions but repackaged political and juridical plays that have been pressed into action before to deal with unhoused people. If the writing of this book has confirmed anything for me, then, it is that houselessness will remain a condition needing attention as long as liberal systems of property constrain our ability to enact different relationships with land. Whether it is status quo attempts at mitigating houselessness by way of punitive policies that sweep and arrest unhoused people or more "progressive" policies affording unhoused people a sense of agency and dignity by helping them self-manage their living environment, the contradictions of liberalism bear themselves out through the material relations surrounding our dominant model of property. This, at least, I hope will become clearer throughout the following pages.

The Injustice of Property

INTRODUCTION
Liberalism, Property, and Homelessness in Portland

On Tuesday, August 15, 2017, Portland, Oregon's Overlook Neighborhood Association (OKNA) convened for its monthly general meeting. At the top of the association's "to do" list was a vote to amend its bylaws. The second of two proposed bylaw amendments, "Revision B," laid out for neighbors what was at stake in the vote. It read:

> The second bylaws amendment for consideration on Tuesday clarifies who qualifies for membership in OKNA and therefore may vote and hold office. Under a city Office of Neighborhood Involvement interpretation of neighborhood bylaws, it is possible that anyone who happens to be in the neighborhood on the day of a meeting could be eligible to vote. This includes houseless individuals camping illegally in Overlook or squatters occupying a vacant building.
>
> This revision reflects the view that a greater commitment to the neighborhood should be necessary to vote and serve on the board. To that end, this amendment would require residents to provide a legal home address to qualify for membership. That would exclude houseless campers and squatters in vacant buildings. However, it would not preclude a houseless village that has [city sanction] from receiving full membership privileges. A city-sanctioned and permitted houseless village would have a legal address, and its residents therefore would qualify for OKNA membership. Alternatively, a houseless village with a nonprofit component could have a designated representative member in OKNA. Businesses and non-profits in the neighborhood would continue to be eligible to have a designated member in OKNA.[1]

While it is common practice to prevent unhoused people from accessing things due to lack of address—for example, the right to vote, a bank account, or health care—anyone who had been following OKNA's public position on houseless camping over the few years prior to the bylaw meeting knew what this membership restriction was specifically referring to: Portland's then-newest self-managed houseless encampment, Hazelnut Grove (HG). At that time, HG had been operating in the Overlook neighborhood for two years and was officially tolerated by the city government, though the encampment did not hold a land use permit to operate on the site. For OKNA members, this was part of the problem. OKNA felt that HG was in the neighborhood "illegally" and that the city was siding with the interests of the encampment over those of the association. The proposed amendment was also a reaction to the increasing number of HG residents who were attending OKNA meetings to talk about the need for the encampment and about houselessness more broadly. The intent behind the proposed amendment, then, given that "a city-sanctioned and permitted houseless village encampment would have a legal address," was that HG residents not be allowed to participate in neighborhood association affairs because the encampment did not have an official land use permit.

The language of the proposed amendment was posted to OKNA's website one week prior to the vote. The story was picked up by local media, which homed in on the bylaw's exclusionary language toward unhoused people. In one local news report, the chair of the OKNA board, attempting to explain why OKNA would require a legal address for membership, stated, "If you're an undocumented immigrant and you rent here you're welcome on the board. But if you happen to plop down on a city park bench for the night, that's not sufficient to say you have a commitment to Overlook. So, in some sense, yes, we're going to exclude some people, and it's those without an address."[2] This was a telling statement that centered the distinction between being housed and being houseless as a litmus test for participating in neighborhood politics, and it did so by establishing a dichotomy between two stigmatized and often overlapping groups: those without formal citizenship status (seen as deserving) and those who lack formal housing (seen as undeserving). In doing so, the association chair made clear that it was specifically *unhoused* residents who were unworthy of upholding the obligations of political participation, thereby affirming that an individual's access to housing constituted the criteria required for "proper" citizenship.

On the night of the vote around 130 people were in attendance, no small feat for a neighborhood general meeting. Perhaps with the city's condemnation in mind, the OKNA board unanimously voted to remove the exclusionary language from the amendment.³ There would be no change to the association's bylaws. Yet the fate of HG's acceptance within the neighborhood was not resolved with this vote. After the proposed bylaw amendment was dropped from the meeting's agenda, a resolution was introduced that furthered the exclusionary project. Rather than using neutral terms to describe proper political subjects like the proposed bylaw had done—for example, "houseless campers"—the new motion directly implicated HG, mandating that the encampment be removed from its site in the Overlook neighborhood. Specifically, the resolution proposed that if no good neighbor agreement could be reached within six weeks from the day of the meeting, HG would be given a few months to relocate.⁴ The proposed resolution had a good chance of passing. For after the bylaw amendment was dropped from the meeting's agenda, HG residents and some supporters of the encampment had left. When the new motion was proposed, a supporter of the encampment still in attendance called HG members, asking them to come back for the vote. They, as well as a few of the encampment's supporters, returned in time to cast a vote against the proposed resolution. When the motion was finally put to a vote, it too did not pass. Once again, OKNA's attempt to displace HG from its site had failed.

Reflecting on the events of the general meeting, OKNA's board chair stated that a spirited debate about houselessness had taken place the night of the meeting. "Neighbors and homeless advocates offered passionate arguments for and against the measure [to remove HG]," he noted. "A handful of disruptive attendees were not able to prevent an excellent show of local democracy and civil debate in action."⁵ The implication was that despite the fact that unhoused people were claimed to be "disrupting" the otherwise usual "civility" of debate at the neighborhood meeting, OKNA was better off by having engaged in the contested politics at the meeting. It had, after all, used the formal democratic process to attempt to exclude unhoused people from its community.

Despite and perhaps because of the fact that OKNA ultimately lacked the authority to remove HG from its site, the very pursuit of this resolution by the association's representatives affirmed a broader sentiment that something needed to be done about the rise of houselessness generally—and especially about the spread of self-managed encampments in Portland. But it also signaled something far more problematic: a political commitment to using one's secure access to property as a source of power over others in political decision-making. As such, the events in Portland's Overlook neighborhood underscore a sentiment expressed in many places throughout liberal-democratic states, namely, that access to, or ownership of, stable housing is the political currency that individuals must possess to be realized and respected as "sovereign" or "self-governing" political subjects.

Properties of Injustice: Homelessness in a State of Liberalism

This book is about the social and political function of property in liberalism. It examines how and why ownership of, or access to, property is fundamental for mediating the livelihoods of people within this system. To be sure, all residents within liberal states are regulated by property to varying degrees. But this book focuses particularly on people whose relationship to property is precarious: those living without traditional housing. For unhoused people, property constitutes a world of constraints, full of rules and restrictions, norms and values that they must endlessly navigate to engage in the "proper" use of space. And what determines a "proper" use of space is at once legal and ideological. Laws regulating and enforcing proper use of land and the values upheld through centuries of land possession make the discrimination and stigmatization of unhoused people not only legible but logical.

But why is it specifically *liberalism* that should be our focus when examining property? Given that no singular set of beliefs defines liberal ideology outright, no singular set of beliefs or practices indicates how to protect and enhance liberty in the abstract. Republican liberals, classical liberals, social-democratic liberals, and neoliberals, to name a few traditions, advance differing though overlapping positions on this matter. As the broad traditions that comprise "liberal ideology" conjoin a host of social, political, and economic beliefs, some note that it may be more useful to speak of *liberalisms*, as various theories and practices compete with one another to gain ascendance in liberal and sometimes illiberal societies.[6] Fundamentally, however, I posit that the raison d'être of liberalism is to protect and enhance individual liberties, regardless of how each variant of the ideology may envision protecting freedoms. Thus, for the sake of simplicity, I use the term "liberalism" throughout the book to refer to a political ideology that generally finds common (political philosophical) ground around strong protections for individual liberty rights and (now) free market enterprise as its economic counterpart, though I acknowledge and draw out some of its ideological diversity to help make distinctions between the historical relationship between citizenship and property (chapter 1). The more general point is that liberalism has dominated political thinking and institutional practice historically and continues to be *the* melioristic approach to organizing formal political institutions in advanced capitalism. It is therefore important to critically examine liberalism because of how it purports to advance the equal freedoms and interests of all liberal subjects.

My purpose for examining liberal ideology as a distillation of values and practices, however, is not to arrive at a narrower definition of what liberalism is or should be. This is not a book seeking to mold a "better" version of liberal ideology. Rather, I seek to critically examine how liberal institutions and liberal political subjects collectively shape our relationship with real property.

The possession of landed property is a primary means through which individuals realize their political capacities as self-governing, and thus "proper," liberal citizens. While rights to landed property secure an individual's material well-being, they also function as a means of attaining the real and idealized benefits of liberal citizenship that enable individuals' "liberty." But rights do not simply exist in the abstract. They are relationships that are realized and respected (or not) when struggles for power materialize in society. As a political system premised upon ideations about what is right and good, fair and just, liberalism operates as a network of institutions and laws through which power is materialized. Perhaps no other material thing represents the power idealized within the capacities of self-governing liberal citizenship more than landed or real property.

To the extent that landed property concentrates and delimits the sovereignty of the liberal individual, liberalism reinforces what can be called "propertied citizenship."[7] Just as liberal ideology proposes that all citizens enjoy equally protected liberties, the notion of propertied citizenship indicates that citizens' equal capacity for self-governance resides within the security of property access or ownership. For individuals without access to, much less ownership of, landed property, however, the capacity to self-govern is not protected absolutely.

The agency afforded to individuals through liberal self-governance is critical for becoming stably housed. For people living without housing, far too often the ability to ensure housing stability is restricted by freedoms that they themselves do not enjoy as individuals advocating for their own interests. Indeed, securing stable housing is nearly always contingent upon subjecting oneself to political and economic systems that tend to reduce an unhoused individual's ability to act according to their own desires. Further, the ability to pursue access to stable housing is not equally enjoyed by all people. Differences in individual and group identities such as one's class, race, gender, ethnicity, and abilities, for instance, substantively shape a person's capacity in this regard. Crucially, liberal ideology assumes away the significance of these differences, creating a continuous tension between the protection of individualism and universalism.[8] The negation of difference is normalized in service to the ideal that liberal citizens remain equal on all accounts, ignoring the ways in which individual differences significantly impact one's agency and thus opportunity to determine how they will become stably housed.

The neutralizing effect of propertied citizenship within liberalism leads to the assumption that the housed and unhoused are on an equal playing field. This assumption is problematic for a variety of reasons. For instance, unhoused people are sometimes assumed *not* to be inhibited by any structural injustice that prevents them from securing stable housing. Arguments denying the existence of structural injustices, or the social processes that constrain unhoused people within liberal housing markets, reify the assumption that unhoused people lack self-determination and as such diverge from the idealized liberal (propertied) citizen subject. Many popular accounts of the recent upsurge in houselessness continue to blame the unhoused for their condition. The effect of propertied citizenship is thus a strongly normative one. It not only demarcates who is considered properly self-governing and thus deserving of housing stability but also shapes how propriety is constituted in any given geo-historical moment.

One of the primary arguments the book advances, therefore, is that property as it is understood in liberalism is *unjust* in the specific ways that it materializes political power and advantage through a set of rights and relationships that are not equally protected for unhoused people. If by injustice we mean that an individual's capacity for self-determination is restricted or eradicated, then the relations maintaining propertied citizenship *enable* injustice to continue, given that property rights and relations deny unhoused people the ability to determine how best to secure stable shelter.

Perhaps nowhere are these struggles more apparent than in the spaces of self-organized houseless encampments and nonprofit-led tiny house villages. Cities have seen an enormous uptick in the sanctioning of organized encampments over the last decade. Within these spaces, we are able to see how people living without traditional or stable housing have begun to confront the injustices of property and housing instability. Even while organized encampments produce spaces of care and dignity, often through democratic practices, they remain bound by structural constraints that not only inhibit residents from exercising their own capacities as individuals but also reify the unjust processes and relations of liberal property systems that liberal ideology promises to protect against. Through the lens of self-organized encampments and villages, I suggest, we can see not only how sociopolitical constraints over shelter and housing stability are worked through by residents but also how these spaces reflect larger political and social constraints of property within liberalism that housed and unhoused people alike are obligated to work through in order to respond to the injustices of property.

The Integral Relationship between Property and Political Power

Although property can be nearly anything—it is realized both in material things, such as land, or immaterial resources, such as some intellectual content—nothing is property unless it is owned. Most simply, then, property can be defined as an individual's or group's *entitlement* to some resource and the benefits it provides them. Entitlements stemming from ownership are significant for different reasons, but all relate to the use of power. Establishing entitlement nearly always necessitates *legal* enforcement; someone or something must intervene to arbitrate entitlements over property. This is ensured through the sovereignty, and thus real force, of states. Though legal administration of property entitlements may often be prosaic, legal entitlements fundamentally shape society by channeling people into relationships structuring their use of propertied spaces. Entitlements establish who is allowed to be in which space and when. Seen in this way, property structures an enormous number of social relationships with varying levels of political and economic consequence.

The idea that landed or real property ownership enables and exacerbates uneven relations of power is not a new one. Scholars have exhaustively assessed the legal contours of property entitlements, explaining how these variously benefit or constrain owners who wish to do this or that with their properties. No aspect of this property scholarship has received more attention than the "right to exclude." The priority of exclusion rights has traveled some distance from its foundation in moral and political philosophy. If John Locke noted in the late seventeenth century that any property an individual puts their own labor into becomes rightfully of their possession, more than a century later, William Blackstone declared a property entitlement to be the "sole and despotic dominion which one man claims and exercises over the external things of the world, in total exclusion of the right of any other individual in the universe."[9] For many even today, exclusion *from* property constitutes the very definition *of* property. As legal scholar Thomas Merrill avers, "Give someone the right to exclude others from a valued resource . . .

and you give them property. Deny someone the exclusion right, and you do not have property."[10] As Merrill's claim reflects, the moral underpinnings of Locke's and Blackstone's oft-cited declarations—while absolutist in defining how property comes to be, and thus, what a right to property is—remain a powerful and popular interpretation of property today, especially as the right to exclude is realized through law. This traditional model of private property ownership based on "fee simple," or what is hereafter referred to simply as the "ownership model," reinforces the absolutist position on property possession as one solely concerned with the power invested in owners' exclusion rights.[11]

Supplemental to such positivist legal framings of property, a multitude of "relational" scholarly approaches examine and emphasize the consequences of the ownership model. Relational property analyses, originating in the work of the legal realists in the early twentieth century, and more recently sociolegal scholars of property, recognize a correlative role of property rights entitlements. Here, property is examined not only for how it enables a right of exclusion but for how it allows owners to grant others access to a property, to transfer a property right to others, or to immunize themselves from harm to, or loss of, a property, for instance.[12] These facets of property can equally implicate uneven relations of power.

While the relational property literature underscores the multifunctionality and thus nonexclusive aspects of property entitlements, scholars have advanced the idea that landed property ownership is also about the social *relations* surrounding use of and access to property. Significantly, this approach to property underscores how entitlement to resources substantiates an owner's political subjectivity and use of power. In doing so, a relational rights approach highlights how autonomy does not derive from individuals' separation *from* society, a foundational claim of liberal rights literatures: rather, autonomy is dependent on an individual's relationship *with* society. Legal scholar Jennifer Nedelsky argues, for instance, that if autonomy "requires the capacity to participate in collective as well as individual governance . . . [then] the constitutional protection of autonomy [should not be seen as] an effort to carve out a sphere into which the collective cannot intrude, but a means of structuring the relations between individuals and the sources of collective power so that autonomy is fostered rather than undermined."[13] A relational approach to examining property necessitates that property rights be seen as socially situated and contingent on social interaction for their realization.

Property rights, then, reveal how power is leveraged between people in relationship to resources. When property functions as "a source of private authority," it enables in individuals a strong sense of autonomy and protection over their governing capacities regarding the use of or access to resources. In this way, property "empowers owners by making their intentions a source of demands on others' conduct."[14] Property rights establish social duties obliging nonowners to respect the authority of owners, in the sense that "nonowners' respect of the owner's right to property is part of the nonowners' respect of the owners' right to self-determination." Contra an absolutist notion of an owner's "sole and despotic dominion" over a given resource, then, a relational approach illuminates various ways in which nonowners also enjoy certain rights upon which property owners cannot infringe.[15] Though owners' rights facilitate the use of power over others, owners who abuse this authority may often engage in unjust relations, by offending "the moral equality prevalent between owners and nonowners by virtue of their shared status as private persons."[16] The notion that property rights draw owners and nonowners into relationships over specific resources brings individual autonomy into political conversation about property rights, politicizing the assumed neutrality or normalization of exclusive legal entitlements to property.

Throughout this book, I apply a relational perspective to illustrate the different ways in which property in liberalism establishes uneven relations of power between the housed and unhoused. By using the term "relational," I understand property to function not only as a set of rights entitlements but also as relationships facilitating a variety of socioeconomic, political, and legal possibilities that affect *all* those encountering a given property's use. As we will see at the end of chapter 1, much of the literature pertaining to houselessness has analyzed unhoused peoples' relationship to property through the notion of *exclusion*. Few scholars, however, have sustained an analysis of property not only in terms of what limits property presents for unhoused people and what progressive potential may exist with alternate property enactments but also from the point of view of how the very maintenance of property relations shapes unhoused people's lives and struggles for stability. To do so, I suggest, requires we look at property not only for how it excludes but for how it necessarily forces unhoused people to struggle *within* property, within the economic, political, and legal structures that maintain property as a sociolegal system. By doing so, we may better see why housing precarity remains a feature of liberalism.

That being said, I caution that a relational approach that does not consider how property ownership has historically shaped political subjectivity fails to get at a core issue with houselessness today: that property continues to constitute liberal propriety, despite and because of democratic reforms that only modestly protect against some forms of structural discrimination. Specifically, I argue that we may better understand these legal and normative tensions dialectically, whereby property and citizenship are understood as mutually reinforcing. A dialectical approach in turn allows us to see how contemporary struggles of houseless encampments, and houselessness more broadly, remain shaped by long-held values about property in liberal ideology. At the same time, struggles over unjust uses of power through property are not only ideological but material in origin. They emanate from spaces where property has been, often long ago, enacted unjustly, and that also remain contested today. Examining how propertied spaces are materially enacted—and curated with intention over time—similarly reveals how "proper" political subjectivity is defined and assigned value.

The book then develops insights into how and why we must not only focus on how houselessness is produced by the logics of capital circulation through the built environment, as absolutely critical as that is to understanding property's commodification and its resulting social and spatial inequities.[17] We must be equally attentive to how houselessness is produced and maintained through the social and political substantiation of unjust systems of property, particularly those relations maintaining property that take conscious and active doing. Seeing property in this way reveals that houselessness is both an intended and unintended outcome of these processes.

Portland's struggles with houselessness reveal much about this dialectic, as well as something about all places whose struggles with houselessness are dire and seem intractable. What the policy strategies of establishing encampments by the City of Portland reveal is that even the most well-meaning and progressive approaches to stabilize the unhoused become necessarily entangled within the constraints of a liberal property system cultivated to perpetuate and justify property insecurity.

Liberal Property, Progressive Portland

Theft *is* property, argues Robert Nichols, discussing the dispossessive function of property in liberalism that turns land into ownable resources. Nichols' inversion of Proudhon's statement that "property is theft" is telling. It locates the historical and active socioeconomic and political function of dispossession of land through property's employment within liberalism, a process whereby used but "unowned" land is unjustly taken. It is in these exact moments of land dispossession, Nichols argues, that land becomes property through legal enactments and is thus realized as property.[18] American liberalism has perfected the legal creation of isolable real property, a strategy used to dispossess Indigenous peoples and others of their land. But it is not just land that liberal enactments of property have taken. Dispossession also denies self-determination to those who do not "own" their person, such as in the case of those enslaved in the United States prior to the Emancipation Proclamation. Such dispossessions name the violent processes enforced throughout history to benefit settler societies. Doing so under the guise of liberty and what is "right," liberalism has endured for centuries by dispossessing lands and peoples from resources and consequently their self-determination. It has done so by enforcing the ownership model as the proper socioeconomic relationship with landed resources.

Such liberal enactments of property, like those facilitated by the U.S. government through the homesteading process, not only physically excluded groups of people from landed resources but also *necessitated* differentiation between people as political subjects. The intention behind and the outcomes of such enactments of property, argues Brenna Bhandar, functioned as political and social means through which liberal citizens were identified and given privileges by way of their engagement with and participation in systems of private property. Bhandar's work more specifically recognizes these as "racial regimes of property," regimes that were premised on the "improvement" of racialized others, such as Indigenous groups, by violently enforcing private property ownership and thus possession as the legitimate means of cultivating the proper civil and political subject.[19] One of the outcomes of such colonial enactments of private property was the normative distinction of the "proper" political subject in contrast to a nonwhite racialized "other."

Such processes of dispossession shaped the development of American urban landscapes writ large. The development of the settler colonial city of Portland, Oregon, is no exception. The city sits on the traditional homelands of the Clackamas, Multnomah, and Cascades peoples, all bands of the Middle Columbia Chinook-speaking Indians, who used the landscape for subsistence prior to Anglo-European settlement. With the backing of the U.S. government, the federal Donation Land Act of 1850 facilitated the process of Anglo-European settler land possession in present day Portland, enabling only white male settlers to claim up to 320 acres of land in what was then the Oregon Territory.[20] Vital to this homesteading process was the settler government's need to survey and plot this "unowned" land. In translating "uncultivated" landscape into plots, the government enacted isolable property deeds, excluding Indigenous groups from these newly propertied spaces through the violent force of law.

The development of the State of Oregon was premised on the exclusion not only of Indigenous peoples but of *all* nonwhite settlers. Though slavery has always been banned there (save for punishment of crime), Oregon was the only "free" U.S. state to constitutionally exclude Black and other people of color from owning landed property at the onset of its statehood in 1859, a decision made by popular (white male only) vote in 1857.[21] This state ban merely updated a set of exclusion laws that had been passed in 1844, which facilitated the violent removal of any Black settlers, as well as Chinese individuals, from Oregon territory.[22] Oregon's exclusion laws are thought to never have been actualized to expel anyone living within the state; small populations of Black, Chinese, and other people of color continued to live in Oregon despite this legislation. Nevertheless, the real threat of realizing the laws' intentions functioned as a barrier to settlement all the same. The prohibitory language of the state constitution was not removed until 1926, effectively promoting Oregon as a white-only state, a space premised upon the interests of white citizens, realized through ownership of newly created property for and by white people.

When people of color eventually gained the opportunity to own property in Portland, they were nevertheless remaindered to specific spaces in the city. Around the turn of the twentieth century, for instance, Black people lived only in downtown Portland near the main railway station and its surrounding hotels. Decades later, Black Portlanders began to move into neighborhoods where Anglo-European settlers previously had lived, particularly in the inner northside district of Albina. Decades of real estate steering practices, coupled with extensive use of racial covenants in many neighborhoods throughout the city, established Albina as the designated neighborhood for people of color by midcentury. While Albina thrived for decades in the midtwentieth century as a hub of Black social life, from the late 1950s to the mid-1970s the neighborhood was instrumentally dissected through a variety of urban renewal projects that displaced thousands of people from their homes.[23] Today, the neighborhoods that make up Albina have been heavily gentrified and are predominantly white and upper class, reflecting the city's demographics more broadly.[24] The history of Albina as a socially liminal space within white-majority Portland and a place reflective of the city's legacy of dispossession reinforces the idea that processes of racialization are not relegated to the past but remain intimately connected to broader regimes of property produced through mostly white, elite interests.

The historical exclusion of Indigenous and nonwhite peoples from Oregon cannot be divorced from the sociospatial landscape of contemporary

Portland. No longer are people of color prohibited from owning property, forced to live in one neighborhood, or denied suffrage. And recent city housing strategies have been aimed at reversing centuries of systemic discrimination in housing policies and policing practices.[25] Nonetheless, the city's development trajectory continues to reinforce the racialized displacement of low-income communities of color, unevenly developing Portland as a white-majority inner city with communities of color residing in East Portland.[26] These racial and economic inequities have become increasingly central to the political discourse of, and social movements in, the city. The city government's complicity in the federal government's suppression of Portland's well-publicized Black Lives Matter protests in response to the murder of George Floyd in May 2020, coupled with its history of racialized police violence and murder and penchant for drawing white supremacist groups in and around the city to antagonize its self-ascribed progressive resident base in the decades leading up to 2020, implicitly and overtly reflect the entitlement of ownership interests of those early Oregon settlers.[27] Such instances remind people of color and other marginalized groups living in Portland that liberal progressivism has found favor there for another reason: the city's rhetoric decrying systemic inequities does not dismantle the ownership model of property as much as it reinforces it. And the city's struggle to correct past inequities is nowhere more prominently illustrated than through its current approach to sheltering its unhoused residents.

Homelessness in the City of Roses

Over the last decade, no issue in Portland has garnered more attention and concern than houselessness. Polls surveying Portland residents find houselessness to be the number one "quality of life" issue in the city.[28] Multiple related issues regularly occupy the headlines of the city's weeklies, the statewide daily newspaper, and increasingly, national news and opinion pieces.[29] For all the praise the city has received for being one of the most livable, environmentally progressive, and well-planned communities in the United States (in large part due to its liberal progressive ethos), by many accounts Portland appears bumbling in its attempts at ameliorating the houselessness crisis.

There is much to be concerned about in the social and economic factors exacerbating the houselessness situation in Portland. In 2023 the city counted the highest number of unhoused people in its history, 6,297, a number that has increased yearly on average for more than a decade.[30] Of the total houseless population, the unsheltered population specifically increased 29 percent from the previous year alone, from 3,057 to 3,944 individuals, constituting "unsheltered" houselessness as the majority condition for unhoused people in the city.[31] In addition, there has been a significant increase in the number of unhoused people of color relative to the general population. For unsheltered people specifically, the number of Black, Indigenous, and other people of color (BIPOC) counted in the 2022 point in time count increased by 21 percent since the previous count three years prior, alongside a 7 percent increase of unsheltered non-Hispanic whites. Notably, people identifying as American Indian, Alaska Native, or Indigenous made up 12.9 percent of Multnomah County's houseless population, despite making up only 2.5 percent of the county's general population. Similarly, people identifying as Black or African American made up 17.2 percent of the houseless population, despite making up 7.1 percent of the Multnomah County population.[32] These numbers come after eight years of housing emergency initiatives attempting to stabilize the unhoused population, efforts that were no doubt hindered by the intervening COVID-19 pandemic.

Reflecting trends across North America, Portland's struggle to provide access to housing and ensure its affordability has become ever more pronounced. From 2010 to 2020, Portland experienced rapid growth, with the population increasing 11.8 percent over that decade, making residents' ability to obtain affordable housing a policy priority.[33] And perhaps the most crucial years therein were from 2015 to 2020, when the city's median household income rose 22 percent, sitting at $103,000 for homeowners and half that for renters in 2020.[34] The city's average rent increased on average more than 2.5 percent each year from 2013 to 2022, with 2015 and 2022 respectively seeing more than 5 percent increases.[35] By 2020 the average rent was more than $1,600, with the largest increases for studios and one-bedroom apartments, at 4.4 percent and 3.7 percent respectively.[36] Vacancy rates for all housing was at 5 percent in 2013 and again in 2022 but rose to 10 percent during the COVID-19 pandemic.[37] Furthermore, from 2015 to 2022 the median sales price for a Portland home increased by about $200,000.[38]

To address the inequities stemming from these trends, the city, county, and state levels of government have done much over the last decade to restructure their approach to managing houselessness. The City of Portland declared a state of emergency on housing and homelessness (SOE) in October 2015, which incentivized the city and county governments to establish the Joint Office of Homeless Services (JOHS) in order to concentrate houseless service provisioning throughout Multnomah County, where Portland is located.[39] Portland's SOE declaration reflected two primary goals. One was to bring new rounds of financial investments into housing and houseless services. For example, the city expanded rental assistance, eviction prevention, housing placement support, and the construction of new affordable housing as well as emergency shelter bed capacity. The second goal focused on institutional reform, with an understanding that speeding up service provisioning helps to bypass time-intensive bureaucratic processes. For example, the city eased zoning and building regulations to more quickly site emergency shelters and encampments as well as to repurpose vacant city-owned buildings. These intergovernmental efforts have plowed tens of millions of dollars annually into various resources helping to shelter more people and prevent others from becoming unhoused. The city's SOE was a critical legal tool and moral means to establish the encampment model itself, as we will later see.

Unaffordable housing and increases in unhoused populations are not circumstances unique to Portland. Many mid- and large-sized cities throughout North America experience similar problems. But there are important aspects of Portland's response to the houselessness crisis that have broader import for discussion about the relationship between houselessness, property, and liberalism. Portland is of particular interest because of its unique approach to formalizing alternative shelter models that appear to conflict with the ownership model of property. Having legalized self-organized encampments and nonprofit-led tiny house villages on publicly and privately owned properties, Portland is at the vanguard of houseless shelter strategies that have largely been repudiated within society up to this point in time. Such liberal progressive strategies seek to remedy the racialized and gendered relations of property that have led to and maintain the houselessness crisis we see today. And in this way, Portland provides a relevant set of circumstances to assess how governments, the public, and the unhoused themselves are responding to the houselessness crisis and where the shortcomings lie in such approaches.

The insights stemming from Portland's approach to addressing housing and houselessness do not merely show us how well liberal policies correct for past injustices that result from enactments of property. As I will argue throughout the book, they also help us see how liberal progressive efforts to ameliorate property insecurity within the legal mandates and social norms of liberalism are ultimately insufficient for untethering political subjectivity from property. Further, we begin to see something else: houselessness is unlikely to be eradicated within liberalism. This is so not only because of how market relations exacerbate economic inequality but also because of how the sociopolitical relations contributing to the injustices of property *necessitate* that the proper social order, and thus the liberal solution to houselessness, is found within the traditional ownership model. As such, Portland is a quintessential settler city whose novel attempts to correct for historical housing and social injustices require sustained attention so that we may better understand how its liberal progressive policies emplace thousands of individuals struggling for property security within a system that justifies their insecurity.

Chapters Outline

This book seeks to reveal how the injustices of property manifest themselves within the social and political relations surrounding unhoused peoples' struggles to use landed property. I have focused particularly on liberalism as a political ideology because of how it uniquely values the individualist ethic of authoring one's own life path largely unencumbered either by state influence or interference by others in exercising one's rights. My goal in this book is not simply to describe how unhoused people fare within American liberalism, however. The point in doing so is to make an argument about the role of property in leveraging and protecting political-economic opportunity and power for some, while justifying the exploitation, marginalization, and dispossession of others. I find it necessary to address how property relations negate the very promises of liberal subjectivity, both ideally and materially, because of how they appear to protect against the various injustices faced by unhoused people without accounting for their responsibility in contributing to them. I seek to show that this has been the case in American liberalism since its founding, in order to advance a political response to the injustices of property that can address the specific problems unhoused people continue to face.

To connect these arguments, I begin by establishing historical context for what propertied citizenship has been, and continues to be, within American liberalism. In chapter 1, I trace three specific ways in which the connection between ownership and political subjectivity has enabled sociopolitical privileges because of how central property is for producing and maintaining injustices. My intent in this chapter is to identify how much has stayed the same in regard to how property mediates political subjectivity and how these relations affect unhoused people today, despite the advance of a liberal ideology that promises to eradicate injustices. Chapter 2 turns the lens on Portland, as I examine the city government's acceptance of organized houseless encampments, which led to the legalization of the current Portland Encampment Model (PEM). The chapter shows how the founding model of self-governing encampments, a model the city rhetorically praises, nevertheless has been consciously avoided through the development of the PEM. I argue that this strategic transition away from self-governance toward "managed" nonprofit-led villages diminishes the self-determination of unhoused people living in both types of encampments. Chapter 3 examines the potential of collectively managed properties by detailing the function of Portland's self-governing encampments, identifying their benefits and constraints. In doing so, it demonstrates how encampments managing property collectively are also undermined within the liberal property model, even as they point toward an opportunity to avoid the pitfalls of the ownership model.

Chapter 4 assesses the findings of the preceding chapters to examine specifically what is unjust for residents of Portland's encampments. I draw from Iris Marion Young's work on injustice to describe how unhoused Portlanders are differently affected by unjust structural processes and the difficulty in identifying whose responsibility it is to enact changes to attenuate these injustices. I suggest that while Young's process of assigning responsibility for correcting structural injustices is useful, it nevertheless leaves us wondering how we may respond to the specific injustices within liberal property systems. By way of a conclusion, therefore, I lay out the contours of how we may respond (and how unhoused groups already are responding) to the injustices of property. I do so by identifying how two different movements to shelter unhoused people enact different types of responses, in order to show how attempts at mitigating against injustices challenge and may be challenged by liberal ideals around proper use of land. Ultimately, I argue it is misguided to ask *how* injustice within liberalism is possible through the lens of property relations—for the injustices of liberal property as shown throughout the book are indeed justified in a legal sense, as problematic as this legitimation is. Instead, I argue we must address *why* claims for justice are necessarily limited within liberalism, given the essential role property enjoys within this political ideology and policy framework, and thus, *whether* liberal property systems can be justified in a social and political sense.

CHAPTER 1

Connecting the Evolution of Propertied Citizenship in American Liberalism with Homelessness

Hazelnut Grove (HG) is a houseless encampment that has been operating in Portland since September 2015. The encampment came to life on vacant, government-owned property set along a hillside in an inner northside neighborhood of the city. A perimeter fence bounds the space, which lies between a bike path, a major thoroughfare, and a light rail line. Looking south from the encampment, one can see Portland's downtown skyline with the city's westside neighborhoods tucked into the hills behind it. Despite its centrality, the services at the encampment are scarce. It lacks running water and electric hookups. Residents sleep in uninsulated tiny houses that cannot be heated due to municipal building code restrictions. Cold, moisture, and mold permeate the structures throughout the long rainy winters endemic to the Pacific Northwest. Though offering only a nominal standard of comfort to its residents, the encampment provides a relatively secure space, which helps stabilize people with nowhere to sleep. And it does so democratically; the encampment is self-managed, run by fifteen to twenty residents and a few volunteers. The residents make decisions about how best to operate their own living environment, a power that is so often lost for those who are unhoused.

While interviewing residents at HG in 2017 and 2018, I met Pete.[1] A white male in his early thirties, Pete had been houseless in Portland since 2011, floating from one friend's house to another until he joined the encampment in the summer of 2017. During my many conversations with him, Pete reflected on the difficulties of living within such an encampment. Once, I asked what HG represented to him. He noted the sense of autonomy he experienced in such an environment, mentioning in particular the benefits that come from the self-governing process. HG members meet weekly to discuss divisions of labor, such as who will take responsibility for maintenance projects, participate in neighborhood association meetings, do security shifts at night, and much more. That resident members largely decide where to commit their laboring energies within the encampment also appealed to Pete. More broadly, he hoped the encampment model would be inspirational outside of the space itself, encouraging "people regardless of their housing situation to be more interested in implementing the methods [of self-governance] everywhere, in all kinds of living and working situations." For him, it was a safer space to sleep, and one that also modeled what a more just and democratic mode of social organizing could be like.

While Pete saw positives in his difficult living situation, he also made clear that there were immanent constraints imposed upon him that made living in a self-managed encampment more challenging. Prior to my interviews with residents there, HG had struggled through two years of attempted evictions, removal attempts initiated predominantly by the nearby Overlook Neighborhood Association, but also by other concerned residents in the city and some members of Portland's City Government. Though the city government allowed HG to operate at its site, some of the public held that the encampment had no "right" to be there. I asked Pete what he thought about these claims. "In a capitalist sense, I see there is a conflict," he said, referring to the encampment's lack of ownership rights to the property. But, he asked in return, "Is there something wrong with people living here, building and improving, and creating the basis for them to be able to be productive or functional?" He continued, "We are trying to be citizens. We are trying to be productive members of society in the ways that are available to us. They are just different ways than what people are used to." Affirming his right to use the space, he stated emphatically, "The city owns the property. The city is the people who live in the city. And we are people who live in the city." For Pete, the encampment was justified, not simply because Portland's government tolerated it as a legal use of municipal property but also because, as unhoused residents of a city with increasingly fewer affordable places to live, the right to maintain residence on otherwise unused land enabled his and others' moral right to the city more generally.

Pete's comments speak to the reality of many unhoused peoples' lives in contemporary America. Whether they live in unsanctioned or sanctioned encampments, or sleep alone on the street, comments such as Pete's reflect a hard reality about being unhoused today. While being human ought to guarantee anyone a secure and dignified place to exist, the structures reinforcing property as a socioeconomic and legal system do not accommodate such human concerns. In other words, there is no enforceable right to housing, a point all too often made by housing activists. As such, legal and moral claims like these, for a right to a space in the city, point to a much deeper tension affecting *all* people within liberal democracies: that property mediates an individuals' relationship to space and thus to one's social, political, and economic relationships grounded within places.

Property has always been fundamental to the ideals and practices of American liberalism. For centuries, property ownership literally defined who could enjoy the rights and privileges protected by liberal citizenship in America. Property ownership no longer formally defines citizenship rights and privileges in such a direct way. Indeed, property is valued in large part for its fungibility or potential value through exchange. Yet, one central idea throughout this book is that property remains crucial to shaping political subjecthood and a liberal social order more broadly. I contend that, despite the appearance that no such determinative relationship exists any longer between property and citizenship, the benefits of liberal political subjecthood remain rooted partly in property ownership and rights of access to landed property. While this may seem rather evident on the surface, I want to suggest that there are profound implications to the close relationship between political subjecthood and property access. For not only does this relationship affect our political and legal responses to mitigating houselessness, it points to concerns surrounding the justification of property within liberalism more broadly.

The idea that property shapes political subjectivity has been conveyed through the concept of "propertied citizenship." Propertied citizenship can be understood as an idealized political subjectivity, whereby property owners or those with secure access to property de facto benefit from liberal citizenship because of how their property security enables them to use power over others.[2] The adjective "propertied" emphasizes the central role of ownership or possession in liberalism, whether historically or in the present day. As Ananya Roy argues, propertied citizenship is so vital to American liberalism that it defines the very elements of model citizenship, so much so that "social groups that do not meet [the model's] propertied mandates are therefore rendered marginal in the discourses and practices of citizenship."[3] Speaking to the plight of unsheltered houseless people specifically, Roy argues that what we find at "the edges of exclusion," or through the struggles over the boundaries of propertied citizenship, is that "the homeless have been trespassers in the space of the nation-state."[4] To the extent that citizenship and political power are contingent upon property ownership, unhoused peoples' political privileges and liberties offer little protection against the power of property rights.

Within modern liberalism, therefore, a set of unique tensions exist for houseless people. Property, on the one hand, is a legal system that regulates exactly how and when unhoused people access spaces and resources necessary for their survival. When excluded from property, unhoused people are denied the freedom to pursue their means of social reproduction (e.g., sleeping), means protected through constitutional rights. Such exclusions are problematic for many reasons, but primary among them is that the continual exclusion from spaces of reproduction facilitates an individual's likelihood of premature death.[5] To benefit from the privileges of propertied citizenship in this sense, unhoused people must have access to property (for all spaces are property of some sort) to have their liberty rights respected. On the other hand, the protections and privileges of liberal citizenship rights are not contingent upon property access alone. Many unhoused people have their political or civil rights "protected" due to having a legal status as citizens (for those fortunate enough to hold citizenship) *regardless* of whether or not they own or have access to property. As such, a primary contradiction within liberalism for unhoused people is that even though property rights deny unhoused people key rights and protections necessary for sustaining livelihoods, denying access to life-sustaining spaces of reproduction does not in itself render void the broader constitutional protections presumed universal to liberal citizenship. Property does not define citizenship outright; rather, it limits basic liberty protections, particularly for those without secure access to property.

But it is not just that property's function within liberal legal practice limits liberty rights for unhoused people. For the unhoused and housed alike, normative ideals coupled with the material relations of ownership influence who is or is not a "proper" liberal subject and thus demarcate and justify who belongs within society. And it is this feature of property that this book emphasizes. There is and has been a dialectical relationship between these two conceptions of property, one being property-as-commodity and the other a more proprietarian understanding of property as the foundation for a proper social order.[6] While "property-as-propriety" was more explicit in past discourse and practice regarding the proper ordering of a democratic public, I argue that property continues to mediate and demarcate propriety and democratic values within liberal American ideology and practice.

This chapter examines how property has maintained a particular sociopolitical order through time. Specifically, it looks at how property has been central to the values imbued within, and the material benefits gained by, liberal citizenship through American liberal ideology and practice. Tracing the dialectical nature of property through a more proprietarian notion of property over time, I suggest, highlights how and why property relations affect the livelihoods of unhoused people within liberal America beyond a simple lack of housing. What such a history illustrates, I argue, is how social and political relationships have maintained property as an exclusive good, one that simultaneously materializes wealth while enabling political power to ensure that property continues to order liberal subjects along economic, racialized, and gendered lines.

A Note on Dialectics

To examine the different ways that property maintains proprietarian orderings of social life requires an analytical framework attuned to the processes constituting socioeconomic and political relations. Dialectical analysis is useful for this reason. Such an approach examines how and where certain processes or practices (e.g., property and citizenship) connect and disconnect with one another and how these interrelations produce or maintain some ideological and material meaning in the world. Things that are dialectically related cannot exist without each other in the sense that the outcome of their relations creates some new form. To form some meaning (propertied citizenship), both things or processes rely upon each other to form meaning and value in the world. For the purpose of historical examination, such an approach analyzes the "emergence" of certain processes and relations to better make sense of how a "new form comes to be in relation with the old . . . [to find] new properties of the old form."[7] Importantly, dialectics is a form of analysis that does not *prove* any particular outcome (e.g., that property ownership defines citizenship outright). Instead, it is a mode of analysis used to explain how certain relations or processes of "mutual dependence" evolve.[8] Normative explanation is required, therefore, to evaluate how certain dialectically related outcomes matter more specifically to an object of analysis.

Dialectical analysis is intended to explain outcomes or forms of specific relations. In this way, it is also useful for indicating potential pathways for change within specific socioeconomic and political contexts. As David Harvey notes, dialectical analysis serves to identify the "dominant social values to which most people willingly subscribe," in a particular set of geographic relationships.[9] Not all relations or practices are of importance in such an analysis, however. Some values or material interests take on more significance than others at particular times and in specific geographies. As such, the task of dialectical reasoning is to "identify those characteristic 'moments' and 'forms' (i.e., 'things') embedded within continuous flows which can produce radical transformations or where, conversely 'gatekeeping' or other mechanisms might be constructed so as to give a 'thing' or system . . . qualities of identity, integrity, and relative stability."[10] Examining *how* such "permanences" or the stability of certain values or practices are maintained within a given social system is precisely the point of this mode of analysis.

Dialectical reasoning is apt, therefore, for analyzing the history of liberal property relations. It helps examine how certain property relations (laws, norms, practices) construct more stable forms of property in practice as well as how values regarding the proper use of property proliferate in particular geographies. The production and maintenance of specific geographies, the socioeconomic geography of a city, for instance, are partly rooted in competing ideas about how property is and ought to be used. In the context of propertied citizenship, what requires explaining is how the social and legal values and material relations surrounding liberal property ownership have shaped and continue to shape political subjectivity.

The account that follows examines different ways in which property has been connected to citizenship in American liberalism. I identify crucial "moments" and "forms" where property has intertwined with citizenship or political subjectivity to show how the valuations of property have evolved over time into a relatively stable normative social order. As we will later see, this "proper" social order matters for unhoused and housed people alike, not simply because it excludes them outright; rather, it matters because it forces them to struggle within the relations maintaining property as a privatized, nondemocratic relation. From this historical account, then, we can better see how struggles rooted in the constant tensions and contradictions between property ownership and political rights as well as subjectivity have been and remain as much about who holds legal rights of ownership as they are about who is able to define whom property is *for*, and along with that, how property ought to be used.

The Property-Citizenship Dialectic

COMMODITY, PROPRIETY, AND LIBERAL SUBJECTIVITY

Since Anglo settlers colonized what is now the United States in the early seventeenth century, property has been fundamental not only to economic life but to social and political life as well. In colonial America, the establishment of landed property titles through the granting of estates to small farmers secured property as a material benefit for white male settlers.[11] Colonial administrators were influenced by English common law practices, which were themselves inspired by Locke's labor theory of property, an ideology reifying the idea that an individual's labor invested into land secured one's natural claim to property ownership. In prerevolutionary America, society was primarily property owning and middle class. It was a time when "economic advancement was within reach of most colonists, and even day laborers could earn enough to acquire land."[12] The broad distribution of small, landed property titles, coupled with settler imaginaries of terra nullius, continued the enactment of landed property as the economic means of wealth creation for much of settler society.

The English common law tradition embracing property as the material means for social propriety practiced in the colonies was highly influential to the U.S. Constitution's framers. In drafting the Constitution, the Founders prioritized the citizen's natural right to own and acquire property.[13] The reason for doing so was not merely to perpetuate modest wealth creation for a largely agrarian society and to protect slavery via the ownership of chattel property. The protection and regulation of landed property was prioritized in order to promote "the public good."[14] As the republican ideology of the Founders affirmed, property ownership established the economic basis needed for an individual to remain free from government interference, which in turn enhanced individual liberty.[15] Republican thought thus constitutionalized the colonial faith in property ownership as a means of properly ordering society, a benefit that was additional to the humble material security afforded to most white owners.

Through the colonial and republican periods of American political history, therefore, property ownership was critical for defining *propriety*. Property ownership was conventional. It exhibited the "proper" social behavior and morals promoted by republican elites. Though ownership of small titles was commonplace and promoted throughout this period, the effect of this political valuing of property also meant ownership demarcated individuals as "proper" political subjects. Gregory Alexander's excellent history of the "proprietarian" tradition of American law illustrates the unevenness of maintaining property as an individual's source of propriety. Late eighteenth-century republicans, he notes, valued property for being "the material foundation for creating and maintaining the proper social order, the private basis for the public good."[16] To the extent that early American *republicanism* did not separate public from private life as sharply as does American *liberalism* today, Alexander notes that early republicans envisioned "property as necessary to facilitate a publicly active, self-governing citizenry . . . [believing] that ownership of property provides the necessary foundation for virtue, enabling citizens to pursue the common welfare."[17] Within the early American republic, therefore, property mattered for its economic benefits just as much as it did for promoting ownership as the pillar of political life and moral virtue.

The early republican framing of "property-as-propriety" is significant for how it emphasized the role of the citizen in society. Somewhat counter to the contemporary notion of citizen as *homo economicus*, civic republicanism understood citizens less as self-interested entrepreneurial agents and more as political beings.[18] As Gordon Wood notes, republican ideology understood that citizens achieved their "greatest moral fulfillment by participating in a self-governing republic."[19] The notion of the self-governing, virtuous citizen persists today, of course. But exactly how such virtue is valued has changed over time. For instance, Woods notes that "public or political liberty—or what we now call positive liberty—[once] meant participation in government. And this political liberty in turn provided the means by which the personal liberty and private rights of the individual—what we today call negative liberty—were protected."[20] Given that virtue was based on liberty and independence during this period, "it followed that only autonomous individuals free from any ties of interest and paid by no master were qualified to be citizens."[21] Nonowners, from this perspective, could not be "independent" in their political judgements. And so it was that only a small fraction of white, male property owners, those with no "ties of interest" and "paid by no master," were recognized as autonomous political subjects in the early American republic.

In short, prior to the extensive industrialization of American society, property was not yet widely realized as an economic asset cherished only for its exchange value. Indeed, among republicans, ownership of landed property was thought to actually maintain "one's gentility and independence from the caprices of the market . . . [protecting] its holders from external influence or corruption, to free them from the scramble of buying and selling, and to allow them to make impartial judgements."[22] Accordingly, "virtuous" property-owning citizens in the Republican era, protected from the "caprices of the market," were obliged to provide for the public good. As Carol Rose notes, republican notions of propriety promoted the idea that "governance and good order always included a duty of liberality to the larger community, for the sake of the common good."[23] And because of this, "the ill fortune of others presented the propertied with a duty to assist, and not with an occasion to revile or shame those in need."[24] The virtuous citizen of early republicanism was thus expected to be a publicly oriented political subject, who, by way of landed material possessions, shaped what the proper sociopolitical order would look like by contributing to the greater good of (white) society.

While republican visions of propriety influenced political practice, it is important to note that there was no singular proprietarian vision of a "properly" ordered society. Multiple competing positions concerned themselves with how owner-citizens could and ought to improve the "public good." Moreover, this competition reflected how political ideals work to shape social practices. As Alexander notes, all proprietarian visions of property shared "a commitment to the basic idea that the core purpose of property is not to satisfy individual preferences or to increase wealth but to fulfill some prior normative vison of how society and the polity that governs it should be structured."[25] Yet, the Founders' general vision of a properly ordered society sought a "social structure within which each person and each institution had a proper role and position," a vision Alexander locates in the Founders' elitist beliefs about property ideally serving as a means of anchoring "the citizen to his . . . rightful place in the proper social hierarchy."[26] Despite a rhetoric of political equality, the republican proprietarian vision for the properly ordered society was one premised upon social and economic division. Women and enslaved Blacks were relegated to the bottom, while white males remained at its peak by policing the boundaries of the proper social order. More precisely then, civic republicanism "divided the populace into rulers and ruled, and the rulers, though they might be called 'the people,' were actually only those citizens who had the property necessary to make them 'independent' and thereby capable of participating in governance."[27] Property was an owners' source of political authority to govern what proper society ought to look like.

By the mid-nineteenth century, the advance of free market values within American society was complicating early republican perspectives on proper citizenship. Steps to promote economic growth, coupled with rapid technological innovation, began to threaten proprietarian virtues of the idealized agrarian, small property–owning society envisioned by the Founders. As new corporate charters were established, ownership opportunities precipitated the exchange potential of property as an economic asset. The expanse of the railroad system, for instance, allowed corporate enterprises to extend their operations across state lines, creating a national market for goods.[28] Though property remained central for enabling individual autonomy of political subjects, the growing influence of more classically liberal perspectives in this period provided new arguments about why property mattered to political autonomy and thus to liberal citizenship more broadly. Republican proprietarian visions were becoming harder ideals to enforce, if they were ever realizable in the first instance. As Alexander notes, the core ideals of civic republicanism—"the priority of virtue (individual and collective) over self-interest, the fear of corruption, the need for stability, property as a material foundation of civic virtue—easily lent themselves to being put into service of expressing doubts about the benefits of a society where the market was the final arbiter of values."[29] As the Gilded Age progressed into the twentieth century, critical ideological tensions between an increasingly antiquated civic republicanism and a more contemporary, classically liberal ideology would prioritize the value of economic rights of property over those cherished for being solely political rights. In many ways, these two streams of political thought reflect broader debates about the coherence of democracy with liberalism—ones that remain as significant today as they did at the onset of the early industrial era.

DISPLACING DEMOCRATIC WITH LIBERAL PROPERTIES OF CITIZENSHIP

The industrialization of mid-to-late-nineteenth-century America reflected a period of rapid economic and political change. And although property remained central to discourse regarding citizenship, the meaning behind "proper" citizenship became less about looking out for the public or common good and more about protecting citizens' economic liberties and interests. Virtuous citizenship was now increasingly signified through one's economic accomplishment, modeled by whether, and accordingly, how much, an individual could earn. During this period, Judith Shklar argues, more value came to be placed on a citizen's "economic independence," specifically their capacity for "self-directed 'earning,' as the ethical basis of democratic citizenship, [which] took the place of an outmoded notion of public virtue."[30] Key to this conceptual shift was growing societal acceptance, or perhaps acquiescence, to the idea that a citizen's economic rights *should* mediate their political subjectivity. The influence of classical liberal ideals espousing socioeconomic utility and individual protection *from* government shaped this valuation of property's relation to citizenship, forcing republican proprietarian perspectives to balance democratic rhetoric with liberal values.

The material realities of industrial capitalism engendered a liberal ideology whereby the potential to earn shaped how the proper citizen ought to be measured. But this shift did not happen overnight. Indeed, the ways in which political subjectivity changed in relation to property during this period reflected the historical transition from a feudal to capitalist society. As Marx argued, the dispossession of communal lands in feudal England throughout the seventeenth and eighteenth centuries facilitated the isolation of property from its producers. This process of enclosure shifted possession of rights to land from those directly working or producing the land—peasant labor—to those simply possessing exclusive rights to the products of that land. This process of "primitive accumulation" entailed "expelling a resident population to create a landless proletariat, and then releasing the land into the privatised mainstream of capital accumulation."[31] Of course, the enclosure process has never formally ended and the piecemeal eradication of communal use rights to benefit from landed property continues today.

The effect of this type of land dispossession and the creation of exclusive property was not only economic but political. Somewhat paradoxically, the large-scale dispossession of property from labor eventually cleared the way for a major transformation of citizenship, via the extension of formal political rights to those who now did not own or have claims to the benefits of landed property. Such formal political rights were all but impossible for those without property during the American colonial and even postrevolutionary eras. However, with the spread of market relations over the following centuries, both the dispossessed wage laborer Marx pointed to and those literally without landed property could now formally hold political rights of citizenship equal to those enjoyed by the capitalist class. What this "democratization" of liberal capitalism would mean for an (white) individual's citizenship status was that it was no longer predicated on their class position.

For classical liberals whose interest in property required prioritizing liberty by further protecting the individual's economic rights, the extension of formal political equality to wage laborers and those without property was fitting. For the relation between capital and labor had long presupposed individuals as formally free and equal. Through the transition from feudalism's dispossessed peasant labor working communal land to the wage laborer of the industrial era, newly propertyless wage laborers were forced to "freely" sell their labor on the market to owners of the means of production. Ellen Meiksins-Wood's thorough analysis of the historical tension between capitalism and democracy is apt here. In respect to the spread of political rights to propertyless labor, Meiksins-Wood notes that the logic of capitalism presupposed that individuals were already "free" in that they were without "prescriptive rights or obligations, without juridical privileges or disabilities."[32] Because of this, wage laborers during America's industrial advance could now be seen as equal political subjects, "self-owning" individuals who realized their political independence through the ownership of their own labor rather than real property itself. Wage laborers and those without real property embodied the "detached" or disinterested liberal individual so revered within classical liberal ideology. Through the extension of political and civil rights of citizenship to those with little or no property, wage laborers and the propertyless emerged for the first time as "sovereign individuals" holding equal political rights to those of the propertied classes.

Such a political-economic shift brought new social consequences to liberal America. If political rights and subjectivity were no longer solely determined by property ownership, economic inequality was now not only formally acceptable but *protected* through the uneven balance of economic and political rights. It is this false equality, Meiksins-Wood argues, that "displaced" liberal citizenship to the purely political sphere. That is, the economic rights central for protecting capitalist property relations were now largely isolated from political and eventually civil rights. For laborers "enjoying" political rights without ownership over the means of production and those without ownership of real property, the extension of political rights had little effect on growing inequities resulting from the protection of capitalist property rights. Isolating the economic from the political, Meiksins-Wood argues, created a forum in which "extra-economic—political, juridical, military—status had no direct implications for economic power, the power of appropriation, exploitation and distribution."[33] For owners of the means of production and corporate property holders, this separation all but ensured that capitalist growth premised on prioritizing and protecting economic rights of liberty (property rights) could not be limited by the political opposition of a democratic majority.[34] For the working classes who were slowly extended formal political equality, then, fewer means existed to ameliorate a widening wealth gap exacerbated by the broad acceptance of laissez-faire economics premised upon private property ownership.

As the rhetoric of democratic republicanism gave way to more classically liberal values grounded in economic liberty and government restraint from intervention in individual affairs, liberalism's ascendancy promoted "equality through liberty, by means of liberty, not liberty by means of equality."[35] The unequal relationship between economic and political rights, similar to that between liberty and equality, has and continues to point to a paradox of liberal-democratic citizenship. As Meiksins-Wood puts it, "Socioeconomic position does not determine the right to citizenship—and that is what is democratic in capitalist democracy—but, since the power of the capitalist to appropriate surplus labor of workers is not dependent on a privileged juridical or civil status, civic equality does not directly affect or significantly modify class inequality—and this is what limits democracy in capitalism . . .

In that sense, political inequality in capitalist democracy not only co-exists with socio-economic inequality but leaves it fundamentally intact."[36] This historical "devaluing" of citizenship, in resigning the scope of citizenship to the purely political sphere, forces a reckoning with how the material and economic relations of property possession have limited, and continue to limit, the rights and privileges of citizenship within liberalism. Particularly as political and civil rights have been further extended into the twenty-first century, property has remained crucial for shaping citizenship, not only on account of class differences but also around racial/ethnic and gender differences. For essential to liberal ideology is that all individuals regardless of socioeconomic differences are equal in the right to liberty, a liberal virtue retained today despite clear inequities among citizens. As the following section will show, the emphasis on liberal individuality, particularly the self-owning individual, is deeply rooted in the relationship between property and citizenship.

PROPERTY AS SELF-POSSESSION: IDEOLOGIES OF RACIAL LIBERALISM

The historical process of severing capitalist property relations from the reach of political power, while not a completed project, points toward another important connection between liberal, propertied citizenship: the ideal of self-possession. In liberal theory, the notion of a self-possessing individual is popularly located in the thinking of John Locke. Writing in the late seventeenth century, Locke understood all individuals (read: only white men) to have property in themselves, because, he argued, individuals own the labor they invest into a resource. Locke argued that any resource that an individual "mixes" with the labor of their own hands gives that person a "right" to that thing.[37] Crucially, individuals do not only enjoy a natural right to properties in resources, they also hold property in their own *person*. In his view, individuals enjoy property as a natural right because they are sovereigns over themselves; related to this, property is by extension the resources an individual owns through the products of their labor. In classical liberalism, so deeply indebted to Locke's thinking, property was long regarded as a natural right exclusive to individuals, and as such, individuals were thought to be in *possession* of their person.

It is difficult to overstate the longevity of this liberal ideal. Republican and classical liberal ideologies both connected property with self-possession, though somewhat differently. As noted, republican ideology cherished the assumed collective political benefits resulting from a society of "self-owning," small landowners. But the notion that an individual ought to hold inviolable rights to own and acquire property to satisfy individual economic preferences resonates more deeply in classical liberal ideology. The shift from politically contributing to the common good to an ideal promoting industriousness through one's earning potential also marked a shift in how citizens were understood to be self-owning.

Critiques of the self-possession ideal have generally centered on the liberal attachment to individuality. Classical liberal ideology understands individuality as a means of cultivating one's innate sense of what it means to be human.[38] Liberalism is also individualist, however, in the sense that "it asserts the moral primacy of the person against the claims of any social collectivity."[39] The effect is to promote *individualism* as a sociopolitical process of prioritizing individual sovereignty in the pursuit of enhancing self-asserted liberty interests. In C. B. Macpherson's critique of liberal theory, he locates the sovereign, self-owning individual in what he terms "possessive individualism." The possessive nature of liberal individualism, Macpherson argued, was rooted in the liberal belief that the individual was "the proprietor of his own person or capacities, owing nothing to society for them."[40] The liberal individual secures their freedom because they own their capacities to labor. It was *ownership* that came to be "the critically important relation determining [an individual's] actual freedom and actual prospect of realizing their full potentialities."[41] Given that the liberal human subject was believed to be free when they were free from the interference of, or dependence on, others, an individual's freedom becomes "a function of possession." From this perspective, the ideal structure of the liberal polity is one premised upon a society of equal individuals relating to one another as proprietors of their own persons, one where self-possessing individuals exchange their bodily and extracorporeal properties in order to satisfy and secure individual liberties.

If we consider the fate of individuals who did not "possess" themselves and had no property in their person but who instead were owned as property itself, the benefits and protections of liberal citizenship were clearly denied to much of American society for centuries. The struggle for women's rights of self-possession and political autonomy, for example, was rooted in relations of property. Until the late 1880s, the concept of "coverture" accepted within common law meant that upon marriage, women ceased to have a legal and thus political identity of their own, a process that necessitated that women give over their possessions to their husband.[42] This oppressive concept reinforced the liberal principle that because women were the property *of* men, they lacked property in themselves in that they were denied possession over their own bodies.[43] That women were subject to their husband's will was rooted in liberal conceptions of the natural place of women within the private sphere, thus reserving the male-dominated public sphere as the natural space for political engagement.[44] Coupled with the denial of suffrage until the early twentieth century, this meant that women struggled against a liberal ideology that placed them outside of the proper role of citizen subject.

Similarly, enslaved Black people were owned as a form of property itself and the law protected and promoted their exchange as chattel and thus individual property.[45] The proprietary relationship between owner and slave reinforced how law regulated and valued the proprietous citizen. Racial differentiation in law and practice colored how and whether an individual would benefit from liberal citizenship. As De la Fuente and Gross note, throughout the Antebellum era, "white identity [was] equal to a set of moral and civic virtues that characterized only white people," so much so that "one had to claim whiteness to qualify for basic rights."[46] Crucially, they note that it was liberal laws pertaining to *freedom*, more so than the laws protecting owners of chattel property, that reified Blackness as a category illegible to proper citizenship. Given that antebellum law "constituted whiteness as a category of social superiority," they note, whiteness was made "inseparable from the privileges of citizenship."[47] The racialized hierarchy constructed by law and realized in practice created the threshold for rights of citizenship, a threshold demarcated by an individual's ability to "possess" their whiteness.

After emancipation, the privileges of political and economic citizenship were in theory extended to Black Americans. The Fourteenth Amendment guaranteed all U.S.-born and naturalized people citizenship rights, which extended to the formerly enslaved.[48] And the Fifteenth Amendment extended suffrage for Black men. In practice, however, Black Americans and other nonwhite peoples were all but unable to realize the privileges that came with these citizenship protections. For instance, though Black males were extended the franchise with the Fifteenth Amendment, Black suffrage was not realized in any substantive sense until the Voting Rights Act of 1965. Despite the repeal of property qualifications for voting, Blacks and other propertyless wage laborers faced other material qualifications for suffrage, for example through poll taxes, an updated form of property qualification.[49] Such restrictive practices denied Black families not just the right to vote but ideologically reinforced that propertyless individuals lacked the capacity to possess themselves as proper self-governing citizens.

If restrictions on Black suffrage from the late nineteenth to late twentieth centuries was one means by which a white dominant liberal polity attempted to maintain itself as racially exclusive, restrictions on owning landed property was *the* means by which a white polity of "self-possessing" citizens was effectuated. By restricting ownership of real property largely to whites, formerly enslaved people were deprived of this primary means of wealth creation. During and immediately following the Civil War, for instance, real property confiscated from Confederate holdings by the Freedmen's Bureau—lands that were promised to and actually occupied by formerly enslaved people (the well-known "forty acres")—were quickly returned to the possession of their former white owners.[50] Returning land to southern whites actively dispossessed Blacks of their newly acquired land after the war.[51] And though Blacks were not banned outright from owning landed property, "Black Codes" enacted and enforced by white dominated society perpetuated a variety of legal and economic strategies to coerce Blacks back into contracted plantation labor, thus stymying the opportunities of Black families to acquire real property and through it the properties of (white) citizenship.

Restrictions on real property ownership for nonwhites were endemic to government practices shaping the geographies of housing in America well into the twentieth century. Today, homeownership is linked with virtuous citizenship in the American political imaginary, a notion of citizenship still influencing owners' voting behavior at the local level.[52] This long-valued norm was engrained into American society during the New Deal, when the Federal Housing Administration (FHA) revolutionized homeownership by insuring private mortgages. The policy enabled many more white Americans to afford homes than in the past. The FHA-backed mortgage inspired a post–World War II boom in homeownership, incentivizing the development of modern American suburbs literally and figuratively built around the single-family home. The newly formed suburban areas of the mid-to-late twentieth century, Kenneth Jackson argues, embodied the essence of American society by way of "conspicuous consumption, a reliance upon the private automobile, upward mobility, the separation of the family into nuclear units, the widening division between work and leisure, and a tendency toward racial and economic exclusiveness."[53] The "American Dream" of homeownership was modeled on the social and political characteristics of the modern suburb.

At the ideological core of the "suburban ideal," however, was the correlative notion of a private place away from the crudeness of urban life.[54] Urban life in mid-twentieth-century America was highly segregated by race. Segregation was not naturally occurring but structured through the practices of the FHA and the real estate industry, which enforced practices such as redlining and the use of racially restricted covenants, systematically excluding people of color from white neighborhoods and segregating them into specific underserved neighborhoods. The legacy of these practices is well known today. The FHA upheld the positions of the Homeowners Loan Corporation, an entity rating neighborhoods for investment risk, which was based primarily on neighborhoods' social and economic characteristics, resulting in the redlining of majority-minority neighborhoods and all but eliminating potential owners of color from accessing mortgages and other housing-related loans.

Although such practices were legally prohibited with the passing of the Fair Housing Act in 1968, disparities in property ownership based on race or economic class continued to be shaped by these practices of racialized exclusion. Keeanga-Yamahtta Taylor recently showed, for example, how the federal government's 1968 Housing and Urban Development (HUD) Act incentivized mortgage lenders and real estate agents to extend homeownership opportunities specifically to Black borrowers who had been excluded from homeownership financing for decades. HUD's "colorblind" lending initiatives were meant to overcome past exclusions and promote low-income Black homeownership. But the effect of these programs largely reinforced the exploitation of low-income Black families through predatory lending schemes, what Taylor calls "predatory inclusion," by incentivizing low-income borrowers to take on iniquitous loan terms that effectively exacerbated the debts of many Black families.[55] Through government programming and practices, Taylor argues, Black property "was marked by its distress and isolation, where value was extracted, not imbued."[56] In contrast, white property was valued as worthy of investment in that it modeled proper homeownership. Though Black homeownership rates did increase in the second half of the twentieth century, structural racism in housing policies and practices reinforced nonwhite homeowners as deficient economic citizens in the broader ownership landscape, a legacy perpetuating large racial disparities in homeownership today.[57]

Such racialized regimes of property demarcated the material and political benefits of ownership for white people. Both pre- and post-emancipation, then, whiteness enabled ownership of real property without much qualification beyond that criteria, while at the same time powerfully shaping for whom possession was available and who it was meant to benefit. As Cheryl Harris argues, embedded into American law was and is a set of unearned privileges and benefits, in which "white identity became the basis of racialized privilege that was ratified and legitimated as a type of status property."[58]

By "protecting settled expectations based on white privilege," Harris argues, law recognizes "a property interest in whiteness."[59] To the extent that whiteness constitutes a form of personal property or self-ownership, Harris argues, then "possession—the act necessary to lay the basis for rights in property—was defined to include only the cultural practices of whites ... [which] laid the foundation for the idea that whiteness—that which whites alone possess—is valuable and is property."[60]

The argument that unearned racial privileges and benefits for whites are secured through a form of status property—one that prioritizes material and political-legal access to the benefits of real property for whites over nonwhites—relates to a broader critique of the neutrality of liberal ideology. Namely, critics suggest that neutral, or colorblind, liberal laws and institutions work to reinforce equality among racialized differences in the abstract but in fact overlook or exacerbate them in practice, perpetuating "racial liberalism." Recent scholarship identifies racial liberalism as an ontological practice of maintaining a political economy that has been actively produced for whites via the exploitation of nonwhite lives in order to advance the social contract upon which liberalism is premised.[61] As Charles Mills argues, by effectively restricting political benefits of liberal citizenship to whites, racial liberalism in effect "restricted full personhood to whites ... and relegated nonwhites to an inferior category, so that [liberalism's] schedule of rights and prescriptions for justice were all color-coded."[62]

This history pertains not only to Black oppression. Racial liberalism, as Moreton-Robinson argues, is rooted in a "white possessive logic" that required the possession of Indigenous lands to relationally produce the nation modeled upon white property ownership forms.[63] Such "racial regimes of ownership," as Brenna Bhandar writes, were not simply the primary means toward dispossessing and appropriating land from Indigenous and other racialized groups. "Being an owner and having the capacity to appropriate ... [were] prerequisites for attaining the status of the proper subject of modern law, a fully individuated citizen-subject."[64] The possessive logics which liberalism has been predicated upon more broadly identify the limitations of a liberal social contract where "the property rights of non-self-owning people of color are systematically violated ... [and] rights, liberties, opportunities, income, and wealth are continually being transferred from the nonwhite to the white population."[65] For this reason, those who have been historically dispossessed not only of property but of themselves, whether they hold citizenship status or not, must struggle simultaneously for a right both to property and to *personhood*.[66] As Ananya Roy suggests, to dispossess racialized others of property and personhood is to enforce a racial liberalism that "banishes" racialized subjects from the proper liberal social order.[67] To understand the contemporary relations of property with citizenship therefore requires making sense of how the historical dispossession of land from persons and people from self-possession remains connected to "propriety" and is struggled over within liberalism. For much of American history, self-possession has been rooted in an ontology of white material interests, meaning that the rights and benefits that stem from personal properties and landed property have been regulated through the legal-political stipulations of white society.

In highlighting how these different points of connection between property and citizenship constitute fundamental features of liberalism, it is important to note that such ideals fashioned from liberal theories must be continually put into practice in the material relations of social life. Ideals upholding property as the means to liberty for citizens have long been contested and reworked over time. Law and social practices have rendered old forms of property qualifications for citizenship rights not only illegal but antiquated and largely unsaleable in contemporary social life. Nonetheless, elements of the proprietarian tradition remain, albeit in different forms both materially and ideologically. The final section of this chapter identifies how these key features of liberal propertied citizenship affect unhoused people specifically and thus why they matter for understanding the contemporary houselessness crisis.

Connecting Propertied Citizenship with Homelessness

We have seen how the relationship between property and political subjectivity and citizenship has changed over time. Given this changing and thus indeterminate relationship, it is useful to examine the durability or "permanence" of these ideals and material relations in the current moment. Before detailing how a propertied citizenship dialectic underscores the specific context of Portland's encampments, I focus more broadly on unhoused people's political relationship to property forms.

Houselessness scholarship examining the relationship between property and citizenship has homed in on how property rights of ownership provide an absolute right to exclude. As mentioned in the introduction, a focus on exclusion has proliferated within legal scholarship on property, often with a particular emphasis on its detriment to marginalized populations. Through this lens, unhoused people are shown to have a "negative" relation to property, where negative means a relationship structured by so-called negative rights. These commonly require only that individuals or governments refrain *from* imposing on other individuals.⁶⁸ More simply, a negative right is a right related to liberty, as it protects an individual's freedom from interference. What follows from this idea as it relates to unhoused people is that people without access to landed property exist in a negative relation to those who possess the power to define when, where, and how unhoused people may be in propertied spaces.

Arguments about unhoused people's negative relation to property have been expressed by legal scholars examining property and houselessness through the notion of (un)freedom. Jeremy Waldron, for example, argues that "there is no place governed by a private property rule where [an unhoused person] is allowed to be whenever [they choose], no place governed by a private property rule from which [they] may not at any time be excluded as a result of someone else's say-so."⁶⁹ "Homelessness *consists* in unfreedom," he insists, because for an unhoused person, "their having nowhere to go *is* their being unfree (in a negative sense) to be anywhere."⁷⁰ Expanding on Waldron's general arguments about this spatial paradox, Christopher Essert claims more forcefully that freedom is not lost simply in those moments when owners realize their power through excluding unhoused people from spaces. "There is a prior issue of freedom that arises even in the absence of any actual denial of leave," Essert writes. "To be homeless . . . is to be always and everywhere subject to others' rights and therefore to the *possibility* of their enforcing those rights. It is to be under the power of others, dependent on them, dominated by them, unfree."⁷¹ The mere capacity of being able to enforce one's authority over the unhoused *through* property, in other words, is what makes unhoused people unfree. In this light, negative rights of property deny unhoused people the freedom to author their decision-making about how they may best survive, because they "lack the normative control provided by property rights."⁷²

Geographers examining houselessness and property have expanded on these arguments by illustrating the ways in which private property rights effectively exclude groups from space and thus from belonging in the political sphere.⁷³ As Don Mitchell has stressed throughout his work on public space, anti-houseless legislation is a tool used to regulate the public order. When implemented, it reflects norms about who can be, and who is, properly part of the public. Use-of-space ordinances restricting or removing unhoused people from public space, Mitchell argues, recreate "the public sphere as intentionally exclusive, as a sphere in which the legitimate public only includes those who . . . have a place governed by private property rules to call their own."⁷⁴ To the extent that restrictive public space ordinances cannot fully eradicate unhoused people from space, the unhoused population can "at least be shrunk down, isolated, and contained so that the public need not feel the pressure of its presence."[75] Indeed, as Neil Smith argues, American municipalities' capacity to remove unhoused people from and for spaces of middle- and upper- class consumption relies on the "revengeful conservatism" resulting from failed liberal policies seeking to solve houselessness in the 1980s.[76] Property, as a medium for forming the public and for eradicating unhoused people from gentrifying spaces, relies upon negation.

A negative focus on property-as-exclusion misses a normative feature of property within liberalism, however. Through this lens, unhoused people are understood to be placed or forced "outside" of property.[77] Such a binary framing underemphasizes the reality of unhoused peoples' existence. For property is a primary mechanism through which individuals are emplaced within differing relations of political and economic power. Staeheli and Mitchell recognize this through their concept of "property regimes"—or the "prevailing system of laws, practices and relations among different properties"—illustrating that although relations of property are always being restructured through social actions, so too are the relations shaping property "systematically structured [and] relatively predictable."[78] Significantly, when regimes of property are legitimated through their enforcement, property becomes "a means of sorting community and social norms."[79] As such, "dissent, transgression, or any disruption or breaking of rules calls into question the social legitimacy of members of the public." The enforcement of property regimes, Staeheli and Mitchell argue, enables something more like a collectively held "power to exclude [which] entails an ability to *reorder* the public."[80] Understood relationally, it is the *collective* decisions by property owners to exclude, not just decisions by individual rights holders, that emplace unhoused people within the various relations comprising property.

A relational approach to analyzing unhoused people and property illustrates, therefore, that unhoused people are not excluded from and placed "outside" of property. To claim that they are would suggest that houseless people have no ties to, or are not affected by, the rights and relations undergirding property after an event of being excluded. It would imply that unhoused people are outside of the proper sociopolitical order until they are once again "let back in" to it by being let back into property. Unhoused people are not outside of property, however, but rather remain *within* the relations of property even as, and especially when, they are excluded from property at particular moments.

This is an argument shared by geographer and property scholar Nicholas Blomley, who has written that there is no inside or outside to property, "only graduated positions of conditional access." Blomley advocates an approach to examining property that pays particular attention to the precarity of individual or group situations to, or relationships with, property. Precarious property relations, he suggests, entail a "power/liability pairing, in which one party has the power to change a particular set of relations, while the other lacks an immunity to such changes."[81] For Blomley, relational property analyses do not just illuminate how property makes certain individuals or groups vulnerable but can show how "the security of the privileged to access and secure shelter produces and depends upon the production of property precarity for others."[82] To suggest that we are always within property, in this sense, means that we are always entangled in the politics related to the production and maintenance of property. And it is incumbent upon us to address how we are differently placed within property, as more or less vulnerable, or more or less secure, in our access to it—something I assess more specifically in chapter 4 through the language of justice and our responsibility for working toward it.

Such a relational perspective begs the following question, however: If there is no "outside" to property, where, then, lie the limits of property? Where can we find the political constraints on people's lives because of their relationship with properties more broadly? I suggest this is where a dialectical approach can be useful. With a historical understanding of the relationship between property and political subjectivity in mind, we are better able to assess how the dialectical tensions of property and citizenship unfold in the social and material relations of the world. In other words, the tensions of property and its constraints on political subjects are seen in specific places as they restructure places in particular ways.

The limits of property, then, partially lie in the struggles for social and political recognition as expressed in struggles to access shelter and secure housing. They are shown in the individual struggles of unhoused people of color, as geographer Deshonay Dozier has pointed out, struggles contesting the historical dispossession of property and personhood for Black people—as well as the policing of unhoused Black people's right to personal properties—by carving out spaces of survival in public spaces where difference is neutralized in order to cohere with the proper (white) social order.[83] They are shown in unhoused Indigenous peoples' struggles for shelter in a society that has historically enacted property over "unowned" land, thereby diminishing Indigenous land uses as nonproperties, when understood in relation to whiteness (as addressed further in the conclusion). A dialectical approach brings to light the variables shaping the long production of propertied citizenship as a normative liberal order and thus how power materializes through relations of property in specific times and places.

This approach also allows us to explain *why* property, when seen as a relationship, is so critical to any conversation about houselessness and liberal policy solutions today. Generally, it means that *all* individuals are affected and implicated at some level in how the normative relations of property continue to marginalize unhoused people. Corporate property owners, homeowners, apartment lessees, and the unhoused are all embedded within and collectively enforce regimes of property in some way; we are obliged to the authority of property rights holders who control material resources as much as property owners are (theoretically) restricted and normatively admonished not to abuse their authority to limit the freedoms of the rest of us. Yet, this does not mean that responsibility for the production of houselessness is equally distributed simply by the fact that we are all within property. *Whose* values about propriety, and *which* rights, matter more (legally and politically) for collectively producing the injustices of property are paramount questions when assessing how unhoused people are affected by their relationship to property.

In Portland, these moments of gatekeeping are borne out through the struggles over self-governing houseless encampments and nonprofit-led tiny house villages. As we will see in the next few chapters, encampment residents are often described as improper political subjects due to their "illegal" or improper use of property. But it is important to recognize that opposition to houseless encampments (and their residents) is not always reflected in discourse about them. While a majority of Portland's population rhetorically supports the existence of self-governing encampments in the abstract, support quickly dwindles when the placement of encampments in particular areas of the city confronts the social and material realties of peoples' lives. Such relations, I suggest, show less about the direct disdain held for unhoused individuals residing in encampments than they do about how individuals and governments acquiesce to the demands of a property system that necessitates property precarity for some so that others can remain more securely housed. To explore this point more fully, it is useful to see how the encampment model began and how its social and physical forms have been shaped over time by diverging interests. When looking at the development of the Portland encampment model, we can better see how unhoused peoples' struggles to access property are challenged by, and can in turn challenge, a property system that maintains conditional access to propertied space.

CHAPTER 2

Developing Portland's Homeless Encampment Model

On April 28, 2021, the City Council of Portland, Oregon, unanimously approved what seemed to be a very ordinary amendment to its zoning code. Yet, the amendment reflected anything but quotidian municipal decision-making. In passing Ordinance no. 190381, the city council ended a decades-long struggle fought by Portland's unhoused communities (and their supporters) to be able to legally operate sanctioned and organized encampments on public and private properties throughout the city.[1] The ordinance is significant because it was the first to codify encampments as an accepted land use, justifying the perpetual integration of encampments into the built environment.

The move was also unusual because, until quite recently, Portland's city government had been opposed to both organized and unorganized forms of camping. City code ordinances prohibiting camping were first implemented in the early 1980s, a restriction adopted by municipalities nationwide in response to the rise of houselessness at that time. The tenor of the city government's position on organized camping began to change, however, when in October 2015 it declared a state of emergency on housing and homelessness. While the SOE intended to ameliorate many things, most significantly, it suspended land use restrictions that had previously prohibited organized (and for a time, unorganized) camping in the city.[2] Because of this, the city not only permitted but promoted organized and nonprofit-led encampments throughout a nearly ten-year SOE period. Today, Portland has gone all in on its encampment model, or "PEM," as an official model of shelter.

Alongside the development of the PEM, there was, and continues to be, conflict and contestation. Members of the public, neighborhood associations, and private entities have put their collective energy into preventing sanctioned encampment communities from establishing these spaces of respite throughout the city's landscape; they have also attempted to stymie the city government's efforts to accommodate these efforts. The reasons for this are many. There has been panic over the assumption that encampments bring increases in crime, concern that encampments will blight neighborhood aesthetics, and fear that homeowners adjacent to encampments will lose value in their properties. There have also been disparaging claims about encampment residents suggesting that unhoused people are not deserving enough to be able to organize themselves as communities, much less on government-owned land. Concern for the health and safety of encampment residents has also been a common narrative driving the opposition to sanctioned encampments.

To better understand the relevance of this shelter model to liberal property systems more specifically, the chapter provides context about the contested development of the PEM.[3] It details the uneven acceptance of organized and sanctioned encampments by the Portland city government as well as by the public. In doing so, it traces the municipality's decades-long history of banning organized camping to demonstrate how the city's stance on encampments eventually moved from one of prohibition to legalization. I argue that it was during the SOE period that self-governing encampments revealed what a model for sanctioned encampments could look like at a larger scale, eventually leading the city to incorporate them into municipal land use code.

The process of legitimizing sanctioned encampments, however, presupposed a "proper" model of sanctioned encampments. By examining the social and technical means through which encampments became legal land uses, the chapter also illustrates how the city transitioned away from self-organized encampments to a more "managed," top-down village model. Part of the reason for this, I suggest, is due to how neighborhood-level political organizing contested the self-governing model. Another reason relates to how government assists unhoused people to become stable through its Shelter to Housing Continuum (STHC), an apt metaphor illustrating how official shelter strategies reinforce the ownership model. I argue that the disavowal of self-governing encampments by government and the public highlights how relations of property are used to control the means by which unhoused people become stable. The chapter thus explains why the PEM came to take its current form and how the shift away from self-organized encampments toward the village type ensures the model's justification within liberal models of property.

Situating Portland's Encampment Model

Before detailing the historical development of the PEM, it is useful to describe what the model looks like at present. Doing so helps to understand what these spaces of respite are and what they are not and should give a general sense of how they feature within the urban landscape. The sanctioned encampments existing in Portland today range in residential size and organizational form. The areal size of sites ranges according to the property's prior use, its capacity for tiny houses and commons spaces, utility hookups (for most sites), and its access to transportation lines. Organized encampments can be as small as ten tiny houses, but many accommodate up to sixty such dwellings. As of 2024, there were sixteen encampments located across the city.

As already indicated, there are two main organizing forms for the encampments, the older self-organized model and the newer "managed" village model. They are distinguished by who organizes them. For instance, self-organized encampments are contracted by the city to manage their own affairs. These encampment communities secure their own membership, manage everyday relations within the site, and navigate neighborhood and government relations primarily by themselves. In contrast, managed villages are not self-organized but are run top-down by local and out-of-state social service

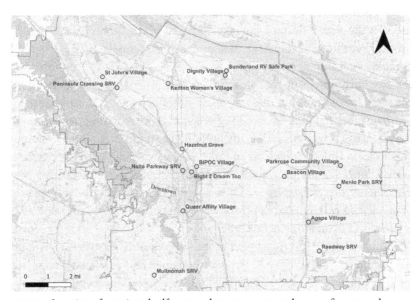

FIGURE 1. Location of sanctioned self-managed encampments and nonprofit managed villages in Portland, 2024.

FIGURE 2. Dignity Village, with its commons building (left) and tiny homes in background.

providers. Village residents have much less voice in the site's operations and perform fewer of the everyday tasks of maintaining the site. Finally, the nonprofits running the managed villages employ onsite social workers to help connect residents with various types of support for housing, employment, and health care. For the most part, self-organized encampments are responsible for accessing these resources for themselves.

Of Portland's sixteen encampments, only three are self-organized. This model is the oldest encampment type in the city and is the organizing model for the first three encampments that established themselves. The first self-organized encampment in the city was Dignity Village (DV). Permitted by the city government in 2001 in response to a protest, DV has operated in the same location on the city's far north side since then. Situated between Portland's international airport, the city's yard waste recycling facility, and a low-security corrections facility, DV holds between fifty and sixty tiny house structures in which individuals and their pets may reside. The village is well known for being the progenitor of Portland's model of self-organized encampments. It is collectively run by its overall membership through the aid of an elected council that ensures bylaws are being followed and updated with respect to their democratic intentions.

Right 2 Dream Too (R2DT) is the second oldest self-organized site and has been operating since 2011. The encampment operates similarly to DV, as a self-organized site with sixteen tiny houses for resident members. It differs from DV and all other encampments in the city in that it also serves as a low-barrier overnight shelter space that is run by the resident mem-

FIGURE 3. Right 2 Dream Too, men's overnight guest tent.

bers. Prior to the COVID-19 pandemic, the space hosted about sixty nightly sleepers. Like DV, R2DT is a registered nonprofit and manages its own affairs through its resident membership plus a board comprising volunteers and resident members. R2DT has fought hard to stay located within the central city and has overcome numerous political and legal obstacles to remain operating as a donation-based shelter.[4]

The third self-organized encampment in the city is Hazelnut Grove (HG). HG also began as a protest encampment, first establishing itself in summer 2015 shortly before the city declared the SOE. The site is located between a light rail line and major north-south thoroughfare connecting the central and north sides of the city. HG holds fifteen to twenty tiny houses and is organized by its resident members, who follow similar bylaws to those of DV and R2DT. HG is unique in that it never has been issued a land use permit by the city; rather, it is tolerated by the city, and receives minor support from the local government for garbage and waste removal in addition to perimeter fencing.

Less than two years into the SOE, the city government opened the first nonprofit-managed tiny house village, Kenton Women's Village (KWV). KWV was similar in design to the self-organized encampments, hosting about twenty tiny houses, but it was also given showers, flushable toilets, and an indoor kitchen with a commons space. Unlike the self-organized encampments, KWV is run by the nonprofit Catholic Charities, which employs part-time social workers to help village residents connect with health, employment, and housing services. As the following section will show, KWV gar-

46   Chapter Two

FIGURE 4. Hazelnut Grove, looking down a path leading to tiny houses.

FIGURE 5. The original location of Kenton Women's Village.

nered much acclaim, particularly in comparison with the self-organized encampments, as it was better serviced and was planned more thoroughly in conjunction with its neighboring Kenton Neighborhood Association.

Between 2019 and 2022, four managed villages opened that operate on church-owned properties. Agape, St. John's, Beacon, and Parkrose Community Villages range from ten to twenty tiny houses each and are organized with a mix of financial support from their host faith institutions and the city and county governments.

When COVID-19 began in March 2020, the City of Portland had to rapidly expand and restructure its sheltering capacities. It reorganized indoor shelters to space out sleeping quarters, opened brand-new shelters, and rented motel rooms for unhoused people. It also opened three more sixty-person tiny house encampments within the span of a few months. The city called upon the expertise of R2DT and other advocacy communities in Portland to develop these new encampments, which were then referred to as C3PO, or "Creating Conscious Communities with People Outside." The C3PO encampments were originally organized by their residents and two (the Queer Affinity and BIPOC Villages) were culturally specific. However, after being relocated in 2021, both of the latter sites transitioned to a nonprofit managed model, while the third site established in the Old Town neighborhood closed without relocating.

Then, in 2021, the City of Portland declared its intent to open six new "safe rest villages" (SRV) managed by nonprofit organizations. Funded by grants from the American Rescue Plan Act, the SRV sites expanded on the village model as an alternative to traditional indoor shelter. The SRV sites were opened throughout 2022 and 2023 and each offers between fifty and sixty tiny houses for its residents with the exception of one site that hosts residential vehicles.

The sixteen encampments spread throughout Portland's landscape are the result of years of planning and struggle by unhoused people, advocates and activists, city and county governments, and some supporting members of the public. The organizing work of the earliest encampments, especially the efforts of DV and R2DT, not only modeled how self-organized encampments could operate rather successfully but also why organized encampments are necessary alternatives to indoor shelter.[5] Of course, these communities did not pop up overnight. Several land use ordinances restricting where encampments can be sited and how they can become sanctioned delayed the process for many extant sites and prevented many more encampments from opening altogether. And when they did manage to organize themselves, community opposition challenged the validity of these spaces. As the following narrative of the PEM shows, these challenges shaped how the city saw the function of the encampment model, one where collective management was disincentivized and where a more top-down, managed style prevailed.

The Uneven Enforcement of Portland's Camping Prohibitions

ORIGINS OF THE CAMPING BAN

Although no systematic count of the houseless population in Portland was made until the late 1990s, historians suggest houselessness has been present in the city for nearly a century. As in many U.S. cities during the 1930s and 1940s, "Hooverville" encampments were prominent in the Sullivan's Gulch neighborhood as well as nearby Ross Island, while general laborers frequently lived without stable housing in downtown's Old Town neighborhood throughout the first few decades of the twentieth century.[6] However, it was not until the 1980s that a nationwide uptick in unsheltered houselessness brought legislative attention to the issue in Portland.

In response to the increased visibility of houselessness in the city, Portland's government passed its first "unlawful camping" ordinance in June 1981.[7] The ordinance prohibited temporary campsites on public property or on public rights-of-way. At the time, Portland's city code defined camping as "any bedding, sleeping bag or other sleeping matter, or any stove or fire . . . whether or not such place incorporates the use of any tent, lean-to, shack or any other structure or any vehicle or part thereof."[8] The 1981 ordinance was not challenged in the courts until 2000, when the Multnomah County Circuit Court arbitrated a case concerning two unhoused men who were cited for sleeping in public.[9] The judge assigned to the case ruled the city's camping ban was unconstitutional on the grounds that it restricted individuals' freedom to move or stay in place and that it punished houseless people for their status. Despite the ruling, the city did not change its practices. "'This is just one decision of one judge,' former City Attorney Jim Van Dyke told the *Oregonian* at the time. 'We've had other decisions of other judges upholding that ordinance,'" he claimed.[10] Thus, while the judge's ruling provided rhetorical support for overturning Portland's anti-camping policy, the city government nonetheless continued to find ways to enforce the ban through other policies.[11]

Despite the apparent ineffectiveness of the Multnomah County Circuit Court decision in changing the city's actions, the ruling nonetheless generated a wave of optimism among activists and advocates, helping to reimagine what more accommodating land use policies could look like regarding collective living for unhoused people. Shortly after the ruling, for instance, Portland activist Jack Tafari wrote an op-ed piece in the city's houseless newspaper *Street Roots* titled "We Need a Tent City." Tafari called for Portland—its bureaucrats, unhoused people, and their advocates—to consider creating a sanctioned tent city. Tafari explained that a sanctioned campsite would allow unhoused people a safer place to sleep and to leave their things, protection from the elements, as well as an alternative to the "sanctimony" encountered in the city's religious missions.[12] As far as the city government was concerned, however, camping was still illegal, and officials continued to take no real action on camping assistance. Within a few months of his written plea for a tent city, Tafari led a campaign called "Out of the Doorways." The campaign convened a small group of houseless individuals who were residing in tents on public property at the time. Employing civil disobedience, the group persisted in camping through a cycle of police sweeps in various spaces around downtown, decrying the very conditions that the Multnomah County Circuit Court had recently opined were unconstitutional.

Out of that initial group of protestors arose a collective called Camp Dignity. For nearly a year, Camp Dignity continued to camp in opposition to Portland's city code while negotiating with the government to find a sanctioned place for a tent city to operate. In 2001 the two parties came to an agreement, which permitted Camp Dignity the use of a city-owned property far outside of the center city near Portland's international airport. It was at this site that the group was refashioned into the previously mentioned Dignity Village, North America's longest-running sanctioned and self-organized houseless encampment.

The newly sanctioned DV was not intended to be permanent, at least from the city's perspective. In February 2004, after several failed attempts at relocating DV, the city passed Resolution no. 36200, which defined DV as a "designated campground." The designation was allowed under state land use regulations, Oregon Revised Statute (ORS 197.746), which allows for each Oregon municipality to establish campgrounds "to be used for providing transitional housing accommodations"; the campgrounds were expressly meant for "persons who lack permanent shelter and cannot be placed in other low-income housing."[13] In this way, the city resolution secured the legal means under which Dignity Village could operate and the encampment has remained operating at the same site ever since.

DV succeeded in securing a legal permit, but this was a one-off event. Camping remained otherwise prohibited throughout Portland and the city's anti-camping ordinance would not be challenged for another seven years. In 2011, in a landmark case for the city and anti-houselessness advocates, the constitutionality of the city's camping ban was considered in the U.S. District Court of Oregon. In the *Anderson v. City of Portland* (2011) complaint, a class of unhoused people sought redress from the City of Portland, arguing that the city's anti-camping ordinances criminalized the status of houselessness in violation of the Eighth Amendment because of how it punished unhoused people for sleeping in a public place even though they had no lawful place to sleep.[14] The plaintiffs claimed that the ordinances were being enforced selectively, only against houseless people. The district court, however, found that the city's camping ordinance was *not* unconstitutional per the Eighth Amendment. It also found that it was not applied unequally to all unhoused people in violation of the equal protection clause of the Fourteenth Amendment.[15]

The district court's decision nonetheless generated some actionable responses from the city government. A resulting settlement from the class action suit effected some changes to Portland's camping ordinances. Importantly, the settlement redefined what constituted "camping" and instructed what constituted proper police engagement with unhoused people. For instance, the changes required that police officers must give additional notice to houseless individuals before sweeping their camps, "no less than 24 hours after and within seven (7) days of [the date and time the site is posted for cleanup]."[16] Additionally, the settlement required that police follow specific procedures when clearing a campsite, especially when taking people's property, such as by photographing and itemizing all confiscated property. Finally, the settlement expanded the definition of "campsite" beyond the more general one found in the original anti-camping ordinance. Now, after more than thirty years, campsites were redefined to encompass more personal property (e.g., shopping carts and belongings within them) in order to ensure that people could retrieve their belongings after police intervention.

Despite these minor changes, the camping prohibition remained in effect. It would not be until the city declared its SOE in 2015 that Portland's anti-camping policies would be drastically reworked.

EXPERIMENTING WITH CAMPING DURING THE STATE OF EMERGENCY

The SOE facilitated a radical regulatory departure from the city's anti-camping ordinances up to that point. The 2015 SOE declaration was intended to relieve many issues related to growing unsheltered houselessness in the city. The main SOE policies were implemented in February 2016, when the city announced its "Safe Sleep" initiative, a set of policies aimed at making it easier for houseless individuals to rest in public spaces throughout the City without being swept or ticketed. Crucially, the policies were implemented in recognition of the large disparity between the number of unhoused people lacking shelter in the city and the limited availability of emergency shelter beds.

The Safe Sleep policies provided houseless individuals with four new options for resting or sheltering. The first option directed people toward traditional emergency shelter. A second option, meant to encourage individuals to shelter in cars or RVs in an "organized" space, never took off. It would later be adopted in modified form by the city, allowing individuals to sleep in their cars without citation.[17] The third option allowed individuals to sleep on sidewalks (while somehow still adhering to the city's sidewalk management plan) throughout the day, though they could do so with only a sleeping bag or tarp, not with a tent or larger structure. From 9:00 p.m. to 7:00 a.m., individuals could erect tents on public rights-of-way or "remnant" municipal property. They were instructed to sleep with six or fewer tents in one location, presumably to avoid the growth of a larger camp. Tents were then to be taken down at 7:00 a.m. and any remaining things were to be cleared out.

The fourth and final option was as controversial as the third. It allowed for self-organized, sanctioned encampments to operate on city-owned properties. Newly created and sanctioned encampments were expected to partner with a local nonprofit that had experience in social service provisioning. New encampments were also to establish and follow a "code of conduct" (as DV, R2DT, and HG had), and the sites would have city-financed servicing for portable restrooms and waste removal.[18] The city's guidelines stipulated that sanctioned encampments were to operate only for the duration of the Safe Sleep period, which at that point had no sunset date.

Some endorsed Safe Sleep as a compassionate approach to working with houseless individuals. An attorney for the Oregon Law Center who had worked on some of Portland's largest cases involving camping stated that Safe Sleep was "the most comprehensive, progressive and deeply rational [policy] that has ever come from City Hall."[19] Supporters of the new policies, who were incensed by the history of sweeps in the city, hoped that the guidelines would eradicate the need for sweeps altogether. So too were then-mayor Charlie Hales and his staff encouraging of the progressive new policies. Announcing the rollout of Safe Sleep, the mayor's chief of staff Josh Alpert argued that the city needed to try out new policy, to experiment. "The simple truth of the matter," Alpert said, "is that we do not yet have enough indoor safe places for people to sleep, which means we must try to accommodate as many people as we can who must sleep outdoors, while we continue to add more indoor space."[20] From the perspective of the mayor and his staff, Safe Sleep was a means of taking the SOE seriously, recognizing it as an extant, on-the-ground emergency requiring an unconventional governing response.

Safe Sleep was extraordinary in that it was the first and only serious attempt at decriminalizing houselessness in Portland's history, if only temporarily. From the get-go, however, the implementation of Safe Sleep faced an uphill battle. The new rules were slow to reach unhoused individuals, who were unsure as to where they could rest. Police also had difficulty educating people about what constituted "safe sleeping" within the SOE guidelines and what was still considered "unsanctioned camping." Further confusing matters, camping in Portland was allowed in many public spaces but was not allowed everywhere and at all times. Understandably, unhoused individuals were confused as to where and when they could sleep and generally took the new policies to mean that camping was now legal almost anywhere in the city.[21] Thus, without clear distinctions between city-owned and other public properties, street sleeping became even more visible within Portland's landscape.

Critics of Safe Sleep denounced the policies for different reasons. One coalition of neighborhood and business groups joined together in suing the city, citing the mayor's lack of authority to unilaterally suspend the city's anti-camping ordinances. These groups argued that Safe Sleep did nothing to solve the houselessness emergency. And, in an important turn of phrase, they argued that Safe Sleep was inhumane in that it "resulted in violence, unhealthy conditions, and pain and suffering for [the city's] most vulnerable residents."[22] The lawsuit was unsuccessful. But the arguments presented in it reflected a broader public sentiment that unhoused people should be encouraged to use indoor shelter in addition to the usual insistence that more affordable housing was needed.

Others supported decriminalizing houselessness but found Safe Sleep to be wholly inadequate. As one advocate-participant on a city government–led Safe Sleep work-session committee put it, "Safe sleep was a net negative. As far as public perception, it was a colossal failure. It wasn't implemented properly. There should have been, across the City, coalition building first. [To do that] you get the police leadership and the union on board. You start town-halling it to the neighborhoods. You connect it to services and public communication. So, you should spend some money . . . [instead, the City] made cards. [Safe Sleep] needed to be better communicated."[23] By most accounts, Safe Sleep came to be criticized as being chaotic and ineffective.

On August 2, 2016, almost six months after Safe Sleep was announced, mayor Hales called an end to the policies. In effect, this meant that individuals living in public could once again be cited for camping in violation of the city's anti-camping ordinance and police would once again be able to ticket groups who were now adjusting to the Safe Sleep guidelines. Still, though Safe Sleep had ended, the SOE remained in effect. And the mayor's ethos concerning camping at that moment was steadfast. Upon announcing the sunset of Safe Sleep, Hales requested there not be a "citywide sweep of homeless camps" and that individuals who lived in peace throughout the city be left alone.[24] "What was true last night is true tonight," the mayor stated the day after the sunset of the Safe Sleep policy. "We do not have enough shelter beds. Some people are going to sleep outside. Some people are going to put tents up."[25] The mayor and other city staff reiterated that even though Safe Sleep had ended, houseless people would continue to be treated compassionately. This was, after all, their primary intention behind Safe Sleep.

Portland's experiment with suspending land uses in order to decriminalize camping was not insignificant. The Safe Sleep period marked a critical shift in the thinking of some government staff about the relevance of self-organized encampments. For instance, during a city council work session on houselessness that took place the first week of Safe Sleep, Josh Alpert articulated the role he saw encampments playing in the SOE and service landscape. "We're offering a structured, organized camping program," Alpert told the council in justifying the loosened camping restrictions of Safe Sleep. Underscoring the newness of working with two unpermitted encampments that had emerged at the beginning of the SOE, he noted there was "an effort to organize and actually create capacity to get people to agree to a code of conduct." It was clear that the city was thinking more structurally about organized encampments. As Alpert remarked at the planning session, "The past two months or so, we've been very hands-on with Hazelnut Grove, on trying to figure out whether even that model was worth exploring to create a system around. I believe the short answer to that is yes. And we've seen really good things come out of Hazelnut Grove. Again, the process of how we got there I know leaves a lot to be desired. But at that time, really trying to figure out just whether it would work or not was what we were interested in doing ... Through some trial and error with the camp itself we, I believe, got to a point that gave us confidence that we should actually get a large group of people together to see if we could build a *system*."[26] Alpert went on to note how officials' engagement with R2DT during this time inspired in the city the confidence that it could "create a pretty comprehensive permit system" to be applied to other encampments. Despite this consideration, Alpert ended by indicating what this new system he was considering was *not*. "I also want to be very clear that it's not envisioned, at least in my mind, that we will have, you know, hundreds of camps around the city. But ... ideally after starting with one, maybe adding a few more around the city."

Although Safe Sleep was largely understood to have done little more than help unhoused people avoid camping citations for six months (as important as that was), hidden from public focus was the slow institutional development of encampment policies during this period. However, while the organizing form of the encampment system was being developed as far back as 2016, the legal means, or the how, was still not articulated within government discourse. For the "proper" model that could be implemented more broadly had not yet been developed.

Formalizing Sanctioned Encampments

TRANSITIONING AWAY FROM SELF-ORGANIZED ENCAMPMENTS

When the Portland city government declared the SOE in October 2015, it was grappling with the consequences of the city's rapid growth over the previous decade. This development made affordable housing increasingly difficult to obtain, rents and median home prices were rising, and wages were not rising along with the rate of inflation. By 2015 nearly half of Portland's unhoused population was categorized as unsheltered, and neither the city nor the county had adequate shelter bed space to meet the need.[27] It was due to these circumstances, coupled with the extant model of self-governing encampments, that the idea of a system of sanctioned encampments gained traction as an alternative to traditional indoor shelter.

Ideas do not always align with social and political favor, however. After the fallout of Safe Sleep, there was not yet a feasible path toward legalizing sanctioned encampments. Though technically permitted by way of conditional review during the SOE, many self-organized encampments that attempted to gain sanction during this time were unsuccessful in obtaining permits and were swept by the city. As a result, almost two years into the SOE, only three sanctioned encampments existed. And all three were the self-organized encampments that had existed prior to the start of the SOE.

While the city tolerated these original sites, Portland's new government was less inclined to support the self-organized model of managing encampments. The reasons for this vary. Partly, this shift was due to the preference of the city and county's collaborative houseless service entity, the Joint Office of Homeless Services (JOHS). JOHS sought to continue expanding traditional indoor shelter space and to get people to use those services during the SOE, particularly as new partnerships came to life between the city and private developers desiring to establish new indoor shelter sites.[28] But it was also partly due to changing preferences of city staff, perhaps influenced by a vocal element of the general public, which saw self-organized encampments as less effective than the nonprofit-led village model.

The city's rather abrupt shift away from supporting self-organized encampments to promoting nonprofit-led villages overlapped with the first mayoral administration to come into office while the SOE was ongoing. In January 2017 Portland's new mayor Ted Wheeler began his first term. Wheeler's administration confronted a housing and houselessness crisis that had become the city's clear policy priority over the previous few years. In contrast to the previous mayor, Wheeler was initially opposed to self-organized encampments and disapproved of Hales' looseness with SOE exceptions for camping. In June 2016, as mayor-elect, Wheeler stated during a public forum on houselessness that while he saw some value in using city-owned property to shelter groups, he indicated that this was only to "get the homeless off the street while bigger projects are in the works."[29] Wheeler was clear that when his administration took over, his approach to dealing with the crisis would not include using public property for "campsites."[30] While "campsites" also meant unsanctioned, single-site tents, Wheeler was clear that he wanted to move away from organized sites like those of R2DT, DV, and HG. In a January 2017 interview, Wheeler said his focus was on "creating as many alternatives to people living on the street or in camps" as possible.[31] At the onset of his term, then, it was unclear how Wheeler's administration would address the burgeoning movement around sanctioned encampments within the broader houselessness services landscape.

Within his first year, Mayor Wheeler seemed to depart from his previous position on sanctioned encampments. At a March 2017 commencement speech for the first city-financed and managed village, KWV, the mayor stated, "We do not see this as an end solution. This is not permanent housing. This is not necessarily supportive housing. But it's a good next step . . . [for] addressing the homelessness situation."[32] Nevertheless, he continued, "assuming that this pilot is successful, then I would expect that we'll see other tiny home villages in the community as well."[33] Though Wheeler still rejected the idea of developing the type of self-organized encampments endorsed by the previous administration, his support for the managed village model was premised on the very groundwork established by the Hales administration, which promoted city-supported tiny house encampments.

The city's preference to no longer enable more self-organized encampments and instead establish a managed village model is rooted in the economic and social differences between the two encampment types. Most markedly, villages receive much more funding from the city and JOHS than self-organized encampments. The newer managed village model is significantly more expensive for the city than self-organized encampments, and is even more expensive than traditional indoor shelter.[34] When KWV opened, for instance, not only was it provided with newly built tiny houses, showers, and a kitchen-commons space, its water and electricity expenses were subsidized by the city as well. HG to this day does not have potable water or electric hookups, while R2DT and DV pay for these utilities on their own. Nonetheless, government staff justified the higher cost of supporting villages in different ways. The original executive director of JOHS put it this way:

> I am trying, when we talk about villages, to recognize that short-term cost savings may not be all that of an important way to think about villages. Because if we get too focused on [short-term costs], we are going to end up paying down the road. Instead of making the necessary investment up front. So, if we are going to have the villages, if we have to upgrade the quality of the sleeping structures now, let's do that. If we are going to need running water, let's do that now. As you do that, it starts to look more similar in cost structure to our [indoor shelter]. But again, you are not doing it because it is cheap. You are doing it because it is a form of shelter that will serve a subset of the population who are otherwise not well served by our shelters.

Though costly, for JOHS it made sense to invest in the managed village model, particularly in respect to the extant model of self-organized encampments. When asked about how self-organized encampments factor into the JOHS's planning for outdoor shelter, the JOHS director weighed the strength of the self-organized model versus the managed village model:

> Not needing a lot of paid staff on site can bring costs down. [But] if the self-governance requirement is such that a big chunk of the population who is out there can't successfully function in the village, then that's a cost. So, you can have a village that has more self-governance, lower costs of operations to the public side. But you have to understand the people who are going to make that work are a subset of the population. So, if you want to serve a higher need population where that level of engagement is too big of a challenge, then you need something that looks like Kenton [Women's Village], where the whole onus of running the village is not on the women who live there. That brings costs up. But those costs are necessary if you want them to be successful.

For the city and county, the financial costs needed to make the village model function well outweighed the potential social costs of supporting self-organizing communities. Implicit in these claims is that self-organized encampments are less deserving of city sponsorship.

To be sure, the city, county, and JOHS recognized value in self-organizing encampments. The original executive director of JOHS acknowledged that the city does not believe that "Kenton [Women's Village] is the only model ... there are others out there already [that] have built their own infrastructure and have demonstrated capacity to serve the people who are in their communities." Particularly in relation to indoor shelter, government staff recognized why self-organized encampments (and villages) can provide better options for unhoused residents seeking shelter. One staff member of Clackamas County (Metropolitan Portland) compared them this way: "Shelters don't make use of any of the strengths of the people in them. They don't even identify the strengths of any of the people in them. They just say, 'oh, you don't have any housing, you need a bed for the night, and see you in the morning—goodbye.' In a village, you are a part of the value of the village. You are the village. You are a cog that keeps the village going. You have responsibility and dignity. And accountability to your fellows. All the things that you lose when you lose housing. You get to build back some of that dignity. And you are providing a service to others by yourselves. No one else is doing it for you." Above all, government staff acknowledged that self-organized encampments provide "a sense of community for the individuals resting there. Flexibility in terms of what is allowed. And also sense of safety, for some," a member of the mayor's staff noted. So too did city staff find value in the "idea of literally building your own thing ... [allowing] individuals to feel a sense of ownership over their structure," which was central to giving many residents of self-organized encampments a sense of purpose.

Government sanctioning necessitates institutional constraints for encampments, however. As the JOHS director went on to say, the encampments have "to be part of the [housing] continuum. And it has to be a partner in the system." And this can be challenging for encampments, he said, because "some of the villages will spring up and organize themselves in opposition to the system. To get the support and sanction of the local government, there has to be this willingness to be a part of this system." Though they were the progenitor of the village model for the city, the utility of *self-organized* encampments nevertheless seemed relevant only to the existing encampments in the city at that time, that is, for DV, R2DT, and HG.

Indeed, the same city staff members who affirmed the benefits of the self-organizing encampment model also indicated their skepticism toward it. Regarding the autonomy of the self-governing encampments, one mayoral staff member rebutted, "You know, Hazelnut can say, 'we are self-governed.' And I am like 'yeah, but we [City Government] pay all your bills.' Or R2DT will say the same thing, but then they will want to ... and this is the funny thing about government, is everybody loves to hate on government. But everybody needs government to pay their bills." In other words, the self-organized encampments were seen not so much as self-governing but as a hidden cost for which the city is accountable and over which it has authority. Similarly, another city staff member working with the villages similarly remarked that although encampments are "self-managed, they're also supported by the City. They're on City-owned property. And they do get some services from the County providers." But beyond those sites, they noted, "there are not a lot of other success stories." From the city's perspective, self-organized encampments were a nice thought, holding a special place in Portland's history, but ultimately one that was not all that useful in helping unhoused people become stable.

It was not just the city that was souring on self-organized encampments. Portland's transition toward the village model was likely influenced by a portion of the public that found fault in the self-organized encampments as well. And no self-organized encampment was more contested than HG. Many of its housed neighbors understood the site to be an illegal taking of space. One homeowner neighboring HG explained that "the neighborhood was against the encampment because it is an illegal dwelling, an illegal taking of property." Many neighboring residents considered the encampment to be illegal because it lacked a formal right to the property, despite the city allowing the encampment to operate there. "I don't think it is right for the City to turn over publicly held property to the homeless camp," another neighborhood resident said. "It belongs to all of Portland." Instead of accepting it as an emergency shelter, many neighbors requested the space be vacated and put to a more "public" use.

The arguments in opposition to HG exceeded its legality alone, however. Moral objections were made about the residents themselves and how they use the space. One homeowner neighboring HG believed that its residents had "no intention of moving on from the encampment." This particular neighbor understood residents of HG as being undeserving of a place to stay. "I've met these people at our neighborhood meetings and they are quite content to live there forever, do whatever the hell they want. Work if they want, not work if they want," she said. Another homeowner in the Overlook neighborhood doubted the sincerity of HG residents' participation in the Neighborhood Association meetings. "[HG residents] do not have the best interest of the neighborhood. They are only interested in themselves. [Housed] individuals in the neighborhood are for the good of the neighborhood. Hazelnut people are not. They care about themselves." In this way, HG residents were rendered unfit for self-governance, painted as unable to conceive of—and make decisions for—the public "good," an ethical feature of liberalism that has for centuries been thought to be inherent to property-owning citizens.

Some neighborhood residents also implied that self-organized encampments like HG miss the mark of legitimate property stewardship because of their economic relation with property. What constitutes legitimate use of property, expressed one homeowner, was one's ability to own or rent it. "I have property because I purchased property. If you want to rent property, you can rent property," she said. By this metric, HG residents could only be deficient, as they did not own or rent the property. This same homeowner continued by arguing that the fact of "being a human being does not give you a right to property. You have to pay for it in some manner . . . the fact that you are human does not mean that you have a right to squat on land. No, not in this country." Similarly, another neighborhood homeowner felt that "it wasn't fair" that individuals "are able to simply say, 'I am homeless, I don't have to pay for property and be part of it all.'" That houseless people "choose" to live in emergency encampments, to this homeowner, reflected the assumption that "[unhoused people] take advantage of the situation by not playing by the rules." To the extent that neighborhood homeowners believed the encampment to be an illegitimate way in which property could be used, the encampment residents were seen as "undemocratic" in their "taking" of property.

All of these aspects of opposition underlay the conflict between HG, OKNA and the city over the encampment's hesitation to sign a good neighbor agreement with the neighborhood association. Shortly after HG moved into its site in the Overlook neighborhood in 2015, OKNA and the encampment began "good neighbor" negotiations. The informal agreement between the two groups was mediated by the city. But the talks lasted for only a few months before falling apart. Different reasons were given as to why they did. The chair of OKNA suggested that HG was going behind the neighborhood association's back and worked "with the City to develop a permit outside of the good neighbor agreement" after initial talks had started between them, a move that OKNA members did not approve of. In turn, HG residents suggested that OKNA only wanted to talk about HG leaving the site during the talks and not about how to integrate the encampment into the neighborhood. In response to the talks falling through, the communications director for the mayor's office stated they would forego an agreement because "the well had already been poisoned in terms of the relations between the neighbors and the camp."[35]

The reasons why the talks fell apart, however, were less important than why they were initiated in the first place. Many housed neighbors in Overlook objected to the encampment moving in without their consent. The then-chair of OKNA mentioned that he was upset that HG formed themselves without first coming to interact with the neighbors. That HG wouldn't talk to OKNA "created animosity from the get-go," he said. "If you don't engage with the neighbors upfront, you are going to have problems."

Other neighborhood homeowners who were privy to the good neighbor discussions observed the process differently. One homeowner mentioned she "didn't feel like the neighborhood was negotiating in good faith." She suggested the talks were somewhat one-sided, more in line with the rhetorical position of OKNA. "There was an idea that the people living at Hazelnut were not participating in the process in a way that was okay with the neighborhood association," she said. And because of that, she felt as if "a system was being set up that was making it very difficult for the residents of Hazelnut to succeed in the process."

In the end, it was HG who backed out of the good neighbor talks because of this seeming one-sidedness. One HG resident stated that "it's off-putting" to hear OKNA say "we don't want you here, we don't want you here." As such, HG continued conversations with the city about the encampment's future without OKNA. In response, one homeowner stated, "I don't think that individuals in Hazelnut Grove have any intention of being controlled." For this homeowner, a good neighbor agreement was a disciplinary mechanism for OKNA. That is, homeowners felt the agreement was necessary to ensure houseless people would live by certain standards imposed by the neighborhood association.

The failed good neighbor talks reinvigorated OKNA's opposition to HG remaining situated in the Overlook neighborhood. Shortly after the talks ended, the chair of OKNA's board wrote a press release to publicize how HG was "excluding" OKNA homeowners from the good neighbor agreement. With OKNA's hopes dashed for participating in good neighbor talks, the chair renewed OKNA's "call for the [City] to remove Hazelnut Grove from its current site as soon as possible," arguing again that the encampment was illegally placed.[36] OKNA and HG never again attempted to negotiate a good neighbor agreement, despite encampment residents becoming more involved in neighborhood association affairs.

It is important to note that not all Overlook neighborhood homeowners opposed HG. Indeed, there were a handful of individuals who donated their time and labor to help the encampment. Some supporters felt that HG was "a practical, if inelegant, solution to getting people into safe living situations when there isn't enough permanent housing for people." Other supporters liked that the encampment was self-governing. "I think that if we normalize [that model] . . . it is good for people to humanize the situation," said one neighbor. Therefore, a small coalition of neighbors contested what the neighborhood organization was attempting to do. Said another neighbor, "I support [HG] to do what it takes to live down there. I am more interested in the collaboration of a community" than bringing an eviction upon the encampment. And it was not just HG alone that found support from neighbors and the community. Many other encampments had volunteer laborers helping with landscaping, building, and donating resources.

The conflict between HG and OKNA resonates more broadly with all of the city's self-governing encampments, even those that never became sanctioned. Perhaps due to HG's struggles to assert their right to self-manage, many homeowners neighboring encampments came to see the then-emerging "managed" village model as more legitimate. One neighbor of HG who was opposed to that particular encampment nevertheless indicated their satisfaction with the city's newly opened women's village. "[KWV] is great. You have [a nonprofit provider] there, and they are connecting residents to job training, and substance use treatment if they need it, and helping to find housing." When asked about producing more encampments in the city, this same homeowner noted that "if the City said . . . they are going to do all things [for HG] like they did in [KWV], that is something I think the neighborhood would rally behind. I would support that." Another homeowner neighboring KWV more directly indicated the perceived differences in accountability between the two models. "People don't want to hear that people are self-governing. If there are problems, who do you sue? You are not going to sell the [self-governing] idea to folks. It's different when you are paying people to work there, like Kenton [Women's Village]." While it is true that not all interviewed homeowners saw the value of *any* type of encampment, the support for the tiny house village model over that of self-organized encampments was clear.

Such sentiments catalyzed the push for self-organized encampments to become city-sponsored villages. In late 2018, Portland's government declared its intention to relocate HG out of its original place in the Overlook neighborhood to a new site with water and electric hookups; it would, in addition, provide new tiny houses.[37] These talks began in early 2018, when JOHS staff met with members of HG to hear their ideas for what they would like in a new village, and crucially, where it should be located. The result was St. John's Village, which opened in May 2021. At the commencement of St John's Village, various city and county commissioners whose planning went into the development received mention in Mayor Wheeler's speech. "Look at what we have created! This village-model shelter is not just a dignified place for participants to stay and receive the services they need to end their houselessness; this is an attractive addition to the neighborhood," the mayor said.[38] Now the village model was not a blighted emergency service, but one that, it was hoped, would integrate into the neighborhoods of the city more smoothly. The appeal of villages also related to what was being left behind, self-organizing communities, whose struggles continued as we will see in the next chapter.

As the COVID-19 pandemic hit the United States in March 2020, one of the ways in which Portland's government attempted to protect unhoused Portlanders was to build multiple outdoor *self-organized* encampments.[39] As previously mentioned, with the help of R2DT representatives, the city funded the development of three new temporary encampments under the banner of "Creating Conscious Communities with People Outside," or C3PO. Each of these villages had approximately sixty tiny homes and government-approved staff helping with housing placements. A year into the pandemic, the self-organized C3PO encampments were no longer self-managed and instead were run by nonprofits as the city switched its service providers.

Reflecting upon the lessons learned by developing the C3PO villages, JOHS endorsed the village model, noting that "not every unsheltered person is willing or able to live in a congregate shelter environment. We believe our shelter system should offer a range of models . . . This village model provides individuals experiencing homelessness with shelter, increased safety, and stability."[40] Along with the praise for villages, the city staff in Portland's Homelessness Reduction Program also shared that having to "set up temporary emergency shelters due to the pandemic . . . has allowed us to start developing a formal framework for creating and operating permanent outdoor shelters."[41] To build on what the former mayoral administration had hoped would become a "system," the new administration was now also on board with legalizing the PEM. Doing so would enable the City to protect the momentum gained under the SOE to establish a managed village model.

REALIZING THE NEW VILLAGE MODEL

By early 2021, the city government's general stance on villages was moving beyond mere support to a desire to allow encampments to become legal land uses. There was a problem, however, in that the clock on the housing SOE period was winding down. The SOE was the legal tool affording encampments to be sited. If the SOE was not renewed and was allowed to lapse, encampments and villages would once again no longer be in accordance with land use ordinances. Despite the continued sanctioning of encampments, the city used the pending conclusion of the SOE to press for the legal protection of not only the existing encampments but of the village model itself.

The formal incorporation of the village model as an accepted city land use was not accomplished overnight. The idea that villages should be integrated into the city's land use codes was evident to the previous administration as well as the original executive director of the JOHS, who, at least as early as 2018, recognized that the impending end to the SOE would be a crucial moment of change through which it would be possible to establish a legal means toward protecting sanctioned encampments. As they put it, "because the SOE will not be with us forever, we want the gains [of encampments] to last. So, we need to do the institutional reform during this period that it is going to take to sustain it. We needed to look at the codes and zoning to allow ourselves to have made the changes necessary to go beyond the state of emergency." And it was this type of structural planning throughout the SOE that eventually brought the city government to its decision to amend zoning ordinances three years later.

By March 2021 Portland's city council had publicly workshopped its plan, which capitalized on the land use easements enabled by the SOE. What emanated from this process was the policy initiative "Shelter to Housing Continuum" (STHC), which sought to update the city code by bringing encampment land use and building requirements into accord with many zoning categories throughout the city. Then, on April 28, 2021, the city council unanimously approved the amendments in the STHC plan, officially revising the city code and bringing Ordinance no. 190381 to life. While STHC addressed issues beyond encampments, such as the citing of traditional indoor shelters and vehicle sleeping, significantly, the ordinance added a category to the city code that enabled sanctioned encampments and villages to legally operate.

Title 33 is Portland's city code for planning and zoning regulating all land uses in the city. The STHC amended Title 33 by adding an additional category of shelter called "outdoor shelter."[42] This added mass shelter and short-term shelter to the previous community service use and restructured the relationship between encampments and the city's regulation of space. First, it exempted approval of outdoor shelters from extended design review.[43] This allowed new developments to bypass what was previously a longer conditional use review, a process that primarily examined the development of permanent buildings, not temporary or changing structures.[44] Now, encampments within all zoning categories—except open spaces and some industrial zones—did not need conditional use review. Second, the amendment waived "system development charges," the fees for new applications, lowering costs and speeding up approval for new shelters. Finally, it formalized something that had already been implemented in practice throughout the city's encampments, namely, that all new encampments must be operated by local government or a nonprofit agency. Amending Title 33 did not only create a quicker and cheaper path for siting new encampments. Significantly, it provided the needed legal protection for encampments so that they could continue operating after the SOE.

Upon casting their final "yes" votes in the meeting to amend the zoning code, Portland city commissioners took a moment to discuss the need for the amendment changes. Commissioner Ryan stated, "Right now, we face unprecedented emergency on our streets. And as the number of chronically houseless individuals has grown . . . our current response is inadequate, as our work to site shelters has been hampered by restrictive zoning codes."[45] Commissioner Hardesty added that she was "proud" of the sanctioned encampments that paved the way for the vote. Amending the land uses to accommodate sanctioned encampments, she noted, provided the "opportunity for people to be able to live with dignity on our streets, while [the City] continues to use every resource to make permanent housing that people can afford to live in a reality." Finally, Mayor Wheeler emphasized why the city's codification of the outdoor shelter amendments was so important. "These ordinances give us the foundation we need to continue our work to address homelessness without the need to be perpetually relying on emergency powers . . . The changes that these ordinances make give us the flexibility to do so [beyond the SOE]." The commissioners' comments reflected the approving sentiment that changing land use ordinances would help make sanctioned camping legitimate, a formal part of the city's push to house individuals in a stable fashion.

Less than two months after Ordinance 190381 was passed, the city announced its intention to develop a network of city-sponsored and nonprofit-managed "safe rest villages." With more locations potentially available as a result of the land use amendment, the newly proposed SRVs could now be sited more easily, as they would be distributed more equitably throughout the city. The new villages would be organized through the managed model, not self-organized sites. The reason for this, the city's policy advisor for the SRVs noted, was because of how difficult it was to get the public to understand the differences between the managed model of the SRVs and those of self-organized encampments. "The biggest thing that I had to fight when setting up the safe rest villages, [was] everybody point[ing] to those self-managed, C3PO camps, saying, 'You're going to bring that to my neighborhood. Absolutely not,' kicking and screaming. 'That can't happen.'" With a lot of groundwork, the city was able to assuage the public's concerns that the SRVs were identical to the C3PO encampments, and by summer 2023, roughly two years after being announced, the SRV sites were selected, developed, and opened for use.

Perpetuating the Continuum

The City of Portland finds itself at the forefront of a liberal progressive approach to sheltering individuals living without housing. What the city has achieved by way of accommodating unhoused peoples' desires to establish community while stabilizing themselves is laudable. The government's policymaking is notable for adapting to the circumstances of what unhoused communities desire throughout their time of housing precarity. To think that organized encampment communities will now apply and undergo expedited review for new developments after the SOE ends would have been almost unimaginable before the emergency period began. It is an unusual outcome of the relational governance that ultimately created the PEM.

Whether this achievement marks progress for houselessness policymaking, however, is less clear. For it is difficult to disentangle what ultimately marks progress and what is merely politically progressive in this case. While it is clear that encampment spaces serve as temporary emergency sites for stabilizing individuals, the encampment model that the city has chosen—the managed village model—ensures that the very rights and relations of property that enable the shelter-to-housing continuum stay exactly as they are: a cyclical loop of precarious housing situations, whereby unhoused individuals get into temporary shelter before getting a chance at temporary or permanent supportive housing and sometimes back again into shelters, on the streets, or doubled up with family and friends. In other words, the city's push to help unhoused people through the shelter-to-housing continuum necessitates that precariously housed individuals compete *within* the liberal model of propertied citizenship.

The primary goal of providing people shelter, of course, is to help individuals become stable enough to move on to permanent and safer housing conditions. And many *are* fortunate enough to quickly secure temporary housing or, even better, more permanent housing. But the reality for so many unhoused people is that securing stable and long-term forms of traditional housing is often contingent upon successfully maneuvering through a web of relations of property that are not as obvious as one might expect. For instance, encampment residents struggle against a housed public that insists upon defining how houseless life *ought* to be, rather than how houseless life *is* for encampment residents. Even when chronically unhoused residents exit an encampment and find temporary housing stability, they may take years or even decades to secure permanent traditional housing. Though a necessary path to take in order to push for whatever opportunities may open up to become housing-stable, unhoused peoples' struggle through this process to find long-term housing stability can seem futile.

The shelter-to-housing continuum is an apt description of the nightmarish process in which a growing portion of unhoused people find themselves. According to JOHS data, in fiscal year 2020, nearly 18 percent of individuals using county-provided homeless services exited into permanent housing and *returned again* to use homeless services within twenty-one months.[46] In fiscal year 2021, the number of individuals returning from permanent housing to homeless services increased to 25 percent.[47] That is, one out of every four individuals who exit houselessness into some type of permanent housing return to being unhoused within less than two years. Perhaps, then, it is more apt to speak of a shelter-to-housing-to-shelter continuum. While JOHS or other government agencies do not keep data on why individuals return to houselessness, interviews conducted with encampment residents who have left shelter, got into housing, and returned again to shelter indicate that it is simply too expensive and that there are not enough resources available for the needs of the unhoused population. Individuals exit from houselessness into permanent housing units that are predominately obtained through the private housing market as public housing has virtually been eradicated from the United States over the last four decades.[48] Even when partially subsidized, the ability to meet rent obligations can often be overwhelming for those with extensive health care costs, those who have families, or those who have been out of the labor market for some time. It seems that for many, the PEM functions as a crucial backstop for their return to houselessness.

Given that the private ownership model germane to liberalism necessitates that unhoused people function within the tenets of property rights and relations, it should be no shock that a continuous cycle of unhoused people find themselves newly, or once again, housing insecure. For the relations of property within liberal capitalism remain unaffected by many progressive initiatives aimed at ameliorating such inequities. This is not to say that unhoused people have not benefited from organizing themselves in encampment communities. Indeed, as the next chapter shows, the city's self-organized encampments effectively model a collective form of property management that convenes communities that, whether intentionally or not, challenge specific aspects of the ownership model within liberal property systems. Yet, while the collective management of property may appear to challenge liberal property *values*, as I will also show, these collective modes of managing property do not effectively transform the ownership model. As such, the enactments of collectively managed property begin to illustrate how liberal property institutions, though legally justified, effectively inhibit unhoused peoples' self-determination.

CHAPTER 3

The Challenge of Collectively Managed Property

I met Nicole when interviewing residents at Dignity Village (DV) in 2018.[1] A white woman then in her late fifties, Nicole told me about her life before arriving at the village. She was born in Portland but raised and schooled in southern Oregon. After college, she returned to Portland, where she worked for nearly two decades. She became unhoused for the first time in 2008 and had been living unsheltered for nearly two years before coming to DV. Throughout those years, she had different means of sheltering. She couch-surfed with friends for short periods of time but would never stay long because she "really tried not to burden them" by overstaying her welcome. She camped in parks and wooded areas, where in a few different instances her belongings were vandalized and stolen. And she also slept in abandoned houses in one of Portland's neighboring suburbs. As a result of doing so, she was arrested three times for trespassing—in one case, she was accused of burglarizing the abandoned house that she and others were sleeping in. It was around this time that a friend told her about DV. About a month after being added to the waitlist, she was finally invited into the village.

When talking about her experience at DV, Nicole spoke with fondness about her time there. At the time of our interview, Nicole was the chair of DV's board. The village chair facilitates weekly membership meetings by ensuring that decision-making happens in accordance with its bylaws. Based on my time at DV, it was clear to me that Nicole was not only at ease with her administrative role there but seemed to enjoy it. Others, in turn, appreciated her leadership. She was highly respected in the encampment, a respect earned from years of experience working with unhoused people. Her experiential and institutional knowledge of DV was vast, the type of expertise that comes from leading sixty residents at Portland's oldest self-governing encampment for a few years.

When I spoke with Nicole about the self-governing process at the village, she noted its importance for organizing the space. Though she felt connected to the village because it gave her a tiny house to sleep in, what was most notable to her about it was the feeling of pride that comes with being a "self-supporting" membership-based community. She felt agency in creating the conditions of her living environment. The fact that DV is self-governing means that "we get to decide how we are going to live . . . [because] membership makes the rules." The "bottom line" with the self-governing process, she said, is that residents have "better self-esteem, better self-worth when we are part of the decision-making." Nicole's sense of accountability and control over the function of the encampment is something quite rare for communities of unhoused people.[2]

As we will see, the benefits afforded to residents of self-governing encampments are many compared with other forms of shelter. As opposed to traditional indoor shelter and even the managed village model presented in the previous chapter, self-managed encampments retain much control over how the site functions. Yet, the extent to which Portland's encampment residents are able to manage self-governed sites as they see fit is limited in crucial ways. In order to understand the benefits and constraints more clearly, more context about self-governing encampments is useful.

Each of Portland's three self-managed encampments—Dignity Village, R2DT, and Hazelnut Grove—can be understood as both a legal entity capable of contracting with others and a collective of individuals responsible for managing the everyday operations and security of their residents. Portland's encampments contract use-of-space agreements with the city government that allow the collectives to govern the operations of these spaces themselves. The use-of-space agreements provide residents with rather basic use rights to the properties. For example, R2DT's land use agreement stipulates simply that the "user is allowed to enter and use the [encampment] and those City-owned amenities placed in the Use Area, for the sole purpose of operating a temporary rest area."[3] Here "User" refers to the encampment itself as understood through its nonprofit status and not to specific individuals themselves. The use of space agreements also demarcate the length of time encampments enjoy use rights to the property, usually for two years. The majority of the contract, however, protects the city against liability, by stipulating limitations on improvements to the property, waiving the city government's liability for damage or injury caused by encampment residents' use of the properties, and requiring that expenses for property maintenance to the sites are self-incurred by the encampments themselves.[4] Given how the contracts are mostly structured to protect the city government, the use rights in these agreements are rather vague, leaving residents' rights to property less defined and more flexible than those traditionally held by property owners or lessees.

Although the set of use rights for Portland's encampments are relatively undefined, there is one key use right the encampments explicitly do *not* enjoy. The encampments lack possessory rights. In general, possessory rights to property allow tenants the right of "exclusive possession," meaning that "tenants have the right to exclude all others, including the landlord (except for rights under the lease to inspect or repair) from the land."[5] In short, landlord-tenant laws provide lessees the right of exclusive possession for their own security and privacy. And although the restriction on encampments' rights of exclusive possession in Portland had always been standard practice, it became formally prohibited by law in summer 2019. It was then that the State of Oregon passed House Bill 2916, which mandated that encampments not be subject to the state's landlord-tenant protections.[6] This has both its perks and its downsides.

Without being subject to landlord-tenant laws, Portland's self-governing encampments function by securing each member's residency through majority consensus. That is, a residents' ability to use these spaces is dependent upon the community agreeing to the individual staying there, rather than through a legal rights relationship (contract). In this way, many residents among the self-governing encampments agreed that the process is one that is fairer, more democratic. And the fact that encampments do not enjoy

FIGURE 6. A "no camping" sign attached to the fence bounding the Hazelnut Grove encampment situated in the background.

rights of exclusive possession also means that when residents are voted out, removals are not subject to legal evictions and therefore do not involve state records noting them. As such, self-governing encampment communities negotiate "evictions" on their own terms. The upside to this is that the state (sheriff or courts) does not intervene on matters of evictions, something that nearly all residents applaud. And given the discursive approach toward handling bans or removals, in addition to restorative justice approaches that help keep members within the encampments as much as possible, removals of members at self-governing encampments are consensus based.

At the same time, not being subject to landlord-tenant laws creates very particular constraints around enforcing collectively made decisions. Such constraints were on Nicole's mind during our interview. Although "we get to make the rules," she observed, it can also be a burden when "we have to enforce those rules." Enforcing rules becomes particularly difficult in membership-based communities when decisions about the members are contested. Because encampments like DV "don't have the legal authority to kick anyone out, it can be a nightmare" to secure the safety of the community, she noted. As we will see, for self-organized encampments, the right to self-govern can be incommensurable with the residents' rights to safety and privacy. As such, the benefits derived from governing collectively cannot always protect residents' personal liberty rights. In liberalism, propertied citizenship guarantees individuals this right above all others. And this is precisely the problem.

Proper Citizenship and the Right Not to Be Excluded

Within the American liberal tradition, citizenship is predominantly realized through the protection of individualized rights.[7] Primary among these is that of property ownership and the pursuit to acquire property.[8] Historically, American citizenship was constituted through property ownership itself, though this right was available only to elite, white males.[9] Property ownership was politically significant in that it engendered an individual's capacity for self-governance and autonomy more broadly.[10] While property ownership itself no longer defines citizenship, property rights and the liberal values associated with ownership remain prominent in shaping citizenship privileges in liberal democracies today.

What follows from this is that claims for rights and privileges by property-insecure people are less likely to be taken seriously or even protected. Without a secure interest in property—that is, in *not* having legal rights to access propertied spaces—unhoused people are denied citizenship privileges essential for securing their livelihoods. Further, the model of propertied citizenship enables those with secure interests in property to leverage their power against those without secure interests in landed property through economic, political, and legal means. For the American "paradigm of propertied citizenship," as Ananya Roy argues, recognizes only formal rights of property that renders informal claims to space illegible, claims for rights that define property insecure people as being outside of "proper" citizenship.[11] In short, to benefit from propertied citizenship is to have one's political and economic interests protected, if not promoted, over those lacking a secure interest right to property.

To view liberal citizenship and thus *propertied* citizenship as merely a rights-bearing status, however, obscures additional constraints inherent in this model. Citizenship is more than a legal status protecting individuals' liberty rights. It is also an ongoing and active process of being or becoming political. Citizenship is cultivated through routine and everyday social practices, which are in turn evaluated through normative ideals of propriety in liberal society.[12] In this way, citizenship is a legally defined status that is also socially "enacted," albeit unevenly in different historical-geographic contexts and shaped through various relations of power and domination.[13] To enact citizenship through social practice enables individuals to claim rights (legal or moral) they feel are not respected by individuals, the state, or law, to draw attention to the inequities of a legislative and normative ordering of social life within liberalism. It is a means, therefore, of contesting legal standings and normative measures that render individuals as improper political subjects.

If the key normative features of liberal citizenship such as autonomy and self-governance are realized through access to and ownership of property, the right for unhoused individuals to exist in some space remains contingent on enactments of political subjectivity to secure a place to be. Accordingly, unhoused people must constantly justify their occupation of propertied spaces—like public squares, malls, parks, and even self-governing encampments—while owners and renters otherwise appear settled in their rightful claims to occupy property. It is precisely these conditional protections of citizenship that liberalism reinforces for property insecure people. In other words, within liberalism, the political geography of where unhoused people necessarily must exist in space matters enormously for determining what the "proper" use of propertied space can be.

C.B. Macpherson pointed to this incommensurability long ago, arguing that the primary contradiction of liberal-democratic life is found in "the difficulty of reconciling the liberal property right with that equal effective right of all individuals to use and develop their capacities."[14] For individuals to recover their capacities as self-determining beings, and to enjoy a "fully human life," Macpherson argued, necessitates that there be a more democratic right to property within liberalism: an "individual right *not* to be excluded by others from the use or benefit of some thing."[15] For the property insecure, to have such a right would ensure that they would not be denied access to necessary resources that provide them stability and the basic means for their survival. The right not to be excluded provides a powerful conceptual counter to the private authority invested in the liberal ownership model.

What the right not to be excluded looks like in practice is anything but straightforward. One ideal relationship with landed resources that could allow for such a right is popularly found in the notion of "the commons." Scholars have particularly touted the commons for its potential to overcome the exclusionary nature of the private ownership model, as well as its potential to avoid the control of an overregulatory state and to establish individuals' autonomy over some place through more democratic relations within liberal capitalism.[16] As an ideal, the commons or commonly held property offers what is fundamentally lacking in liberal democratic capitalism: the right not to be excluded from resources necessary for human flourishing. And much work within critical geographic and urban scholarship seeks to realize these aspirations, for example by drawing attention to the restrictive control over resources germane to the private ownership model exhibited within the contemporary neoliberal city.[17] From this point of view, commonly accessed property provides a means of bringing people back in from "the outside" of property, to include them once again within it.

An idealized commons is a useful normative model for forming political goals around autonomy-enhancing actions. Yet, there is a certain risk in treating common property as "an autonomous space."[18] As Blomley argues, idealizations of the commons often miss the relational implications of how "the experiential force of exclusion and the salience of the right not to be excluded are socially differentiated."[19] That is, despite the potential benefits of not being excluded from a common resource, the land on which an encampment sits, for instance, it is those same relations producing property norms and regulations that can also reify the exclusionary logics of property and possession. While the actions or practices of "commoning" work to realize the sociopolitical right *not* to be excluded, these practices often become bound through the legal limits of property, conflicting with the spatial demarcations of owned landed resources, despite a collective's intentions to include a broader public.[20]

Less attention has been given to the rights and duties related to commonly or collectively managed and accessed properties in terms of how these relations of property shape political agency, especially for those whose existence is made precarious because they are *within*, not excluded *from*, liberal property systems. As commonly managed properties, Portland's self-governing encampments illustrate critical tensions undergirding collectively accessible spaces of shelter. For these collectively managed spaces suffer from the same limitations that all "commons" do: the authority of the collective can exclude individuals from sites of resources.

As this chapter will show, rather paradoxically, the lack of the right to exclude denies residents at collectively managed encampments a guaranteed right to remain within encampment spaces themselves. And what follows from this is that encampment residents ultimately are not free to "eliminate their subordination" and remain free from control by others over themselves—an ethical foundation of liberal ideology.[21] It is important to understand the struggles of Portland's encampments, then, in order to see not only how collectively organized models of property struggle to maintain themselves within the dominant model of liberalism but how resident's enactments of citizenship meant to realize the benefits of self-governance are rendered improper within and contingent on liberal property relations. Critically, it also begins to show us why liberal property systems and the rights that structure the relations surrounding resources require continuous justification.

Self-Governing Encampments

REALIZING THE BENEFITS OF SELF-GOVERNANCE

Self-governing encampments are organized with the intent of providing unhoused people access to a common resource or good: a safer place to sleep. They are open to the unhoused public and are collectively managed, making them akin to a "commons property." But they may be defined more accurately as collectively managed *state* properties, ostensibly marking them as open to all of the unhoused public, as the properties on which most of the city's encampments sit are owned by the municipal government. Although government owned, they are not public spaces in the sense that all members of the public are allowed to recreate there. Unlike publicly accessible green spaces, for example, the city government requires use-of-space agreements for each encampment. Usually, these are entered into with the nonprofit associated with the encampment, which then enables managing authority over the space itself to the collective residing there. The nonprofits often comprise the members of the encampments themselves, along with a few outside board members. As the contracted managers of these government-owned properties, residents of Portland's self-governing encampments decide to whom these resources are available. In theory, self-governing encampments are open to all individuals needing this resource for shelter stability; in practice, however, they remain "limited to members of the group, but exclusively vis-à-vis the outside world."[22] Self-governing encampments are thus like collectively managed properties that apply commoning *practices*, in that no unhoused person can be denied access to these spaces assuming accommodations are available.

Portland's three original encampments operate as collectively managed spaces. DV, R2DT, and HG are collectively managed in the sense that resident members decide on how the space will function. Self-governing or self-managed encampments organize themselves around collectively constructed rules of conduct, codes laid out by encampment-specific bylaws. Residents decide who performs what type of labor and when, as well as how various laboring initiatives contribute to the collective. And existing members collectively work with incoming residents to help them establish connections to better understand encampment culture. In what can so often be an isolating and fragmented existence for people living without stable shelter, such collectively organized spaces model what alternatives to traditional shelter, and even the ownership model of property, can look like.

It may not be surprising that almost every individual residing in a self-managed encampment who I interviewed articulated how the process of self-governance benefited them throughout their struggles with housing precarity. Most immediately, encampments provide a sense of security that housed people often take for granted. To be able to "lock the door on your tiny house is everything," as one DV resident put it. Feeling secure that you will still have your belongings at the end of the day, as a HG resident shared, "gives you the one thing that everyone else in society gets to have, which is a sense of ownership over something." The relative security that encampments provide for their residents inspires a sense of dignity that is often lost when staying in traditional shelters. This is true even of managed villages. As one Kenton Women's Village (KWV) resident noted, the village helped her reconnect with her sense of self again. "Once you feel like you are nothing, it is hard to get your sense of worth back," she said. When women would come into the village, she noted, many seemed to be down on themselves, grappling with feelings that "stem from relationships, abuse, from being on the streets and feeling and looking like crud." In this way, encampments enable people "to be together in a situation which gives them strength."

FIGURE 7. The home of a Hazelnut Grove resident.

Although encampment residents use these spaces primarily for their own grounding and stability, the longer they remain, the more likely it is they will become involved in actively shaping the conditions of their own environment. When individuals are introduced to the self-governing model, they often feel a sense of agency through collective participation in the group. One DV resident recalled seeing a chronically unhoused person come into the village and eventually gravitate toward participating in the governing process there. The individual was "houseless for 22 years prior to coming to [DV]," he said. "They went from not trusting or speaking to anyone, to conversing and participating within the village before he obtained his housing." To this resident's eye, the self-governing model helped to ensure that even the most property insecure were able to "have a place . . . that they are counted and that they are seen." Many residents lauded the self-governing model for how it naturally draws in individuals who tend to feel that their voice does not matter and shared how engaging in small ways allows them to shape their immediate living environment.

The self-governing process, therefore, is a means to engage residents in the immediacy of direct action politics. For instance, one HG resident specifically appreciated how the encampment had organized itself. "We dictate ourselves how the daily [routine] goes and how things are run. The people living here are deciding what directions their lives are going to take. And it's not some outside source dictating that you have got to do A, B, and C to stay here, and if you don't, well, good luck finding your way otherwise." Instead, many encampment residents felt that being part of the collective inspires cooperation. For instance, a resident at DV noted his purpose at the village was "not so much to do what is good for [yourself], but for the community." He went on, "I never thought that way before [coming to DV]. Everything that I do now is based around what's good for the village. It's all about what is good for the village." For many, then, these spaces engender a sense of belonging and inclusion, and for some, a sense of responsibility and accountability within the informal relations of the site.

As should already be clear, perhaps the most significant feature of self-governing encampments is their ability to give a sense of agency to residents who otherwise feel they have none. Though it may seem simple or quotidian, to convene community in these small ways can be socially and politically affirming. The political engagement within self-governing encampments, as Tony Sparks observes, can produce "localized practices of informal citizenship and governance that simultaneously rejects and seeks to remedy homeless stereotypes of pathology and dependence." Such informal enactments of citizenship work to "resist stereotypes of homeless unfitness for rational self-governance by producing a self-consciously democratic and collectively operated space."[23] In this way, self-governing encampments materialize as more than "homeless shelters," and not only as inclusionary spaces but as political spaces of possibility.

Unhoused people's political agency is, of course, not relegated to the spaces of encampments alone. Residents enact practices of citizenship by making claims to unrealized rights and privileges through their relations with individuals and entities outside the spaces of the encampment as well. Indeed, it is in the spaces where interactions with neighbors, neighborhood and business associations, and local government happen that encampment residents in Portland make claims for, and are denied, the privileges of liberal citizenship.

Due to the relative stability of life in Portland's houseless encampments, some residents have become politically active within their neighborhoods and throughout the city more broadly. For one R2DT member, participating in the decision-making process within the encampment inspired her to engage in politics outside of the encampment. She was encouraged because of the interactions she had during the encampment's weekly meetings, engagement that eventually led to her becoming a board member there. During her early time at R2DT, she "was the quiet type, just doing what I was supposed to do" as an encampment resident. "As far as talking with the city [government]," she said, "I didn't think I would ever speak at City Hall or go and meet the mayor. But here I am, [going to] City meetings, to good neighbor agreement meetings, neighborhood association meetings, meetings with the police. I would have never done that before." The result, she reflected, "opened me up and I have found my voice to say, 'hey, you know what? This is wrong.'" The very process by which encampments democratically organize themselves empowers many residents to want to change the inequities they see within the broader community.

Actively engaging in wider community or government affairs is difficult to do when houseless. Despite the barriers, many of those I met in the encampments engaged in some level of civic or political engagement to try and change the inequities that have contributed to their housing precarity in the first place. For instance, one resident of R2DT, who has since moved into traditional housing, was motivated by the R2DT mission to effect social and political change outside of the encampment. He recalled that living at R2DT opened his eyes to "want to do more to help people in the similar situations." During his nine-month stay at R2DT, therefore, he began organizing for the rights of unhoused people. He volunteered with the national Poor People's Campaign, was active in organizing at the state capital for Oregon's Homeless Bill of Rights, and supported local groups in Portland advocating for the rights of houseless people, such as Sisters of the Road. Local activism was not uncommon among those at HG either, as many residents met one another at different political actions throughout the city.

The case of HG is particularly illuminating in terms of how self-governing communities integrate themselves into wider political communities in the city. Many residents of HG attended the Overlook Neighborhood Association (OKNA) meetings from 2016 to 2018, as mentioned in the introduction. But their reception there was often controversial, as the official position of OKNA on the existence of HG was clearly in opposition to the site. This makes the contribution of HG residents to OKNA that much more remarkable.

Shortly after the unsuccessful attempt by the neighborhood association to remove HG, one resident of HG was voted in as an OKNA board member. Her initial reason for running for a board position was to defend the right of the encampment to exist against a largely hostile neighborhood association.

However, as a voting member of the association, she advocated for unhoused peoples' rights beyond those concerned directly with her own encampment (HG) and tried to use this platform to shape OKNA's planning process more broadly. Along with others in the neighborhood, she helped establish an association committee for houselessness issues whose purpose was to conduct better outreach between OKNA and unhoused neighbors. As one neighborhood resident put it, the outreach committee sought to "improve communication, build relationships, and maybe kind of challenge the neighborhood association" on their initial position regarding HG and houseless issues more generally. It is with these types of political engagements in mind that one HG resident had come to realize that self-governing encampments could act as "a stepping stone for those who have never had a say." Without having lived in the encampment and having had that experience with the neighborhood organization, they said, "I wouldn't have had that opportunity to participate with [the neighborhood organization]." The benefit of participation, they noted, was that it often introduced residents to more formal political discourse and the practice of claims-making.

Beyond enacting citizenship informally within the spaces of the encampments, residents struggled for recognition by making claims to those outside the encampments who did not necessarily see the self-governing model as legitimate. Indeed, encampment residents engaged in political work at the neighborhood and city levels to justify their right to exist in the encampments. Even though the encampments were formally allowed to operate due to land use agreements, many residents still felt it necessary to make claims for their right not only to exist in particular encampments but also to advocate for the larger rights of self-governance that the Portland encampment model was originally intended to provide. In this way, encampment residents are not "passive" recipients of citizenship rights but are active in making claims to realize the expected benefits of the self-governing encampment model guaranteed by the municipal government.

To the extent that claims for citizenship privileges and political recognition was enabled by Portland's self-governing encampments, the model allowed for houseless groups to actively shape the discourse around how they benefited from this type of shelter. Indeed, the very reason that Portland's government began sanctioning encampments was due to the rights claims of unhoused individuals who demanded not only a place to exist but a place in which other unhoused individuals could collectively manage day-to-day affairs themselves. As one DV resident remarked, many self-governing encampments like Dignity Village "started as civil disobedience . . . it was a political movement. Hazelnut [Grove] was a political movement. We and the other newer camps are saying, 'Look, we're here. We have the same rights as everyone else. Listen to us.'" And it was this rhetoric that influenced city administrators early in the SOE to find a legal pathway for formalizing encampments.

At the same time, the sociopolitical privileges deriving from encampment self-governance do not mean that residents are guaranteed the right to any specific place. The right to collectively manage this commons-like space merely allows the process of self-organization and decision-making to remain within the collective purview of its residents. Thus, while the right to self-governance provides residents a degree of autonomy within the property, it does not provide individual rights over the space. Instead, the right to use property is given to the encampments as *collective*, legal entities, not individual rights. And it is here, in between the legal and political relations of property, where residents' citizenship is constrained.

ENFORCING SELF-GOVERNANCE

While residents clearly value self-governance, some noted that the process was constrained in ways that diminished their personal rights and freedoms. According to my interviewees, the most intractable issue concerned figuring out how to remove unwanted residents from the community with due compassion and safety. A further challenge stems from the fact that the encampments cannot fully establish privacy and security in relation to the greater public. Given that the social and physical infrastructure of encampments necessitate that residents live their lives in a public and visible way, residents can still feel unsafe, on edge and worried about people's access to the space and their intentions in wanting to enter.[24] The right to privacy and security cannot be guaranteed in these spaces. This is not because of a deficient self-governing process, however. An encampment's lack of the right to exclude prohibits these communities from following through on their decisions about which members of the public are authorized to be present on site.

That the self-governing process is so closely connected to property rights and relations is well represented in the dilemmas that arise when encampments deal with voting out members. Short-term bans and permanent removals happen for various reasons. Bans I observed were meted out for things as minor as stealing someone's lighter, but theft of another's personal property, violence toward others, and drug use are the most common reasons for removing guests and members from these spaces. Exactly how the process of temporarily banning or removing members happens is different for each encampment based on its bylaws. For instance, bans that I observed at R2DT were somewhat routine. There, I observed both overnight guests as well as resident members being banned from the space. Temporary bans were addressed at weekly meetings, which were led by a small board comprising resident members and volunteers and guided by its bylaws. When a ban was being considered, a board member would read off anonymously written "incident reports" that the encampment had received from residents or other guests pertaining to the actions of a particular person or set of persons. The process was deliberative and the person implicated in the report was expected to describe their own understanding of the situation. In turn, an open discussion with residents would be held, after which collective votes would be taken on whether to ban or allow that person to stay. Those who were banned were given the opportunity to appeal and after a certain amount of time, depending on the severity of the incident, were allowed to return. At R2DT, twenty-four-hour bans were common, given that hundreds of overnight sleepers used the space each week. Guest sleepers who were banned generally accepted the reasons why they were being asked to leave and would be welcomed back a few days later. Although bans were somewhat commonplace at R2DT, conflicts did occur. Mostly, this took the form of people shouting and pointing fingers and sometimes contesting what they felt were unfair accusations. Nevertheless, almost all residents and guests appreciated the ability to discuss measures with the collective, an opportunity that is rarely available in traditional shelters.

Permanent removals of resident members were less frequent at the self-governing encampments. But when resident "evictions" did happen, they were often more challenging for the communities. One member of HG described to me how issues arise that lead to removing people. Though the "methodology" is "dicey and kind of hard," he said, "ultimately, when a person's behavior becomes more dissatisfactory to the entire group, it wells and wells and wells. And eventually something will happen that, by itself, wouldn't be that big of a deal. But after months and months of continuously sustained behavior, it's just like the final 'Fuck you. You need to leave.'" It should be noted that many residents of self-governing encampments I spoke to cherished the more democratic and humane potential of the removal process. Many were given verbal warning for behavior that much of the community found harmful with the hope that residents could change in a positive way. Often, this could be for behavior of mundane consequence, such as when an individual did not show up for their security shifts over a period of time. I observed countless residents at HG appeal warnings successfully, ensuring their place at the site if only for a few weeks or months.

At the same time, when members are finally voted out of the community, it can be challenging to actually enforce those eviction decisions. The reason for this, as one HG member put it, is "because we don't have the ability to pressure people out of the space really, because we don't own the property. So, we can't trespass them." Member removals at encampments therefore may seem (for some) to lack the seriousness of state-sanctioned evictions. In the event that encampment residents refused to comply with their eviction, they contested the decision by simply remaining at the site or returning to it frequently. There are two options to remedy this situation, one HG resident noted. You can either "shame" individuals into leaving, or you physically remove them. Ruminating on these options, he indicated how they affect the rest of the community. "You *can* just make them go and physically handle them out," he said. "But at that point, you are no worse than some of the people we rally against the hardest." The result, he lamented, is often "a group shaming." And that was unfortunate, he said, because "there is a lot of resentment by the end of it." Shaming involves continually reminding a person of the reasons why they were voted out and ultimately not wanted in the community. Ideally, he said, the "person who is getting mobbed realizes, 'Oh, well I don't really fit in here and I don't want to be here. So maybe I should just leave.'" Continued discussions do help convince some as to why they are no longer welcome on site. The best-case scenario in these circumstances is that ex-members will line up another place to stay and negotiate remaining on site until they are able to move on.

FIGURE 8. The commons space at Hazelnut Grove, with members shown in discussion during a general assembly.

Reasoning with an individual does not always work, however, and highly disputed refusals can lead to extended conflict and even violence. One eviction I observed at HG was representative of the incredible difficulty and stress that encampment collectives can experience as a result of being left on their own to implement evictions. The situation involved a man in his early twenties who had been living in the encampment for approximately two months. Around the time of his eviction, he had just started full-time work and was unable to complete his required weekly labor hours for the encampment. He was also beginning to be verbally combative with residents who were making note of his absence from the encampment. Because he worked on the weekends, he stopped coming to the general assemblies on Saturdays. As a result of his extended absence and his inability to contribute to the collective, the rest of the residents decided to give him his first warning, per the encampment's bylaws, reminding him that he needed to complete his labor hours. He was not at the assembly the day this was decided but he did show up shortly after the meeting had finished. Upon hearing that he was on "probation" and may need to leave, he became upset. He began verbally attacking certain residents, which escalated into a larger physical confrontation with several of them. The fight was eventually broken up but left the evicted resident severely injured. Based on the violent interactions of that day, the collective decided to give him notice of an expedited removal from the encampment. The rest of the residents declared that his actions represented the violence prohibited in the encampment and expressed worries for their safety should he remain in the encampment.

Still, violent conflicts are exceedingly rare in these spaces. What should be distilled from this situation is that the evicted resident felt he was being "ganged up on," that the other residents seemed to not empathize with his situation, and ultimately, that he had no recourse for being removed from the only space that he had any sense of "ownership" over at that time. On the flip side, the remaining residents felt that they used the democratic process legitimately to secure what was then an unsafe space for them to be in due to this resident's behavior. And it was exactly these unpredictable situations that residents mentioned distress them the most about the self-governing process.

The fact that the encampments are managed as residency-by-majority contributed to differing levels of precarity and risk for residents and guests of the encampments when such decisions were made. And this power was not lost on resident members. As one longtime resident of DV lamented about the removal process, "To pass a sentence on someone is hard. Not that that sentence doesn't need to be passed. But it is very difficult." To use such a power could be emotionally challenging for encampment residents who still worried for ex-members' well-being. The same DV resident nevertheless noted that the self-governing process offers a more humane approach than the legal system. "[The police and the courts] don't know the person involved in eviction proceedings," he said, "so it makes it easier for [the legal system] to come and do these hard things. But that doesn't help the person who it is being done to." For the members in these communities who know the person being removed, he said, "at least we think about the person who we are passing judgment on. Like, how is this going to affect them?" This more directly democratic decision-making has helped prevent many encampment residents from being not only thrown out but spared legal punishment that can stymie their future housing options.

Making judgments on member removals and even short-term bans was thus often divisive for the residents remaining in the encampment. While many admired the fact that the self-governing process enabled extended discussion over removals, the process was nonetheless imperfect. For many residents, however, the fact that encampments struggled to enforce member removals was due not to the inadequacy of the self-governing process but to the lack of a legal right to evict. As one DV resident complained, in the end, "we can vote [someone] out, but if the person won't leave, the police won't help us remove them." The reason that encampments "can't evict people is because that would mean, for the city, that we are defined as an intentional community . . . and the city doesn't want that."[25] Unfortunately, he lamented, "we have to resort to strong arming people if it should come to it. And I think that sucks. That the people who know they are not supposed to be here won't just up and remove themselves because they know that nothing is going to happen" if community members do not physically remove them.

It is worth noting that nearly all encampment residents adamantly wish to avoid involving the police in encampment evictions because of the potential violence involved in state-backed evictions; they also don't want to draw unwanted attention to already stigmatized residential communities. Regardless of whether encampments did enjoy police support in seeing out contested removals from these sites, encampment evictions were still difficult processes for residents. The difficulty lies primarily in the fact that encampments operate as collectively managed spaces whereby enforcing evictions brings risk and personal hardship into this process. It can be an almost impossible task for unhoused people to remove other unhoused people from a relatively safe space to sleep. As one DV resident reflected, "I once had to look a friend of mine in the eye and say, 'You cannot live here anymore. You cannot come through the gates. You're barred forever.'" He continued, "The village has done me so much good. I hate having to do that . . . And that's the downside of self-governance. You have to enforce." These tensions force us to look not only at how property affects unhoused peoples' ability to self-manage but also how it affects encampment residents' self-determination to not be subjects of domination by way of property rights restrictions.

No Right to Remain

The liberal ownership model in which Portland's self-governing encampments operate necessitates a trade-off for the precarious situation in which encampment residents live. While self-organizing engenders for residents a greater sense of agency over their living situation and often induces political engagement with neighborhood and city politics, these benefits can be overshadowed by other restrictions on collective decision-making. As we have seen, the lack of a right to exclude impacts the self-governing process, particularly when member removals are contested. In these moments, encampment communities cannot ensure safe and peaceful living conditions. Ultimately, they have no legal property right to control access over the space. In that encampment property rights restrict the ability of self-governing communities to see through decisions over who is allowed in the space either as members or the visiting general public, the insecurity resulting from these restrictions also limits residents' basic individual freedoms. By restricting the ability of encampment communities to *enforce* their own decisions, the self-governing process is unable to ensure safety, privacy, and stability for the community. It is no coincidence, then, that residents of Portland's self-governing houseless encampments depicted these spaces as simultaneously helping them realize rights claims for a safer, more dignified, and representative living environment and compromising these liberty rights protections through the eviction process.

These seemingly disparate concerns embody contradictions central to property systems in liberalism. They are concerned with how and *whether* liberal subjects are able to enjoy a right to remain not just in a specific property but *anywhere*. For unhoused people, the right to be anywhere must nearly always be negotiated, as property rights holders authorize who may be where, and when. In this sense, the unhoused are unfree to control their ultimate placement in space. And the only way to eliminate this lack of control, this condition of unfreedom, is "to ensure that each person has somewhere in which they are not subject to anyone else's' authority about what they can and cannot do."[26]

The right not to be excluded is often considered an antidote to this dilemma, as expressed in much common property literature. As previously noted, C. B. Macpherson argued that the rights protecting the private property model within liberalism are difficult to reconcile with personal rights due to how the right to exclude is prioritized over individual liberty rights. For Macpherson, the right not to be excluded is ideally an *individual* right, to better ensure that personal rights are not only commensurable but protected from the private authority of owners within the ownership model. So too, if realized, would the individual right not to be excluded be commensurable with the right to be included in or access commons properties.

The right not to be excluded constitutes a *positive* right, however, a right offered as a collective good to the public rather than an individual or negative right. As such, a right not to be excluded would simply provide individuals an *opportunity* to access commonly owned property, though it could not guarantee that collective ownership would not still exclude individuals from the property. To say the least, the ownership model challenges alternatives operating within it, like state-owned, collectively managed properties.

The case of Portland's self-governing encampments provides insight into the dilemmas of collectively managed property within the liberal ownership model. It shows us that because there is no legal property right with which to exclude people from these spaces, there is consequently no legal right to remain in these spaces. The fact that there are no legal rights *guaranteeing* that individuals can stay on site means that residents do not actually enjoy a right not to be excluded. The downside to this is that without an individually held, legal right not to be excluded from property, individuals have no legal recourse for reentry into an encampment when removed, placing them further into housing precarity if they are unable to access other properties. More significantly, given that the right to remain is socially mediated, not legally backed, *all* residents, not only those who are banned or evicted, are not guaranteed an individually held right to access the space. There is no legal right to remain for any resident and thus ultimately no right to immobility.

And this is partly what is unjust about the ownership model. Because they lack a right not to be excluded, encampment residents do not have rights to prevent themselves from being controlled by the authority of others (e.g., police, city government, the public). For encampment residents do not have a core right meant to be equally enjoyed by all property rights holders or lessees, an "in-rem alienable right that others not enter or interfere with some physical space."²⁷ To justify this specific inequitable property relation for Portland's encampments, all residents would need to equally enjoy the normative liberal feature of property that authorizes owners the right to have control over others' use of propertied spaces. But encampment residents do not enjoy the normative capacity to ultimately control their space of residence, despite their personal and collective capacities to organize themselves within these ultimate constraints.

At the same time, to suggest that legal rights to property are the only means of securing an individuals' tenure within a collectively managed encampment denies the awesome potential of self-governing communities such as those found in Portland. Although encampment residents ultimately do not enjoy a *legal* right not to be excluded, they do enjoy a social right to remain in a collective that is negotiated through the self-governing process. Such an organizing structure, particularly when seen through its relationship with property, is not merely capable of maintaining order, security, and privacy for its residents: it may also better accommodate the more democratically made decisions of unhoused communities. The model of collectively managed properties for unhoused people is premised upon the decisions crafted *by* unhoused people *for* unhoused people, which in turn is premised on residents' collective lived experience. It is here that antiracist, gender-inclusive, and disability-amenable solutions to property's neutralization of these differences can be reworked, if only informally within the spaces of the encampments. Enabling a sense of agency through collective management provides for unhoused people that which is so often taken away from them in any other shelter or propertied space, namely, a right to self-determination.

It may appear, then, that there is no strong reason to suggest that providing legally enforceable possessory rights to encampments would do anything other than protect for individuals the sociopolitical benefits that derive from this democratic model. The significance of guaranteeing encampment residents' right to access property is that it would ensure that individuals are able to continue producing these spaces according to their own particular needs throughout their time of housing precarity. An individually held right to access collectively managed property—a right not to be excluded—would not be a panacea, but it could provide a floor of protection for the most precariously housed and is worth striving for. The Portland encampment model exemplifies what such a right could look like in practice.

Yet, the idea that conferring rights of exclusion on Portland's self-governing encampments would be a legal move to end the hegemony and injustices of liberal propertied citizenship seems like wishful thinking. Private property rights remain fundamental to liberal democracies because they ensure there will be uneven power relations between those who have access to property and those who do not. Moreover, the encampment model exists within, and thus would reify, the exclusionary rights relations germane to the ownership model. The social-legal system producing and maintaining the ownership model holds little space for adaptations like collectively organized encampments that do not reinforce property's commoditization and exchangeability in the market.

Rather than downplay the benefits of self-organizing because of how residents' liberties are diminished, we should address the specific ways in which this democratic model constrains residents' ability to flourish, not because of how it is organized but because of how property rights and relations limit their ability to do so. This requires focusing on the ownership model's inability or adamant refusal to incorporate the collectively managed practices of the encampment model. Such an assertion, however, does not mean that we should wish to see that encampments remain open in perpetuity. Rather, it is a desire to show how the ownership model of property diminishes the political subjectivity and rights of unhoused people residing in Portland's encampments. It also is a claim insisting that our attention remain on how this property model produces varying levels of precarity for all individuals, albeit far more for those insecure in housing tenure.

More specifically, we ought to be examining how relations of property produce experienced injustices. To the extent that liberal property regimes enmesh us within the power relations of rights holders' private authority, the mere fact of this relationality requires that we advance normative assessments of how and which relations of property are more unjust. This requires uncovering and explaining how relations of property structure disadvantage for some based on the relatively privileged actions of others. However, if we see the relational production of precarity for unhoused people as unjust, as I argue we should, an incredibly complex question presents itself: Whose responsibility is it to mitigate these injustices? With this question in mind, the following chapter addresses the specific ways in which unhoused Portlanders experience unjust relations within liberal property systems to explicate how actually existing injustices are structured into, and structure relations of, property. In doing so, the chapter identifies how liberal theories of property justify such inequities, setting up a discussion in the conclusion about how we ought to respond to structural injustices of liberal property.

CHAPTER 4

Locating Responsibility for the Injustices of Liberal Property

Given that property rights establish relations of power between individuals, property must be justified. Individual rights holders whose entitlements provide them control over the use of resources must be able to account for, and ensure against, abuses in their privately held authority in relation to others' personal and property rights.[1] This is what makes liberal property relational. But few theories of justice expressly identify how the relational nature of liberal property is *essential* to property's justification. One such recent justification by Hanoch Dagan is intriguing for this very reason—it identifies relational justice as a required principle for liberal property systems to be justified.[2] Dagan's liberal theory is exceptional in this regard. It recognizes that systems of liberal property cannot be justified within the tenets of liberal ideology and property law without accounting for property's potentially harmful effect on others.

Like much justice theorizing, Dagan's theory develops upon liberal precepts to explicate how property should function in perfect or ideal circumstances. Ideal theories seek to establish criteria by which to assess what more just relations could possibly be or become. John Rawls' liberal theory of justice exemplifies well how ideal constructs establish perfect principles, which, if followed, ought to lead to just conditions within his hypothetical society.[3] There are, however, empirical trade-offs to ideal theorizations of justice.[4] In contrast, a *nonideal* account of the world generally begins from the assumption that a moral ideal like justice "is not fully realized in a certain social setting," and as such, "tries to explain how the ideal in question could be more fully realized."[5] Thus, despite its strengths in underscoring the relationality of just property systems, and thus holding the ideals of liberal tenets to account, Dagan's conceptualization of how liberal property can be justified only goes so far (see below). Ideal theories may identify how just relations of property *could* be, but they are less useful for explaining how actually existing unjust relations are experienced within actually existing systems of liberal property. If our intention is to assess the material relations of liberal property and how these relations produce and maintain injustice, I argue we ought to focus our attention on theorizing and explaining how property relations are unjust in real or "nonideal" circumstances. At their best, nonideal theories allow us to address "the distinctive experience of the oppressed while avoiding particularism and relativism."[6] As such, a nonideal theorization of liberal property aids in identifying the specific circumstances by and in which unhoused people find themselves and thus what ought to be done to make these relations more just.

This chapter examines how liberal property is unjust specifically for unhoused residents of Portland's encampments. In doing so, it moves away from perfect theories of justice to explicate how unjust relations of liberal property variously affect unhoused people. As a first step, I draw from Iris Marion Young's conceptualization of injustice as a connected set of oppressions to structure my explanation of how unhoused people are unjustly affected by property. After explaining the unjust circumstances that Portland's unhoused experience within liberal systems of property, I assess how we may respond to the injustices of property more generally. Here again, I draw from Young's development of the notion of "structural injustice" and examine her suggestions for how we may account for injustice by addressing the question: Who bears *responsibility* for ameliorating these injustices?

Young's contribution to assessing injustice, especially as developed in her "shared model of responsibility," usefully explains not only how injustice is structurally produced and maintained but why it is incumbent upon us to locate *political* responsibility for those producing and contributing to injustice. When we consider the predicament of unhoused people within liberal systems of property, Young's model of shared responsibility forces us to deal with the fact that responsibility is more broadly shared than what is perhaps commonly considered in public discourse surrounding houselessness. Young's location of responsibility for the relations of property that unjustly produce and maintain houselessness in the hands of private capital and government (in)action logically extends to bring small property owners and even renters to account. Promulgating the notion that all bear responsibility for contributing to houselessness seems an unlikely political strategy if it means effectively demanding that those who bear more responsibility for their contribution to injustice care or know how to correct for unjust processes to which they contribute. For as I will argue, justice requires establishing a *duty* to bring any contributor of injustice to account for their responsibility for structural injustice.

The shortcomings in Young's model do not derive from her nonideal theories of shared responsibility, however. Young's typology is insightful for how it allows us to locate responsibility for houselessness as an experienced set of oppressions related to property, thus letting us see how political pressure and social accountability *ideally* mitigate structural injustice. To reject Young's insistence that we can account for structural injustice would not only enable but affirm the uneven relations of power that reside within and derive from relations of property. Rather, I argue that Young's model is likely to be ineffective in action not necessarily due to flawed precepts but because of how the material demands of liberal institutions require that some duty first be assigned to contributors to injustice for any legitimate claim of justice to be realized and for them to be corrected. Put another way, and perhaps more significantly, Young's nonideal theorizations of injustice and the responsibility of correcting for it illustrate exactly how (and where) liberalism limits our individual, though not institutional, capacity to respond to the injustices of property.

To the extent that Young's model unintentionally demonstrates the limits of liberalism as it relates to injustice borne out of property relations, I argue by way of conclusion that the model leads us to a more politically useful question: In the face of such liberal limits to justice, *how do we respond*? The answer to this question must be generated by assessing the actual relations through which property is produced and unevenly maintained in order to explain how responses to sensed injustices can potentially make relations of property more just.

Before addressing how unhoused Portlanders experience the injustice of property, I briefly detail what ideal theories of liberal property offer us. Doing so illustrates why focusing on injustice can be more politically relevant for analyzing houselessness in American liberalism and how it may identify pathways for enabling more just property relations regarding unhoused people.

Justifying Liberal Property

Addressing how liberal property is justified through ideal principles is normatively valuable for assessing how injustices are experienced. Several legal scholars have sought to explain why the "ownership model" of private property germane to liberalism restricts freedom of unhoused people to be somewhere without someone else's say so, and therefore, why liberal property is unjust in that it necessitates that unhoused people will "always and everywhere be subject to others' rights . . . [and] to be under the power of others, dependent on them, [and even] dominated by them" (see chapter 1).[7] With this critique of property in mind, Hanoch Dagan's recent interpretative theory of liberal property provides a thorough explanation of what it would take for liberal institutions of property to be justified.

Dagan's theory attempts to reform liberalism by advancing an ideal theory of property relations that, if properly followed, would be justifiable. It is a fundamentally liberal theory, as it prioritizes individuality in the sense that individuals hold an equal opportunity to be the "authors" of their own livelihoods and not be subject to illegitimate constraints on, or experience domination of, their person. As such, Dagan echoes much liberal ideology, which understands property as an autonomy-enhancing right. Like many relational property scholars, Dagan recognizes that rights to property are power conferring. That is, property rights grant right holders an authority over other owners and nonowners, establishing duties that others must respect regarding the use of specific resources. Because property rights are power conferring, property relations must continually be justified, given how they affect an individual's self-development or capacity for "self-authorship." For property relations to be "just," therefore, laws must ensure that the social relations between owners and nonowners do not detract from the self-determination of liberal subjects.

The substance of Dagan's theory is that liberal property must be pluralistic in form and relational in engagement. It states that ownership must be pluralistic, not monistic, in structure, to encompass the different ways in which individuals can and want to be self-determining. For instance, cooperative ownership agreements allow individuals a sense of collective self-determination that they may not experience within single-family ownership structures. Additionally, his theory recognizes the *relational* power of rights. Particularly intriguing is that Dagan identifies the centrality of justice to property relations. Here justice is understood as interpersonal, between individuals, rather than an issue of proper distribution. This means that when owners enforce a right to exclude from their property, it is necessary to evaluate whether they are overextending their authority when determining the use of or access to resources for nonowners, to prevent them from "abusing the institution of property for a purpose that contravenes its *telos*."[8] Such a view of just property relations understands that there is a duty imposed on owners themselves to respect the rights of nonowners as well as other owners. At the same time, the self-determination of nonowners "need not, should not, and indeed does not, override the self-determination of owners," as that would undermine the autonomy-enhancing protections inherent to owners' property rights. Further, just property relations occur between *private* individuals, which for Dagan would mean that owners should be "required to comply with relational justice in their private capacity instead of as citizens of a particular state."[9] For relational justice to be achieved, therefore, owners' reflexivity is necessary so that the authority of private individuals vested in rights of property does not disabuse others of their ability to self-determine their life worlds. As such, the relational aspect of this liberal property theory attempts to balance the right to exclude with rights of *inclusion*, those meaningful rights that protect personal or civil liberties.

To summarize, Dagan argues that there are three requirements for a liberal theory of property to be justified:

1. Circumscription of owners' private authority to ensure that it follows property's contribution to self-determination;
2. Creation of a structurally pluralistic inventory of property types offering people real choice;
3. Compliance of owners' powers with relational justice to verify that property does not offend the principle of reciprocal respect for self-determination substantiating its legitimacy.[10]

Taken together, these three tenets outline the relational responsibilities that follow from ownership, a demarcation that must be understood reflexively to ensure that an owner's power does not diminish nonowners' self-determination.

Dagan's theory underscores the notion that property mediates an individual's ability to author their own lifeworld. This directly implicates the inviolability of personhood within liberalism. As such, he argues that the substantive import of liberal property systems and laws that regulate them is that it allows owners the "possibility of developing their own life plans rather than the plans imposed on them by other persons or by society at large."[11] Accordingly, property is just when it allows liberal subjects to pursue their own version of the good life.

Dagan's liberal theory of property is idealist and consequently does not explain how people find themselves within unjust relations of property.[12] As such, it underemphasizes a few key challenges to the justification of actual liberal property relations. The first regards how inequities are reproduced by the continuous acquisition of property by extant owners—which is still justified according to these principles—while those without ownership or access rights find their capacity to be authors of their lives diminishing in respect to owners' accumulation. The enormous disparity in wealth related to property ownership is not hypothetical or a future risk. It already exists. Dagan accounts for this by suggesting not that rules around liberal property be reformed but rather that there should be principles requiring pre-distributed property to all individuals so that the autonomy-enhancing function of property would still hold.[13] While this type of egalitarian distributive scheme would certainly reduce economic inequality, the idealism of what it *could* do does not account for the actually existing distribution of property found in contemporary societies. As such, Dagan's theory leaves unaddressed the unjust relations that produce unequal distributions in the first place.[14] The unequal distribution of material goods that currently exists in the world results from the historical maintenance of a free-market system of property premised on the ability of some to obtain property while many others cannot afford to do so. Redistributive justice ultimately enables an exploitative system of production to continue unabated.

A second issue with a legal theory of property premised on autonomy enhancement for private individuals is that it is difficult to monitor and therefore correct for the diminishment of liberal subjects' capacities to be self-determining. How do we know when private owners abuse their authority as owners and constrain individuals from self-development? A reasonable solution within liberal or common law would be to use the courts to adjudicate abuses in this sphere. In many instances, this may help nonowners have their rights respected by the state. Dagan notes, however, that relational justice pertains to the "interactions of private individuals rather than as citizens or as subjects of state institutions."[15] That is, property relations matter between private subjects, interactions that are apparently extra-political and of concern not to liberal citizenship but rather to market relations. It is clear that many nonowners cannot use the legal system or even political forums to ensure their ability to occupy spaces needed for survival, for example when they are unsheltered, much less to establish a right to communal property uses, like in Portland's encampments, which have limited rights of access.

Most significantly, ideal theories like Dagan's do not show us how property relations contribute to injustice; they only show how property could be just in ideal circumstances. To better understand the injustice of property, and how unhoused people are affected within liberal relations of property, we need normative assessments that identify how injustice presents itself. In other words, we need to turn away from the question of how can property be ideally just and instead ask, how is it that property is unjust? The following section addresses how we can identify injustice before detailing what injustice looks like within liberal property systems, particularly for unhoused residents of encampments.

Assessing Injustice in Liberalism

Liberal theories are mainstays of justice theorizing. And as previously mentioned, much liberal theorizing has also been premised upon the construction of ideal principles. That is, theories of justice have commonly sought to define what justice should look like in "perfect" circumstances. The most famous case of this is Rawls' "justice as fairness," though many liberal egalitarian approaches have been and remain founded in similar idealist constructions.[16] Ideal theorizing is useful to account for how inequities may be defined, and as such, can offer useful premises for correcting power imbalances within and among societies. Ideal or perfect theories of justice generally identify specific principles that, if followed, ought to ensure a just state of social relations.

Given that ideal theories of justice define the contours of what justice should be, ideal justice theorizing deemphasizes what injustice looks like. Typical idealist perspectives of justice assume that injustice exists when justice appears to not be present, as an aberration from the standards of proper justice. Such an assumption is insufficient for understanding the substance of real injustices, however. As Judith Shklar argues, the substance of injustice within ideal moral theory is conceived of as "simply the absence or opposite of justice." As such, ideal theories of justice assume that "once we know what is just, we will know all that we need to know."[17] This assumption carries itself into contemporary social justice research as well. Much of the geographies of justice scholarship, for instance, applies perfect or ideal models of distributive, participatory, and recognitional justice to assess cases of injustice.[18] Within this literature, injustice is often expressed as the mere absence of equal distribution, constituent participation, or group recognition. Arriving at injustice by way of subtracting how actually existing inequities fall short of perfectly just relations can be useful for identifying power inequities. But the mere subtraction from perfect models of justice often means that the normative assessment of why some process or relation is unjust is lacking.

Attending to the injustices of liberal property requires turning away from a reliance on ideal theories of justice. Instead, I suggest it is more important to examine how the property insecure experience injustice. How injustice is defined is a matter of judgement, but the substance of injustice can be assessed in relation to criteria that explain how individuals or groups experience specific harms related to their condition. So, what constitutes injustice and how do we know it when we see it?

Perhaps no general criteria to identify the substance of injustice have been discussed more than those identified by Iris Marion Young. Young understands that if social relations are to be "just," then what must be secured is "the institutional conditions necessary for the development and exercise of individual capacities and collective communication and cooperation."[19] Socially just institutions promote two general values that enable individuals the opportunity for a good life, Young notes. The first is to have the ability to "develop and exercise one's capacities and expressing one's experience."[20] The second is to be able to participate "in determining one's action and the conditions of one's action." In turn, Young's definition of *injustice* corresponds with the extent to which these two values are reduced or eliminated through institutional constraints on self-development and self-determination, or what she terms as "oppression" and "domination" respectively.[21] Though the two overlap, domination connotes how individuals have decisions about their own condition made on their behalf without having the ability to reciprocate that decision-making capacity, while oppression refers to the fact that even though individuals may have some authority over their decision-making, they nonetheless are constrained in different ways by institutions. In liberal societies particularly, oppression is omnipresent, experienced in everyday relations and through well-intentioned policies. It is Young's intention to show, in short, how liberalism and its institutions deliberately and unintentionally facilitate oppression.

Young identifies five "faces" of oppression: exploitation, marginalization, powerlessness, cultural imperialism, and violence.[22] I contextualize these criteria in what follows, examining how the institutions and relations of property specifically constrain the self-development and self-determination of unhoused people.[23] Rather than affirming that the inequities of property result solely by way of exclusion from it, I analyze how encampment residents experience harm through the power inequities of the institutions regulating, and social relations validating, unjust relations of liberal property. Doing so establishes a means to evaluate the ways in which life for encampment residents is unjust and to assess how unhoused people more broadly are forced to navigate the injustices maintained through liberal property systems.

EXPLOITATION

Exploitation has been thoroughly conceptualized as injustice. For Marx, exploitation is the process of capitalists appropriating surplus value through the labor of workers. While Marx never framed exploitation specifically through the term injustice, a critique of injustice was nevertheless latent in his analysis. As Neil Smith argues, Marx's analysis of exploitation was "*simultaneously* a judgement about social *in*justice *and* a measure of economic productivity; the calculation of the capitalist's rate of surplus value was simultaneously the calculation of the worker's rate of exploitation."[24] For her part, Young argues that exploitation as injustice can also be understood more generally. The injustice of exploitation, she writes, consists in social processes that "bring about a transfer of energies from one group to another to produce unequal distributions, and in the ways that institutions enable a few to accumulate while they constrain many more."[25] This more expansive notion of exploitation then is understood in contrast to ideal theories of distributive justice, suggesting that unjust relations cannot be made more just by mere redistribution of goods alone. For redistributive theories could reinforce unequal distributions in the longer term, leaving untouched the institutions and social relations that enable such exploitation. *How* exploitation operates as a form of injustice becomes a point of focus then when institutions and social relations enable the unjust transfer of energies from one group to another.

Exploitation is therefore central to the processes of making housing unaffordable and access to shelter precarious for so many. The inequities of the housing market are well documented. As noted in the introduction, the average rental price for housing in Portland has increased by 2.5 percent each year over the last decade, and the average purchase price of houses has increased by over $200,000 over the last five years. It is perhaps not a surprise that the most common reason that people living in Portland's encampments become unhoused is due to the increasing difficulty of affording rent or mortgage payments because of loss of employment or underemployment.

Consider Renee's story, for instance.[26] I met Renee on my first day at Hazelnut Grove in 2017. Renee was then fifty-nine and identified as white with mixed-race parents. She was raised in California but lived all over the American West. She is a veteran of the U.S. Air Force but also worked in the service and social work industries, including a job with housing management in Denver prior to moving to Portland. She arrived in Portland in 2009 and was housed there until 2014, when she became unhoused for the first time in her life. Multiple reasons led to her being unhoused. She was unable to work as a result of her uneven recovery from cancer and the medication she used to manage her pain. Not being able to work, of course, led to not being able to pay bills. When we talked about how she became unhoused, she remarked on her great renter's record. "I have always been told that I leave a place better than when I came. I have always paid my own rent. I have always taken care of myself," she said. But she became unhoused due to a rent increase when the building she was living in was sold to a new owner. Emphatically, she said, "I lost it because of the high cost of housing." Though she had trouble with irregular income for years before she lost the apartment, she noted that it was not until around 2014 that she saw how limited her income from disability support was in relation to the rising cost of living in Portland. "What I get [per month], I could hardly get a cheap place to rent here. It would take all my income to pay for rent . . . plus the cost of utilities. It just became impossible." After the building sold, Renee finished out her lease but was unable to find another place to move to, pushing her into houselessness.

Property acquisitions in commercial real estate frequently lead to the exploitation of low-income and often racialized renters. Given that Oregon did not have a statewide rent control mechanism at the time of Renee's rent hike, landlords were able to increase rents as they saw fit, regardless of whether they had just acquired new properties.[27] What is more, such profit-seeking transactions are legally justified in state law. The struggle to keep up with increases in rent can exploit the already stretched resources of low-income renters, as renters give over much of their monthly income to landlords. But it was not simply that Renee was unable to afford rent. There was no further system of support at that time to prevent Renee from being evicted. Thus, despite her having government support through supplemental disability income, the limits of institutional support constrained Renee's ability to find stable housing, thereby reinforcing the legal right of landlords to exploit this rent-seeking behavior. Renee was harmed like all those within liberal property markets who exhaust their income on rent, through an "exploitable hierarchy" reinforced by law, forcing those who cannot pay their mortgage or landlord-mandated rent to exit housing against their will.[28]

MARGINALIZATION THROUGH DISPOSSESSION

The claim that unhoused people are marginalized within society should not be controversial. Many have shown how the conditions of being unhoused, forced to live one's life in public, invite stigmatizing and criminalizing actions toward individuals in this situation.[29] Marginalization is a relational process, one where individuals are marked by allegedly productive society as less valuable or useless.[30] For Young, marginalization is "the most dangerous form of oppression," as those experiencing it are often "subjected to severe material deprivation and even extermination."[31] The fact that some lack material resources necessary for stability and survival highlights an imbalance of distribution. And the welfare state plays only a minor role in helping individuals mitigate this imbalance, as Renee's case shows. But Young stresses that *being* marginal within liberal societies is as much a result of economic maldistribution as it involves being deprived of the "cultural, practical, and institutionalized conditions for exercising capacities in a context of recognition and interaction."[32] Social and institutional processes that reinforce the marginal status of aspects of individuals' identity—for instance, one's race and ethnicity, gender and sexuality, physical and mental abilities, or one's religious beliefs—exacerbate the ways in which individuals are deprived of value as humans. Within a sociopolitical system that defines itself through the normative ideals of autonomy and self-determination, being marginalized from dominant liberal society enables injustice by way of political, legal, and social misrecognition. That is, those deemed less valuable economically, socially, or politically may have basic rights to privacy, security, and decision-making capacities protected unevenly or not at all.

People become unhoused for many reasons, but all connect back in the end to a lack of resources necessary to secure stable housing. That unhoused people who are forced to live their lives so publicly can be stigmatized and thus rendered marginal in liberal societies belies the reality that for so many, the devaluation of their personhood *facilitated* their entry into houselessness in the first place. And while people are marginalized for a variety of reasons, one material form that oppression takes is through acts of dispossession. As discussed in chapter 1, the historical process of accumulation by dispossession enabled the privatization of property germane to the ownership model today. We can usefully connect dispossession with marginalization through what Ananya Roy terms "racial banishment," which refers to "state-instituted violence against racialized bodies and communities."[33] Such a definition links well with Young's conception of marginalization as a racialized form of oppression that leads to material deprivation and the disempowerment of racialized persons. From this perspective, marginalization through dispossession is unjust in that the enforcement of land use regulations requires racialized unhoused people to simultaneously struggle to securely emplace themselves *somewhere* and struggle to be recognized as self-determining persons within a liberal property system historically valuing whiteness as criteria for proper self-possession. What is oppressive and thus unjust about racialized banishment is not only that there has been an absence of institutional recognition of and support for mitigating the marginalizing effects of property on people of color but also that marginalization *requires* institutional enforcement to enact unjust relations of property in the first place.

Marginalization through dispossession shapes the lives of many unhoused people and Portland's encampment residents are not excepted from its effects. Take Angela, for example.[34] I met Angela at R2DT in summer 2023. She was then in her late forties and had been staying at the shelter off-and-on for two weeks at that point. She identifies as Native American and though she was born in a rural area near Santa Rosa, California, she left there to attend school on her tribe's reservation. She admits that her living situation on the reservation was less than ideal, noting that while technically she could own a small plot of land on her reservation, she never had enough money to purchase or build a house there. As such, she and her mother lived in federally subsidized housing during the years they spent on the reservation.

Angela left for Sacramento shortly after finishing school, partly because of the opportunities that an urban area can provide. This would also mark the start of her experiences with being unhoused. As an adult, Angela had bouts of houselessness in several cities. She first moved to Oregon in 2005 with her then-partner and their newborn child. Upon arriving, she experienced domestic abuse, which made her quickly leave her partner. For three months, she and her child stayed in a shelter for victims of intimate partner violence. She then moved into temporary housing in the Portland suburb of Gresham but lost it three months later during a custody dispute with her ex-partner. She lived on the street for a while after that, then moved back to her tribe's reservation in California to live with her mother. Her housing situation there was similar to the previous experience, and she had no money to purchase her own place. She returned to Oregon in 2021. This time, she resided in several shelters, stayed with friends, and camped on the street. During her first year back in Oregon, she guessed that she camped alone on the street for about eight months, spending the rest of the time in shelters or with friends.

I asked Angela about her experience obtaining stable housing throughout this time. She said that she had been on different waiting lists from local service providers over the course of the year. And she understood that the wait times on these lists can be long, sometimes extending to years. Sometimes when she would ask about housing opportunities, she was told by service staff that she was ineligible for some of their different housing programs. When I asked why they denied her, she replied, "I have no idea. They won't tell you. They just say that I'm not eligible for certain types of programs that they have sponsored." However, when we talked more specifically about how her Indigenous background affected her housing situation, she noted that with some social service providers specifically, she felt like she was being passed over for access to temporary housing. "They tend to do more for certain groups of people," she said. More broadly, she also noted feeling a certain familial expectation as an Indigenous woman to remain rooted with family at home on her reservation, despite her struggle with being housed there.

Angela's story is complex, and the painful aspects of her life that she shared with me depict what it can mean to remain marginal within property. How Angela has survived through such extreme precarity over the last two decades illuminates how marginalization through dispossession does not take place through one historical instance of exclusion from property. Instead, when we understand how relations of property maintain, and continue to force individuals to navigate within its regulations, Angela's story helps us see how dispossession remains active while still being informed by past exclusions.

Being unhoused (and precariously housed) for eighteen years is what marginalization looks like within liberal capitalism. As Roy argues, dispossession has been and continues to be foundational to liberalism, by ensuring that the racialized "subject whose claims to personhood are tenuous and whose claims to property are thus always a lived experience of loss."[35] It is not simply unjust that people of color and low-income people are disproportionately displaced from housing. It is also unjust that many individuals are *disempowered* within liberal property systems, unable to ensure that the decisions they make about where they want to live, who they may want to live with, and how they want to spend their lives largely cannot be determined by themselves. Within liberal systems of property specifically, therefore, this dispossession is unjust because of how it denies unhoused people the agency of voluntary mobility, enforcing the continual loss of security and privacy of being emplaced. It also denies self-development, the process of being able to conceive of and act upon your desires without institutional constraint.

For Angela, many of her decisions about where she would sleep were not of her own choosing but rather resulted from institutions constraining her access to property. As a resident on a reservation for long periods of time, her ability to ensure for herself a living situation based on her own choice has been historically mediated through U.S. federal and state government constraints, as enactments of property forced tribes onto reservations while also starving them of adequate resources to broadly realize self-determination. In cities, Angela fared similarly, finding temporary housing that she could never keep for long. Though there is choice within the private housing market system, without institutional support, the injustice of free market housing within liberalism necessitates that people with no income rely upon only temporary housing situations. Thus, when Angela moved for opportunity, there was no system except the traditional shelter system that she could rely upon. Angela's path through liberal property is not colored by one moment of eviction, therefore, but reflects a sustained confrontation with unjust policies that deny the very self-development that liberal citizenship promises to protect. She is marginalized because she is forced to remain within this state of circumstances without being altogether excluded from them.

Consider another example of how being marginal connects to dispossession. One of the first people I met during my fieldwork in Portland was Simone.[36] Simone was a resident at HG and had been living there since the community's inception in 2015. They were especially active in HG's encampment politics, but also with neighborhood association meetings and in the city's planning for HG's site relocation to what is now St. John's Village. As if it was planned this way, when I returned to Portland in 2023, Simone had just moved into their own subsidized apartment the day before we met, and they were glowing. They were one of the fortunate ones. A recent diagnosis of congestive heart failure placed Simone at the top of the list to receive housing so that they had a consistent electric source for their CPAP machine. The fact that they were finally in more stable housing was almost impossible to imagine because of their experiences within the housing system.

Simone identifies as mixed race, half Black, half white, as well as transgender. How these aspects of their identities feature in their housing precarity is significant. They grew up in a Black majority neighborhood in Cincinnati, Ohio. Before reaching their teenage years, Simone had already lost their father and brother in a house fire, leaving them, their mother, and two sisters temporarily displaced. While these experiences were traumatizing, Simone pinpoints "trans oppression" as a teenager as their motivation to leave the city. They recalled verbal attacks, like being made fun of on the bus for dressing in women's clothing. But Simone was also physically attacked; they were once shot in the stomach while walking in their neighborhood back home, and the scars from surgery were still visible when I met them. Before arriving in Portland in 2010, Simone had lived in a few other cities, Miami the longest, where they found rent difficult to afford. After some time in a Miami shelter, Simone thought that Portland might be a good place to go next, for they had heard that it was generally transgender-friendly. So, Simone and their then-partner moved to Portland and found a cheap apartment to rent. When their relationship ended, Simone found themself unhoused again. They were unhoused for about two years before eventually being led to HG in 2015, where they lived until summer 2023.

Simone recalled one instance when they were denied access to housing due to discrimination. While Simone was still living with their partner, a friend offered to connect them with a landlord they knew who had a cheaper space to move into. The offer was to rent an entire house, out on the Oregon coast in a small town, a break from Portland that Simone was looking forward to. The friend who connected Simone with the rental opportunity told them that the landlord had heard about the couple's struggles with housing precarity and seemed pleased that they could help them get into housing. But shortly before they were to sign the paperwork for the house, Simone's friend called to explain that the landlord did not want to offer them the apartment any longer. As Simone tells it, the friend said that "I told the landlord you were gay, and were trans or whatever. [But] I failed to mention that you were Black." The friend defended the landlord's decisions by saying, "Oh, it's not [what the landlord wants], it's what her neighbors might do." This type of discrimination by private individuals is routine, as landlords do not have to publicly declare why they do not want to rent to people. It was only through Simone's friend that the couple found out that it was not ok to be Black and rent from racially discriminatory landlords. Unfortunately, this was nothing new for Simone, who had been denied other apartments many times without any indication of the reason.

While this event was unjust specifically in that it can be attributed to individual racism, it nevertheless reflects a more *systemic* pattern of discrimination that racialized and unhoused people face in seeking housing stability. In theory, the unhoused have a right to rent and own housing. Far too often, however, the most marginalized simply cannot choose with whom, where, and under what conditions they get to live. It is also unjust in the way that it dispossesses individuals like Simone of a sense of self, particularly when they are forced to perform an identity that is more palatable to dominant society just to get access to a necessary resource like housing. Simone notes, for instance, that they began code-switching when applying for apartments, like the one they had just moved into when we met again in 2023. "I straightened my hair and presented myself, you know, with wearing overalls, pulled my hair back, put some eyeliner on, to make sure I'm especially feminine or whatever, because that is desensitizing. Being a Black male . . . I'm doing multiple things." The goal, they continued, is to let potential landlords or property managers "know that I am trans, know that I am nonbinary . . . and to not be . . . that 'aggressive Black male'" stereotype. For Simone and so many others, a "lived sense of loss" permeates their relation to property.

POWERLESSNESS

Exploitation and marginalization by dispossession render individuals powerless in overlapping ways. If exploitation unjustly transfers energies from one person to another, marginalization relegates individuals to be of little value to dominant society, and dispossession diminishes individuals' decision-making authority, then it is also true that the unhoused or precariously housed who are remaindered within liberal property relations lack the ability not only to make decisions about their own lives but to *act on* such decisions. In general, the powerless are those "over whom power is exercised without their exercising it," as Young puts it.[37] Power, of course, is relative and relational. And my claim here is not that the powerless have no ability whatsoever to affect any decision-making about their life. Rather, it is that some individuals more so than others lack "significant" power, or the ability to "regularly participate in making decisions that affect the conditions of their lives and actions."[38] It is oppressive and thus unjust to not be able to enact decisions for oneself that matter most for one's well-being.

For unhoused people within liberal capitalism, powerlessness permeates everyday existence. To varying degrees, when and where unhoused people access resources for survival is based on who says they can be in specific propertied spaces and what opportunities are made available within liberal property markets for unhoused people to exit out of housing instability. Put another way, unhoused people's power to act on their own decisions is highly contingent on the power vested in other people and institutions. And Portland's encampments provide an interesting case to analyze the relational nature of power and powerlessness affecting many of its residents.

Returning to the dilemma of the previous chapter, we can see how a lack of substantive power limits the capacity of encampment communities to protect themselves in that they are unable to see through decisions about who may enter the space of the encampment. Here, their powerlessness is most notable not in their ability to decide to ban certain problematic members, or to keep out strangers and the public who have unknown intentions. These decisions are often quite clear and consensual. Rather, the powerlessness is highlighted in their diminished capacity to enforce, that is, act on and see through, the decisions they have made about removals. For encampments like R2DT, HG, and Dignity Village, institutional constraints are in place to ensure that these encampments lack the power to fulfill their desires to remove unwanted individuals. Not only did the State of Oregon pass legislation making encampments and villages exempt from landlord-tenant law, meaning they have no possessory rights to exclude, these constraints were already informally practiced for a decade leading up to the 2019 Oregon State legislation based on the city's agreements with these communities. Overlapping systemic constraints are thus in place that delimit how encampment residents may enact these types of decisions, decisions most immanently about their safety and privacy and their involuntary movement from spaces of respite. The residents' powerlessness here is unjust because of how it inhibits them from ensuring their own safety and ability to secure a right to remain in propertied space.

Compared to nonprofit-led or "managed" villages in Portland, however, self-governed encampments hold moderately more decision-making authority. As detailed in chapter 3, self-governing encampments enable residents the ability to develop their social and especially political capacities. Residents' self-development is not relegated to the spaces of encampments themselves but may be enacted through wider sociopolitical relations throughout the city. There is no simple binary for residents' relations outside of the spaces of the encampment (or within), where one's agency is denied or affirmed absolutely. Residents do enjoy moderate agency in their daily life, particularly in the encampment. And in this way, residents are not entirely powerlessness in making everyday decisions about what they will do to become housing-stable. However, the city government's transition away from self-governing encampments toward a nonprofit-led village model illustrates one instance wherein power is enacted over the relatively powerless without leaving the latter much capacity for effective response. As Young notes, the powerless are "situated so that they must take orders and rarely have the right to give them."[39] The inability to reciprocate orders and control one's immediate circumstances is germane to most top-down traditional shelters, but this is so even in nonprofit-led villages to varying degrees.

Residents feeling powerless or ineffective in making decisions about the encampment where they reside is a feature of many nonprofit-led villages. As the city's preferred model of alternative shelter, these types of communities have proliferated throughout Portland. Perhaps more so than with the self-governing villages, residents I interviewed felt less agency in being able to act on or affect the everyday decisions around the village. In Kenton Women's Village (KWV), for instance, some residents did not feel that their voices were heard or that they even had the opportunity to participate in the organization of the village. It is also true that most of the KWV residents liked that the village was largely organized for them, as the KWV model had far more institutional support than self-governing villages. Many residents enter this community "in survival mode," as one resident told me. For many reasons, then, nonprofit control made the residents' lives there easier.

Nevertheless, some residents noted their lives were determined by the nonprofit running the community. A few residents said, for instance, that they did not initiate the general assembly meetings but rather were told by the nonprofit when they were going to meet. To them, it felt like the meetings were really just information-sharing sessions led by the social worker on site, where residents could share their opinions about the ongoings in the village afterward. One result of this organizing style, as another resident told me, is that residents "have to get [the nonprofit's] approval before we do anything." Where this lack of decision-making authority can become an issue, one resident noted, was with new member intake. Unlike the self-governing encampments, KWV does not get to make a final decision about who the new members of the community will be. "We really can't say yes or no, unless we know there is a problem with a person," one member said. This extends to Portland's six new safe rest villages, where members do not get to reflect on new members. Instead, the nonprofits in charge do all referrals, a highly controlled process that selects primarily those sleeping rough on the street near where the safe rest village is located. Much more so than KWV, the safe rest village intake process closely mirrors that of traditional indoor shelters.

As I argued in chapter 2, the decision by the city to transition away from self-governing encampments toward a nonprofit-led model concretized the relative lack of decision-making authority for village residents. Residents of most of the nonprofit villages understand, therefore, that by agreeing to live there, they have less control over their living conditions. There can be a sense of powerlessness, then, for new members who accept a spot to live in the newer villages. The injustices of powerlessness here relate to how the rights and relations of property surrounding encampments inhibit the ways in which residents can exercise their own judgement and authority in decision-making, and not only when deciding who resides in the encampments and villages and therefore how their security and privacy may better be protected. Injustice here also lies in how residents are and are not able to act on their own decisions about what everyday life looks like in collective communities.

CULTURAL IMPERIALISM

Exploitation, marginalization, dispossession, and powerlessness are oppressions that identify how power is realized, directed at, or taken away from some groups in relation to others. These oppressions are institutional and structural, Young notes, in that they "delimit people's material lives, including but not restricted to the resources they have access to and the concrete opportunities they have or do not have to develop or exercise their capabilities."[40] As such, they can inform us about relations of power affecting unhoused people residing in encampments, as they highlight who is authorized to benefit from an individual's or institution's power over resources, and on what terms. While these oppressive relations are often expressed materially, more cultural forms of oppression function through idealist rhetoric pertaining to how the unhoused ought to be dealt with in liberalism.

Young's fourth type of oppression, therefore, addresses how "cultural imperialism" establishes norms through a dominant group's valuation of social relations and institutions. Cultural imperialism is defined as "the universalization of a dominant group's experience and culture, and its establishment as the norm."[41] Cultural oppression partly takes place when a dominant group expresses its own experiences, values, and ideas about what is good in the world as a reference for society more generally.[42] Groups who do not fall into these social norms become marked as "other," straying from what is normatively expected of an individual. The injustice of cultural imperialism, Young argues, resonates in the reality that groups marked as other in relation to dominant society struggle to have their experiences and ideals considered and acted upon, while at the same time, the cultural norms of dominant society are imposed on those demarcated as deviant.[43] For Young, these processes of othering are about concealing difference, subsuming the totality of cultural experiences and values into those belonging to dominant society alone.

As argued in chapter 1, the normative "propertied citizen" occupies a culturally dominant position within liberalism. Given that the ownership model remains dominant within liberal states, one's ownership of and access to property assumes the fulfillment of liberal ideals and values of just and proper relationships with landed resources. Despite unhoused and housed people sharing complimentary desires to be stably housed, cultural dominance is nonetheless shaped by the property-secure and the institutions supporting them, by articulating and determining what property is and how it should properly be used. Property relations, in this way, reveal cultural values of dominant society concerning not only what is considered good and fair but also what is considered just in relation to the dominant norms in liberalism.

Cultural oppression thus arises through various relations between the unhoused and those more secure in their property interests. Discrimination by way of racial othering, ableism, and on the basis of sexual orientation, for example, significantly affects unhoused people's treatment in society. These reductions of difference present themselves in the different ways that dominant society—comprising the property-secure—shapes the values inherent to "proper" citizenship through the use of landed resources.

For Portland's encampment residents, proper citizenship is most notable when the property-secure seek to control how unhoused people become stable. That the property-secure attempt to determine what is best for encampment residents was a commonplace in my interviews with housed people. One homeowner who lived in the same neighborhood as HG stated that their irritation with HG stemmed primarily from the fact that the space is self-managed, and consequently, that its residents are purposefully skirting an assumed liberal social contract. "[Hazelnut Grove residents] have no intention of moving on. I've met these people at our neighborhood meetings," she said, and "they are quite content to live there forever, do whatever the hell they want." For this homeowner, that HG was self-managed came down to social deficiency, implying that unhoused people deviated from what is proper, if not expected. More than that, it was about how individuals at HG resisted being "controlled," as mentioned in chapter 2. For this homeowner, the proper way for unhoused people to engage with dominant (property-secure) society was to submit to traditional shelter; otherwise, she worried that HG would incentivize other people to want to camp. "You can't allow camping," she stated. "Once you do that, everybody's going to come and put their tent up wherever they want. And I am not saying that you have to arrest them and jail them. But we need to have a facility where people can go." For her, HG was not just the material representation of social deprivation, it was *the* source of further deprivation, in that these unhoused people were not following social norms. It was a space that should not be allowed to exist, lest it further degrade the social conditions of her own status as a property-owning citizen. What was needed, she said, was for the government to "force people to do stuff they might not want to do" by banishing the encampment. Otherwise, she feared, "there is a whole chunk of people . . . not doing their end of the bargain for the good of society."

This homeowner's views are exceptionally deprecating of the unhoused and do not represent all property-secure people. Indeed, many homeowners I spoke with who neighbor self-governing encampments and villages saw them as assets to the neighborhood. Nevertheless, the above homeowner's views represent a popular perspective that has gained currency in the cultural discourse around houselessness in U.S. cities, and one that is narrated by some housed people: that unhoused communities do not know what is best for themselves and housed society ought to determine their path toward housing stability. These types of prescriptive relations between the housed and unhoused are culturally oppressive in that they define and uphold ideals of propriety, values assumed to be deviating away from core liberal ideals and property's role in maintaining them.

Though merely ideal perspectives, such values reinforce the types of institutional support encampments do and do not receive. For instance, as the opening vignette to this book reveals, the Overlook Neighborhood Association facilitated a two-year campaign to disband HG. Though unsuccessful, the association's political organizing around the matter involved constant engagement with the city government to incentivize it to remove HG from the neighborhood. In particular, the good neighbor agreement that OKNA was pushing for HG to sign during this time underscores how housed people seek to determine how unhoused should become stable, on housed people's terms. Similar processes occurred with the development of KWV, where the neighborhood executed a good neighbor agreement and highly regulated the conditions of the encampment's existence. The same can be said for many of the city's encampments and villages.

If the opposition of the property-secure constitutes one form of cultural dominance toward unhoused people, so too must it be considered cultural dominance when the city government decided to transition away from self-governance as an organizing approach to becoming stably housed. The fact that the city has moved away from self-governing encampments toward larger villages led by nonprofits suggests as much. As chapter 2 detailed, city government staff involved in the city's new encampments saw some value in the self-governing encampments, but not enough to justify their expansion. One result of this policy shift is the very recent expansion of mass outdoor encampments in Portland, a response intended to push the increasing number of unsheltered people out of public view. Such moves appeal to a property-owning and renter class of Portlanders who also seemed to have turned on the city's general practice of enabling, not eroding, unhoused people's self-determination. In this way, the values of liberal property articulated throughout this book frame the cultural idealism driving the social and institutional constraints on Portland's encampment communities.

VIOLENCE

Young's final criteria of oppression is found in the injustice of violent relations. The oppression of violence, Young argues, "consists not only in direct victimization, but in the daily knowledge shared by all members of oppressed groups that they are *liable* to violation, solely on account of their group identity."[44] Violence, then, is not simply physical attacks on groups, though as we saw in chapter 3, this threat is very real. Violence is also systemic, a social practice that requires maintenance. Systemic violence more broadly encompasses the contexts—the institutions and relations that make them possible—in which groups are targeted for or made susceptible to attack, harassment, intimidation, and physical harm.

Violence marks the circumstances for so many unhoused people in that they are subject to processes of physical and rhetorical othering. For Samira Kawash, unhoused people embody the failures of the liberal project to ensure equitable access to recognition as part of the public.[45] Here the unhoused are products of violence, social processes that more systemically lead to the exclusion of unhoused people from the "proper" public. Such exclusive publics result from institutional failure because of how they open up, rather than close down, opportunities for more systemic types of violence by which unhoused people are particularly affected.

The City of Portland has made strides to reduce the systemic injustice of violence that maintains houselessness as a condition. As chapter 2 suggested, encampments do increase the safety of residents relative to living rough on the streets or within the shelter system. And the recent additions of culturally specific villages like the KWV, the BIPOC, and Queer Affinity Villages, were developed to minimize the different types of violence that push many of their residents into houselessness. Dedicating safer space to support unhoused people who identify with marginalized identities has been enormously beneficial for encampment residents living in these spaces. In the broader context of liberal property relations, whereby people of color and women have faced and continue to face discrimination within the housing market, and again when they are pushed out of housing, culturally specific spaces of reprieve help reduce systemic violence for oppressed groups.

At the same time, the institutional support for encampments that seek to remedy the violence experienced by the unhoused population is not the same as redress for the violence generated by liberal systems of property. As indicated in the introduction to this book, the slow violence of property and possessive culture within liberalism produced and maintained centuries of individual and group-based harm and destruction. And the geo-historical consequences of liberal property relations are borne out today in the experiences of those residing in Portland's encampments.

Consider the story of Beth, a white woman in her early fifties, who had been living at KWV for almost a year at the time we spoke.[46] Beth has lived in Oregon nearly her entire life and has experienced and suffers from horrific traumas throughout her time there. In 2010 Beth was shot in the face by her then-fiancé, who died from a self-inflicted gunshot wound after attempting to take Beth's life. As if to prove her story, she showed me where bullet shrapnel remains lodged behind her jaw. After she stayed two months in the hospital and endured many surgeries, her father took care of her for a year. When she recovered enough to begin working again, she found only precarious employment, mostly as a personal caretaker. Her income was enough to afford rent and she roomed with a friend for a few years. Unfortunately, the house they were living in caught fire and she lost all of her belongings because she did not have renter's insurance. As a result of the fire, she lived on the street, sleeping in a tent in out-of-the-way spots as well as in her car, which once was broken into while she was sleeping. She lived rough for about two and half years until she heard the news about the opening of the women's village. Shortly thereafter, she applied with her friend and got in on its opening day.

By the time I finished fieldwork in 2018, Beth had found housing and moved out of the village thanks to the support of the nonprofit running KWV. Her story is remarkable in many ways. And while her past has been shaped by terrifying physical and psychological violence, to varying degrees, Beth's experience reflects the vulnerability to violence that unhoused and precariously housed women face more broadly. Nearly all the women I spoke with at KWV identified different types of intimate partner violence as a primary reason that they became unhoused and were seeking safer spaces to sleep. For these women, being precariously housed or unhoused meant being predisposed to violence. Fortunately, KWV provided a sense of community and safety for women like Beth. Yet, the oppressiveness of violence that affect them are often produced through the tenuousness of their relationship with property security. What renders such violent oppressions as unjust, and not simply harmful, is both physical and structural. For Beth, her near-death experience facilitated a years-long relationship with access to housing that is hard to even call precarious. While the direct physical violence to her person is clearly unjust, her inability to maintain a secure living environment despite being employed ought to be seen as a type of structural injustice. The institutional constraints of being impoverished within the free market, and especially within urban housing markets, exacerbated the psychological violence she experienced living on the street.

These five overlapping types of oppression identify how injustice is more specifically experienced by unhoused people in liberalism. By analyzing how encampment residents experience injustice from their own telling helps avoid relying upon perfect or ideal theories of justice. It avoids an impossible measurement of how far these injustices aberrate from "perfect" justice. While a liberal theory of property that encompasses relational justice, like Dagan's, provides an intriguing set of principles to identify what just property relations could be, it can only model shared ideals about maintaining the equal moral worth of individuals and the moral efficacy of not inhibiting an individual's self-development. Constructing idealized relations of property in liberalism cannot describe and therefore explicate how it is that individuals are affected by unjust property relations.

We cannot know what is unjustifiable regarding liberal property systems without real accounts of the harm enabled by such a system. Analyzing the substance of experienced injustices, therefore, enables stronger normative critique and judgement about how relations of property within liberalism are specifically unjust for unhoused people and what may be done to lessen them. To do so, it is useful to analyze how property in liberalism is *structurally* unjust, not merely for the unhoused but for all liberal subjects differently placed within liberal property. Drawing from Iris Marion Young's conception of a responsibility for injustice, the final sections of this chapter identify how injustice connects all subjects within liberal property relations, an account predicated on identifying the locus of political responsibility for attenuating the injustices of property for houselessness.

Structural Injustice and Responsibility

The conceptual arch of Young's work on justice—which begins by identifying types of oppression and moves to explaining how we are variously placed within and affected by the structures that reproduce these oppressions—is generative for making scholarship on injustice not only more analytically robust but politically advantageous. To claim that some thing or process is unjust, Young notes, "implies that we acknowledge the circumstance as grounded at least partly in institutions and the social processes they generate."[47] What follows from recognizing the causes of social harms and suffering, then, is that we "recognize an *obligation* to try to improve those social processes" that enable injustice.[48] Thus Young not only defines the contours of injustice but also identifies how it is structural, in service of implicating all those connected to the production and maintenance of injustice and to provide a political means of rectifying them.

Structural injustice exists when "social processes put large groups of persons under systematic threat of domination or deprivation of the means to develop and exercise their capacities, at the same time that these processes enable others to dominate or to have a wide range of opportunities for developing and exercising capacities available to them."[49] It locates the causes of injustice not in individual actions per se, as the legal system commonly does. Rather, structural injustice is the outcome of "many individuals and institutions acting to pursue their particular goals and interests ... within the limits of accepted rules and norms."[50] Significantly, the notion of structural injustice understands that many injustices like houselessness are the product of social structures and relations that often result from *unintended* actions. While individuals or organizations clearly do act in ways that are directly unjust toward others, the purpose of identifying structural injustice is to focus on how individuals' positions in relation to one another contribute to unjust social processes that constrain some while benefiting others.

Defining what constitutes structural injustice is only part of Young's project. Her later work develops a means of identifying responsibility for correcting unjust social processes. To do so, Young suggests a "social connection model of responsibility" to identify with whom responsibility lies for attenuating structural injustices. The connection model holds that all those who share in contributing to or benefiting from the processes producing injustice share a responsibility to change them. Given that no one individual can (usually) be held liable or blamed for structural injustices, the connection model instead locates responsibility in shared political participation. It is a shared responsibility in that structurally unjust processes can only be altered if "many actors from diverse positions within the social structures work together to intervene in them to try to produce other outcomes."[51] Interestingly, Young suggests that those who may be identified as "victims" of structural injustice are also responsible for transforming unjust structures, as they may have more insight into their constraints, even as they share this responsibility with those who are in more privileged or advantaged positions in relationship to them. Further, Young argues that individuals have "different kinds and degrees of forward-looking responsibility for justice," orders of responsibility determined by an individuals' differences in power, privilege, interest, and collective ability in relation to their contribution to unjust social processes.[52] As such, individuals along with organizations must consider how differences in their positions can work to undermine structural injustice.

Young's social connection model avoids the moralism present in much ideal justice theorizing by prioritizing *political* action and transformation. At the same time, by arguing that individuals are unjustly affected by social structures and that a given injustice is caused by social processes, Young suggests there is a moral obligation for all who produce injustice to contribute to eradicating the unjust aspects of these processes.[53] For Young, the political responsibility to act is an obligation that ought to be facilitated not through blame but through criticism of those benefiting and contributing to structural injustice. No one contributing to injustice is exempt from working to change unjust structures. Political pressure must be applied to ensure that individuals and organizations who contribute more to unjust processes take responsibility for changing unjust structures. Such obligations are not only political but something like an ethical requirement for those invested in and benefiting from the maintenance of these structures.

Young's framework for theorizing injustice provides conceptual guidance for analyzing the injustice of property in liberalism, particularly as it relates to unhoused people's condition within it. Far too often, the unhoused are blamed for their condition based on the choices they are *assumed* to have made to end up in that position. Young's model does not deny that people's lives are shaped by their own choices but stresses that it is neither fair nor accurate to blame individuals alone for their disadvantaged positions. Instead, Young embraces the idea that the unhoused and housed alike, real estate developers, city, state, and federal governments, and landlords, among others, hold differing levels of responsibility to change the unjust processes that produce and maintain the conditions leading to and perpetuating houselessness. From this perspective, the most powerful actors benefiting from the commodification of housing hold far more responsibility for changing unjust social processes leading to houselessness. At the same time, Young notes that those who benefit most are heavily disincentivized to change their privileged positions on their own accord. The only means of accounting for one's responsibility for changing unjust structural processes is political pressure.

Such a model supports a relational approach to analyzing property—one advanced throughout this book. As I argued in chapter 1, a relational understanding of property emphasizes not that unhoused people are excluded from property but that they are forced to navigate the various social processes maintaining barriers within property. Again, a relational analysis "reveals that the security of the privileged to access and secure shelter produces and depends upon the production of property precarity for others."[54] To apply a shared responsibility model of injustice through relational property analyses allows us to assess and explain how the social structures contributing to unjust relations for houseless people implicate society more broadly and oblige contributors to amend unjust structures.

Taking Young's model of shared responsibility seriously when considering the lives of Portland's encampment residents, therefore, means understanding not only what the substance and experiences of injustice looks like but identifying and criticizing the individual and organizational complicity in maintaining the unjust relations of property that contribute to and maintain houselessness and that constrain the opportunities of unhoused people to be uninhibited by them. When doing so, it may seem like there are easily identifiable actors who hold a larger share of responsibility for injustice. The Portland city government, for instance, contributes to unjust social processes by limiting the property rights of self-managed encampments. As argued in chapter 3, this restriction diminishes the ability of these collectives to exercise their capacities as self-determining individuals. Similarly, the State of Oregon is also complicit by enacting legislation ensuring that encampment residents have no rights of exclusive possession. Looking historically at the decades of decisions that have gone into maintaining Portland's socially and economically iniquitous housing market, it may also seem like we can also attribute a larger share of responsibility to housing developers who have chosen and continue to choose *not* to develop affordable housing because doing so often does not earn them as high profits without government subsidy. Given that housing development decisions are reviewed by government planning agencies and are incentivized through tax abatements, housing developers, city and county governments, and the landlords who contribute to the social structures maintaining exploitation in the housing market also bear responsibility for changing these unjust structures.

These are the usual suspects who we may intuitively expect to bear more responsibility for producing the houselessness situation we see in U.S. cities. That there are easily identified actors overlooks those who are perhaps most responsible for houselessness in the aggregate: the renters and homeowners who collectively perpetuate the unjust processes of liberal property markets. In the abstract, property owners and renters of property are clearly the largest group herein, with vast economic and social differences among them. But does the fact that nearly everyone in Portland who owns or rents mean that *all* then bear responsibility for contributing to the structural injustices of houselessness? According to Young's model of shared responsibility, it does. And herein lies the primary shortcoming of Young's model.

Young is correct to argue that we should share a collective responsibility as owners and renters to change the unjust processes contributing to houselessness in the city. A first step in taking accountability in this model is understanding how we contribute to the unjust aspects of liberal property in different ways. The second step, taking responsibility for changing these unjust structures, is the challenging part. The shared responsibility model, again, asks all who contribute to structural injustice to understand their role by acknowledging their positionality, their privilege and power *relative* to the unhoused, other low-income renters, the city government, real estate developers and the banks that fund them and to apply political pressure to those who contribute to the injustices of liberal property. Young argues there lies a collective obligation to ensure that our political action eradicates these specific social processes to attenuate the injustices of liberal property. For renters or owners must first recognize they have some role in contributing to the specific unjust structural processes maintaining houselessness before they can attempt to make any substantive change. This accords with a relational model of property by connecting how the relative privileges of some are gained by the production of processes leading to the unjust circumstances experienced by others.

While Young's model perceptively recognizes that structural injustices require taking responsibility despite any singly liable actor, the idea of shared responsibility for justice leaves unaddressed one crucial component motivating real action. And that is that we, the responsible, do not know what, precisely, our response must be. Part of the limit to action here emanates from the fact that we cannot fully understand our position relative to others. Measuring our share of obligation for changing unjust social processes is thus difficult to do. It is, however, fairly reasonable to judge that large real estate corporations have much more to gain by maintaining unaffordable housing markets, and assigning some larger share of responsibility would not be implausible. But there is a more stymying aspect of Young's shared responsibility model. It avoids liability. If there is no "blame" or liability assigned for structural injustice, I argue there is logically little natural *duty* for individuals, governments, or corporations to respond and account for their contribution to structural injustice.[55] More specifically, the shared responsibility model offers no specific mechanism ensuring that those responsible for contributing to unjust structures will attempt, or may even be morally responsible for, attenuating their actions, an aspect of liberalism that is not an unfortunate exception to but a normative feature of its ideology and legal structure.

Duties of Justice

Young's model does not effectively establish a duty of justice due to how she envisions the response to injustice. Given that Young avoids a liability model for collectives, the shared responsibility model does not establish that collectives must be *obliged* to correct for the injustices resulting from social structures. One shortcoming of the shared responsibility model, then, is that no direct means of coercing collectives to act exists. Indeed, because Young's model recognizes that "social structures do not constrain in the form of direct coercion of some individuals over others; they constrain more indirectly and cumulatively as blocking possibilities," the model avoids legitimating the idea that the iniquitous outcomes of social structures are in fact coercive, if only indirectly.[56] This does not negate the intent behind Young's model, but it does make locating clearly defined responsibility more difficult absent any clearly identified form of coercion to rectify injustice.

In a constructive critique of the shared model of responsibility for injustice, Jeffrey Reiman argues that Young's model cannot clearly define responsibility because of how it reifies the concept of "social structures," effectively erasing the human agency behind collective actions. Reiman notes that this is a logical misstep. He argues that "if we grant that a social structure is a pattern of human behavior in which human beings indirectly coerce one another into positions with limited possibilities, then the behaviors that constitute social structures have the features of unjust behavior: *they are acts of potentially unjustified coercion.*"[57] In contrast, Reiman argues that when one takes a "de-reified" view of social structures, "it does not matter that we cannot disentangle causal relations between different people's actions and the structural injustice they lead to ... *everyone* who is not in active resistance is contributing to social injustice."[58] To the extent that a de-reified view of social structure gets us closer to understanding how collective actions produce unjust social relations, even if indirectly, then there exists the potential to conceive of a means of attributing *collective* moral responsibility for injustice.

Reiman notes that Young's model assumes that "people have a moral responsibility for monitoring the social institutions within which they live, and a duty to join with others to rectify injustices that those institutions cause."[59] This is what Reiman calls the "strong form" of moral responsibility operating in Young's model. The strong form of responsibility "expands the notion of guilt, and thus of blame, beyond the normal insistence that people only be held guilty of and blamed for acts they did knowing and intending that they would cause evil."[60] What follows from the implication that people have a moral responsibility to hold institutions accountable and act to correct them is that individuals can "be held guilty of and blamed for acts that contribute to structural injustice even if they did not knowingly or intentionally bring about evil, *because they failed to monitor and correct for the institutions that led to it.*"[61] The strong form of responsibility holds that individuals can be held guilty for contributing to structural injustice "without knowing that they were . . . *because they ought to have known.*" Just like laws that hold individuals responsible for causing harm to others "with hazardous materials if they acted without knowledge that they ought to have had,"[62] Reiman argues, so too does the strong form of responsibility in Young's model allow us to extend responsibility to individuals for other structural injustices, say for houselessness.

The "weaker form" of Young's moral responsibility that Reiman identifies finds that guilt and blame can only be attributed if individuals *knowingly* contribute to injustice, which would hold individuals "prospectively morally responsible" and not "retrospectively guilty or blamable for actions that led" to a given structural injustice.[63] In other words, only once an individual is made aware of—and understands that they have and continue to contribute to—structural injustice can they then be held responsible. By locating moral responsibility through these strong and weak forms, Young's model could identify collective moral responsibility for rectifying injustices to individual and institutional actions.

Though a de-reified view of social structure helps identify who may be responsible, Young's model still overlooks the means through which collectives can be held morally responsible for rectifying structurally produced injustices. And this is the crux of the issue with the model. When we normatively attribute responsibility but do not demand a duty be acted on, there are some negative responses that are likely to follow. One is that those identified as being responsible, even when they are made aware of their contribution to systemic injustice, may simply deny their contribution to injustice. Indeed, a few Portland homeowners I interviewed who purchased their home in a neighborhood with already high, and quickly rising, housing values saw no connection between their contribution to either the rising unaffordability of housing in the city or the increasing numbers of unhoused people sleeping outside. A more likely response, however, is that an individual who recognizes that they are contributing to structural injustice may simply state that the problem is too big for any one individual to rectify and therefore take no action. This sentiment was far more common among the homeowners I spoke with regarding their contribution to rising housing costs and to economic and racial displacement; they understood that housing prices were difficult to afford not only for unhoused people but even for themselves *and* that their ownership contributed to the affordability crisis the city was experiencing at that time. Indeed, this type of response is entirely understandable and renders liability nearly impossible to assign. It is important to ask, then, whether by using Young's model we can reasonably locate responsibility for the injustice of houselessness on renters and homeowners, or even governments or corporations. And if so, should we define this responsibility as a *duty* with which they must comply?

When we speak of a "natural" duty to rectify injustice within liberal democratic states, the question arises of how and whether "deficits" in justice are the responsibility of individuals, institutions, or both. For the question of duty necessitates we consider whether it is ethical to coerce individuals to rectify their contribution to structural, not individually identifiable, injustices. Indeed, some suggest that it may be wrong to coerce individuals into rectifying structural injustices to which they contribute. For, and as mentioned earlier, it is difficult to position oneself relative to others' level of responsibility. It is for this reason that Laura Valentini argues that when individuals "can reasonably foresee that doing their fair share will not get them any closer to justice *due to others' non-compliance*, it is wrong to insist that they ought to comply."[64] From this vantage point, if renters and homeowners understand that they are collectively contributing to the inequities of the housing market but see that taking action to lessen the oppressive structures maintaining property is likely to do little to rectify the situation for unhoused people, then individuals do not hold a moral responsibility to take action beyond their "fair share." For, as Valentini argues, "the greater the injustice due to widespread non-compliance is, the 'lighter' the demands of the natural duty of justice become."[65] Individuals are not responsible for picking up the slack of large justice deficits, like in the case of houselessness, because individuals alone cannot be under any natural duty to "do more than one's fair share," unless, that is, there exist "some *relational* normative structures—such as contracts or role responsibilities—that require it."[66] This is not to say that individuals have no moral responsibility to *attempt* to rectify an injustice to which they knowingly contribute. Absent any relational mechanism requiring a natural duty to rectify one's contribution to structural injustice, however, there is *no institutional mechanism* to enforce that any action be taken.

For Valentini, then, responsibility for large structural injustices like houselessness may not be considered an obligation or duty of justice, but rather, a function of beneficence. Here, individual contributors to structural injustice have *no* natural duty to do more than their fair share to help the unhoused, they have only a moral responsibility to "assist others when this is not too costly to them."[67] For absent any "solidaristic role responsibilities, compliers' duties to pick up the slack are a matter of beneficence, not of justice."[68] Put another way, without an established and institutionalized duty requiring that an individual do more than their fair share, what may be morally expected of individuals to address structural injustices like houselessness ends at making charitable contributions to the unhoused and/or taking political actions to persuade those in power to reform institutions to rectify the issue.

If we are to apply Valentini's arguments about duty to Young's shared model of responsibility, then, we are hard pressed to find that individuals who collectively contribute to producing and maintaining structural injustices cannot be held morally accountable for more than their fair share, which, absent any relational "contract" between others, largely amounts to charitable contributions. Ultimately, this looks a lot like the status quo today. Individuals may volunteer at houseless shelters or donate to nonprofits that assist unhoused people. And they may even show up at city council meetings and demand that the city build more affordable housing and challenge the government to stop sweeping unhoused people off the streets. All of these actions may be incredibly helpful and even lifesaving. But to the extent that this has already been the manner through which liberal society has attempted to mitigate houselessness, it seems less likely that Young's model of shared responsibility will hold individuals responsible for their contribution to structural injustice, as it may not be morally justified to establish a duty for individuals to rectify the myriad issues related to housing instability.

These more normative examinations of Young's shared model of responsibility help us see how morally and politically complicated it may be to actually realize justice for the unhoused through this paradigm. Nevertheless, I find conceptual and normative value in extending Young's model in this way. Specifically, I argue it helps glean insight into the sociopolitical means through which liberalism enables structural issues like houselessness to remain relatively unaffected. And we can also derive insights into political responses to identifying duties for rectifying injustices.

If we find that we cannot reasonably place moral responsibility on *individuals*—renters and owners—to rectify houselessness, this does not mean that we cannot more directly establish a duty to rectify structural injustice for *institutions*. Again, absent any relational role responsibilities holding individuals to account for rectifying structural injustice, a clear duty to act is not identified. In this case, beneficence, not justice, according to Valentini, is the only moral responsibility that individuals have to rectify structural injustice. But this pertains to circumstances where there is no institutional mechanism that coerces individuals to hold institutions responsible for rectifying injustices in the first place. To take the example of Portland's government, it holds no duty to rectify houselessness. It only holds responsibility for maintaining the welfare services that it can reasonably offer.

If a duty was established requiring institutions to rectify structural injustices—to alleviate poverty for example—individuals can then be held morally responsible for ensuring that institutions rectify structural injustices. As Valentini puts it:

> What justice demands in cases of institutional reform—beyond the default requirement to do one's fair share—is partly mediated by one's *role responsibilities* as a member of the relevant institution. When institutions are voluntarily joined, those responsibilities are acquired through voluntary action. When institutions are not voluntarily joined, but morally mandatory (e.g. the state), those responsibilities are grounded in the *natural* duty of justice... [H]ow we should interpret the natural duty of justice is not independent of our associative role responsibilities. By default, the duty requires us to do our fair share in reforming unjust institutions that "apply to us"... Whether it requires more is determined by local rules of association, by the responsibilities attached to one's role as a citizen in a given community.[69]

Valentini thus establishes here that there *is* a natural duty that may potentially be placed on individuals to hold institutions to account for rectifying structural injustice. This is true *if*, and this is crucial, there exists an established duty to ensure that institutions must rectify structural injustice in the first place. Unfortunately, no claims of duty against the state exist that can rectify the injustices of houselessness because there are no established natural duties for the state to do so.

As I have argued through the book, the injustices experienced by unhoused people are mostly structural, produced through relations of property that collectively and indirectly limit unhoused peoples' possibilities to become stable in certain ways. Absent any role responsibilities for individuals to hold institutions like the state to account for their natural duty to rectify these injustices, there is (currently) no relational mechanism to enforce more just relations within liberalism. If justice is about establishing duty, locating responsibility for the injustices of property is not going to be easy, though this is not to say impossible, either. And it is precisely here that I want to conclude this chapter by breaking from abstractions to address how the challenge of justifying duty actually limits our ability to challenge the injustices of property.

There are two important insights that follow from discourse on responsibility and duty for structural injustice within liberalism. The first and most politically strategic insight is that if we establish a duty for institutions to rectify structural injustice, this opens up a pathway to develop a legally enforceable claim against the state for a right to obtain housing.[70] As long as there remains no institutional mechanism or duty for the state to rectify an individual's lack of housing, the state will not do so. Given that the City of Portland does not have an established duty to provide housing for the unhoused, forcing the city to rectify houselessness is not justifiable. It would be justifiable, however, to coerce the city to rectify houselessness if a duty was established in law that obliges it to act. Such a legal strategy already exists as a call to action elsewhere in the world, and certainly the fight for a legally enforceable right to housing would go further in reducing houselessness. Unfortunately, no such legislation has been enacted that may establish a duty for the U.S. state to actualize this right. And it seems unlikely, given the historical arch of property rights and relations in the United States, that such a right will be forthcoming, as critical as this political struggle could be for mitigating and ending houselessness.

The second insight is more normatively significant given how liberalism limits the capacity to enact duty-creating responsibilities for rectifying injustices of houselessness and of property. And that is that however well intentioned any one individual or government may be in helping unhoused people, no matter how sincere and genuine they are in their resolve to ensure that people will not go unhoused within liberal capitalism, the limited duty to rectify the many injustices of houselessness renders inconsequential these actions to the scale of need that exists in the United States to effectively end houselessness. For if property rights and relations structurally produce and maintain houselessness, as I argue they do, anything short of such an established duty for institutions to rectify houselessness seems unrealistic when it comes to making legitimate moves toward ending houselessness. And certainly, the beneficence of well-off donors will not solve the problem, for as Mitchell argues, eradicating houselessness would halt the ability of capital to reproduce itself through a reserve army of unhoused labor.[71] While this may seem pessimistic, over four decades of liberal democratic policies indicate that beneficence at best may quell houselessness for brief periods of time and in certain geographic locations.

I suggest that the intractable nature of this normative and legal dilemma necessitates not that we throw away the intuitions and political intentions behind Young's shared responsibility model but that we read its shortcomings another way. For it seems that Young's failure to definitively establish moral responsibility for rectifying injustice resides less within the model's theoretical limitations than in those presented by the sociolegal and material circumstances in which such a conceptual model is applied. Put another way, the shortcomings of the shared responsibility model become readily apparent only when they are applied to the extant material constraints of liberalism and liberal systems of property. For within the dialectical relations of propertied citizenship, struggles to effect greater change for unjust structural processes do not need to be proportionately shared or even rectified by all of the contributors to them. And this, I argue, is exactly why houselessness will remain within liberalism until we are obliged to coerce institutions into rectifying the injustices of property that result in houselessness.

As such, while the question of who bears responsibility is helpful to implicate contributors to structural injustice, I suggest we must reformulate Young's question for the purposes of political expediency. Given the legal and moral limitations of liberal duties of justice, it may be more useful to ask not who bears responsibility but *how* do we respond to the structurally produced injustices of liberal property? And what does an effective response look like within these constraints? How do we respond in a way that requires accountability and even responsibility for the injustices that unhoused people face? As argued in the beginning of this chapter, ideal theorizing will not usefully lead us to practical answers here. Only by assessing how unhoused communities attempt to produce new material relations surrounding land and property can we identify where responsibility actually lies to correct for structural injustice in liberalism. And this requires that we return to the struggles for shelter stability that illustrate the unjust dimensions of property in order to build the foundations for more just relations with land that refuse liberalism's limitations.

CONCLUSION
Responding to Injustice

This book's examination of the injustice of propertied citizenship seeks to show what life is often like for unhoused people and how opportunities to become housing-stable are constrained within liberal democracies. Beyond creating more affordable housing, too often, the question of what to do about houselessness becomes mired in a finger-pointing contest. Some blame individuals for their own precarity within the housing system while many more condemn the actions of the state, and its acquiescence to capital's desire for profit, as the predominant reason for producing and maintaining houselessness. I do not disagree with the latter criticism, and the arguments throughout the book promote a supplementary way of assessing the conditions maintaining houselessness in liberalism. For while houselessness as an economic condition is produced by the inequities of a socially differentiated economy, the circumstances that maintain houselessness are thoroughly political.

I argued throughout that unhoused peoples' political subjectivity—the ability to feel a sense of agency and authority over the decisions individuals make for themselves as well as to be legitimated as part of the public sphere—is heavily mediated by property within liberalism. Liberalism does not merely promote property ownership as a means of securing a livelihood; it is equally the case that property secures and enables for individuals the private authority to be self-governing and self-determining within this political system. Ownership begets political power. I argued against the notion that, due to the relative expansion of civil and political rights over the last half century, ownership no longer secures one's participation as a "proper" political subject. Such a conception misses the mutually reinforcing features of property with citizenship. Particularly when we understand the relationship between property and citizenship dialectically, a relationship whose history has intertwined in many ways over the last few centuries, we are able to see how one's relationship to property remains a primary indicator for how an individual is able to flourish by living a life on terms that they themselves are able to determine.

When looking at property relationally, I suggest we are able to better see the ways in which houselessness is unjust. It is true that for Portland's encampment residents, having access to property is a necessary and lifesaving good. Especially when collectively managed property is organized democratically by unhoused people for other unhoused people, these types of encampments illustrate how alternative property forms work against the constraints of the liberal ownership model. Yet, as I argued in chapter 3, because of how Portland's self-governing encampments are restricted in their possessory rights, the encampments' authority to realize their collectively made decisions are diminished, while "managed" tiny house villages enjoy even less authority over determining their environments.

But it is not only that the property rights of encampments diminish the collective political capacity of their residents. Liberal relations of property also push people into houselessness for many more reasons. I argued in chapter 4 that unhoused people's circumstances within liberal property are oppressive and unjust. There I showed how property relations exploit renters and wage laborers to transfer their finances and energies to those who financially benefit from owning property through commodified housing, benefiting from others' precarious relation to property. Property is further oppressive in that it marginalizes individuals who have been and remain dispossessed on account of their divergence from a historically white-dominant society of propertied citizens; it is oppressive in the way that it ensures that those without ownership or access rights are powerless to make decisions about how they want to become stably housed; and it is oppressive because it increases unhoused people's likelihood of encountering violence, emotional and physical, because of their inability to secure safer spaces to exist. Most significantly, I argued that when we do not recognize the structural processes contributing to unjust processes producing and maintaining liberal property, and houselessness specifically, we leave unaccountable those perhaps seen as not responsible: individuals owning and renting property, in addition to governments and corporations, whose varying levels of economic, legal, and social contribution to maintaining property result in the structural injustices experienced not only in Portland but in many other places.

My analysis in chapter 4, however, indicates how challenging it is to account for and rectify one's contribution to houselessness. There I argued that the shared model of responsibility that Young rightly urges us to employ is unlikely to engender individual or institutional action rectifying the injustices of houselessness and that of liberal property broadly. Given the absence of established duties that can legitimately ensure that action be taken to rectify the structurally produced injustices of houselessness, liability is virtually impossible to assign to all those who contribute to the inequities of property. As useful as a politics of responsibility is that advances a collective response to the injustice of property by intuitively identifying who contributes to and may be responsible for these harms, the model seems less effective for legitimately disrupting the oppressive features still structuring propertied citizenship today. And that is not because it fails to normatively configure what a useful political response *could* be. It does this well. Rather, our collective responsibility for rectifying injustice is mediated by the material constraints of liberal property systems themselves. These mediations pit homeowners and the state largely against the unhoused, as unhoused groups' enactments of property by way of encampments threaten the "value" of homeowners' possessions and, more ideologically, the proper means of controlling what being a virtuous political subject within liberalism looks like. And yet, alternate enactments of property, like those of self-managed encampments on collectively managed property, show us bit by bit how the ownership model of property is not inevitable or indomitable.

Alternatives to the ownership model have long existed, however thoroughly policed their existence is in the logic of liberalism.[1] They show us how liberal property remains in dialectical tension with political subjectivity, at once open to different forms of land uses at some times and in some places, yet vigorously constrained by social and political norms in others. Collective struggles like self-governed encampments allow us to rethink what property is or could be, and how the relations maintaining it serve to simultaneously leverage more advantageous and less just processes for differently positioned people within liberalism. In light of this, the most pressing question remains: How do we respond to injustices of liberal property? What would a response look like, considering the myriad and overlapping barriers produced by a system that legally justifies the oppression of unhoused (and housed) people within it?

How we come to know what our response should be ought not to be articulated through abstract ideal principles. Though political responsibility can certainly be shaped by ideal accounts of why injustice must be corrected for, the struggles and movements of unhoused collectives offer extant circumstances to assess what actions can be taken. For the struggles of unhoused communities show us the rigorous organizing that groups are engaging in to confront these injustices and how their responses are met with hostility and political responses that in turn limit their ability to realize autonomy and a sense of justice. More generally, the movements behind encampments show how the sociopolitical act of responding reveals new geographies of justice within and against liberal property. Instead of turning to normative theories to help identify more just property relations, therefore, I elaborate on and assess two situations of houseless struggles in Portland attempting to carve out more just relations to land within and against liberalism. The examples help make sense of what groups are doing to respond, how their responses are received, and what the political mechanism of shared responsibility offers us as we seek to lessen unjust relations of property.

The AfroVillage Movement

The first example informs our understanding of how we may respond to the injustice of houselessness maintained by relations of property, if only to learn by way of example how much the fight for material relationships with land is central to these struggles. The AfroVillage (AV) movement in Portland is not a literal space where unhoused people can become stably housed.[2] At least, not yet. Rather, the AV is a concept that its founder LaQuida has been working toward realizing for years. The idea behind the AV is to provide housing and health care support for Portland's most vulnerable populations by specifically focusing on those who are racially marginalized.[3] As LaQuida put it when describing the movement to a popular Portland weekly, the AV movement is not just "about a tiny village, I'm talking about a cultural center for community that has been displaced from all over, so that we can see ourselves in the City of Portland." The AV is intended as a space of collective repair for Black and other people of color in Portland, for both the unhoused and housed. Having lived in Portland for the better part of the past two decades, LaQuida understands that AV will be about "connectivity," a social and physical space where those who may feel they have no place in Portland can reconnect.

As mentioned in the introduction, Portland's unhoused Black population has increased disproportionately to the general Black population in the county. And though the BIPOC Village of Portland offers people of color a safer space of shelter, few other encampments or traditional indoor shelter spaces throughout the city offer culturally specific resources like this. When I spoke with LaQuida, she traced this absence back to multiple things, like the racist founding of the state and the ways in which anti-Black policies shape the demographics of Portland today. "[Black people] come to a place like Portland, Oregon, where it's being recognized as . . . 'Keep Portland weird' or 'the whitest city in America.' And, often times, even the people who grew up here don't really feel like they have a connection to community, because in order for us to get together . . . it just can't be random." The lack of connection for many Black people in Portland, she noted, requires that social spaces exist "where we all feel welcomed." The AV is an attempt to build the physical foundations helpful for realizing this opportunity for connection, by serving Black and other unhoused Portlanders of color who have been disproportionately affected by the historical development of the city.

The AV model is premised on the pillars of self-determination and relational justice to underscore its mission of self-empowerment. The model identifies that the AV will be a space of safety for people to heal and rejuvenate, one especially intended to support Black women who are experiencing houselessness and were formerly incarcerated.[4] Where the village will be located has not been determined, but the terms of stewardship are definite. The village will be self-governed by its residents, with the intention of having the land owned by the villagers themselves. "If you don't own anything, you can't make a decision," LaQuida noted. This puts thrust behind AV's desire to enact a trust in land to better secure the empowerment of the villagers involved. "If it's a land trust, then it's within the community . . . it's ours until we say that it's not ours," she said. Land trusts are desirable for how they can maintain housing affordability for low-income inhabitants by separating the costs of ownership of land from the cost of improvements on the land, thus permanently removing the property from the speculative risk of the housing market.[5] And for LaQuida, this is exactly the point. Whether AV develops into a tiny house village or takes the form of a building, to remove the village from the inequities of the market, she notes, is first "about affordability" and then about "maintaining it for the folks to have within their inventory for their family." AV's vision is a reaction to contemporary and past exclusions from ownership and access to land, one centered on remaking relations of property in order to help make Portlanders of color less vulnerable than those within the traditional housing market. The significance of a land trust, in turn, would be to enable unhoused people of color a sense of agency over how they want to become stably housed.

The plan for AV speaks volumes about why such a village is necessary within the liberal property landscape. The values of self-determination and authority over one's own living environment outlined in AV's vision emanate from the historical relations of property within liberalism. To the extent that property has mediated one's political agency and authority over one's ability to exercise decisions about being housed safely and permanently, Black people have been violently precluded from the benefits of this relationship. AV desires to remove itself from those historical relations to land and property, for its members understand that political subjectivity and personhood partly become conditional upon the social, economic, and legal relations that maintain liberal property systems.

To speculate about how AV will be realized materially is fruitless. But we can learn from the values that AV embodies in its years of organizing to realize the village physically in the world. AV shows us why alternative enactments of property are needed for unhoused people whose housing instability has been highly predicated on being racially differentiated through the proprietarian logic of propertied citizenship. More just relations for AV, then, require not only alternative ownership structures for access to land and thus housing but also require, as LaQuida puts it, "reinvestment in people" as a form of reparations for the unjust relations of liberal property systems. That the village has been slow to secure funding, unlike other villages and encampments in Portland, may be equally telling. For a model of property relations like those envisioned by AV, which seeks not to ascribe, but respond, to the dominance of the proprietarian logic of a "properly" ordered society, has been shown difficult to materialize for people of color within liberal capitalism.

Land Back for Barbie's Village

Barbie's Village (BV) is a tiny house community for unhoused Indigenous people living in the settler city of Portland. It was founded to honor Atwai Barbie Jackson Shields, or Barbie, who passed away from a brain aneurysm in 2018, leaving behind a husband and four children. Barbie was a member of the confederated Tribes of Warm Springs, a band of Indigenous peoples traditionally living near the tributaries of what is known as the Columbia River before they were forcibly resettled on the Warm Springs Reservation located southeast of what is known as Mt. Hood National Forest. Barbie lived in the Portland metropolitan area, and though she and her family were precariously housed themselves before her untimely passing, she was nonetheless invested in helping other unhoused Indigenous peoples in the area become stable through health care outreach. Established in her honor, BV is a means of recognizing her contribution to healing unhoused Indigenous peoples from the socioeconomic and political harms frequently experienced within settler societies.

What makes the case of BV instructive for informing a response to the injustices of property is that the land that the village sits on is not owned by the city government or a private owner, unlike all of the other encampments and villages in Portland. Instead, BV is owned by the village itself. Significantly, the property on which BV sits was formerly owned by the Westminster Presbyterian Church located in Portland's Laurelhurst neighborhood. Through the work of the Indigenous organization Future Generations Collaborative (FGC), the nonprofit behind BV, the property was bequeathed to FGC, transferring the full title in March 2024. Given the historically violent relations that Indigenous peoples have had with the church, the transfer of title reflects an uncommon but meaningful approach toward repair for past and contemporary injustices against Indigenous peoples. When the village is completed and running, BV will host around ten tiny homes on site for families with children in addition to the use of the buildings on the property that were formerly used by the church. BV will appropriate the buildings in service to helping the broader Indigenous community in Portland, providing childcare, kitchen and gathering spaces, and the capacity to host cultural events.

For the organizers of BV, receiving title over the property was an incredible moment, one they did not think would happen. And for good reasons. The FGC had been negotiating with the church for over two years, discussing what the terms of such a transfer would entail. One of the main facilitators behind BV, Jillene, told me that the process had been at times fraught. "For two and half years we have been working with the church, trying to prove ourselves because some people in the church still don't trust us and they think we're going to fail." Part of the problem was a semantic dispute over what was being transferred. The issue, Jillene said, was that the transfer was not universally understood as "land back," but rather, as a "gift." "We call it land back. This is a part of the Land Back movement," said Jillene. But not all members of the church agreed with the wording of "land back," though the confederation of the church that established the title transfer did recognize the transfer of land as reparations for harms to Indigenous peoples by the church. Another related issue that developed through the process concerned the details about the use of and control over the property. BV already had been leasing the property from the church for two years prior to the title transfer in March 2024. Without knowing that the village would actually acquire title to the property, however, BV was hesitant to put funding into the village in the event that the church decided not to transfer the property title to it, despite a funding pledge from Multnomah County to help sustain the village.

Beyond such a historic transfer of property from the church to an Indigenous-operated nonprofit to aid the unhoused, the case of BV is particularly illustrative of how "gatekeeping" functions as a means of maintaining the values of propertied citizenship. The decision to transfer title over the property required approval from the Presbyterian church's regional congregation, the Presbytery of the Cascades (PC). Portland leaders in the PC who worked with the BV task force had drafted a motion for approval at the meeting of the PC on November 3, 2023. In full, the motion read, "In recognition of harm caused by the Christian Church to indigenous peoples through historical and ongoing practices of settlement and conquest, Presbytery of the Cascades transfers the property (for the consideration of $1.00) formerly owned by The Presbyterian Church of Laurelhurst to Future Generations Collaborative for the creation of Barbie's Village, a tiny home village for unhoused families with children and an early childhood center for the Native community."[6] The rest of the PC document briefly describes why the church was considering the property transfer, further acknowledging its role in the historical dispossession of land from Indigenous peoples, among other harmful relations. Indeed, the document indicates that the property title transfer to BV was being done in the "spirit of Land Back."[7]

When the PC congregation met to discuss and vote on approving the title transfer, however, the very spirit of Land Back was challenged. During discussion, one member of the PC introduced an amendment to the above motion for consideration. The full amendment read, "If Grantee [FGC] becomes insolvent, if such real property is no longer used for charitable purposes, including education, transitional housing, and any ancillary uses in furtherance of such charitable purposes, including storage and office use, if such real property is vacant for more than one (1) month, if Grantee is no longer an active nonprofit corporation in good standing, or if Grantee sells or proposes to sell all or substantially all of its assets or its interest in such real property, *then the real property described herein will revert back to Grantor.*"[8]

The amendment proposed multiple contingencies that should not be taken as simply legal protection of the church's vested interests in the real property that was then in question. The issue was not only that the agreement proposed reverting ownership back to the church pending several conditions, rendering the contract contingent on how BV used the property. Rather, the amendment to the motion, if passed, would have fundamentally denied the intention behind Land Back in the first place. It would have denied the *unconditional* transfer of land as an act of repair for the injustices of the past. The conditions that this amendment attempted to establish, therefore, must be seen as an example of how propertied citizenship is used to protect the social and legal norms around what "proper" use of real property ought to be and who has final authority to establish these conditions. The proposed amendment thus implied a different sense of Land Back, one where the transfer of title would revert to its "proper" owners if the original recipients of the "gift" could not properly organize themselves within the norms of liberal property systems.

After an hour of discussion on the amendment, including a motion by PC membership to move to executive session to discuss it privately, the membership voted against the amendment. And with a total vote of 135 in the affirmative to 24 in the negative, the PC approved the property title transfer to FGC to take ownership of the land to create BV.

When I spoke with Jillene of FCG and BV before the vote, she said that the multiyear process leading up to the vote was insightful into how race and property intersect. "The whole process has been interesting," she noted. "Just ... literally seeing the ways that white supremacy plays out," referring to how many cultural and legal barriers presented themselves along the way as FGC sought to get their vision across and be taken seriously as agents capable of exercising their own service for the unhoused. The legal process and barriers that presented themselves over those past two years, Jillene said, ultimately "goes back to the whole land thing. When we tie land to voting, that ties land to power." A feeling of powerlessness had been a constant for Jillene and FGC through their relations with the church and settler society more broadly.

It is important to note that Jillene and other FGC representatives did not use the specific term "property." For them, what was being transferred was *land*. The difference between property and land is significant. FGC was channeling what the burgeoning Land Back movement has catalyzed in their calls for the return of land stolen from Indigenous peoples. For many, Land Back is not merely about Indigenous peoples receiving a property title, because land presupposed property.[9] Only through settler colonial enactments of property was land turned into isolable entitlements over such resources, thus establishing legal title over landed property. Instead, Land Back provides a means of more broadly establishing not just title to land within settler property systems but the potential for "the full restoration of Indigenous land relationships."[10] In short, the vision of Land Back is not only about acquiring title to real property, it is about restoring more holistic connections to once unowned landed resources.

For BV, getting land back matters on different levels. Within the context of settler-Indigenous relations, it remains ever present that the dispossession of land has effectively destroyed and marginalized Indigenous peoples and cultures. The result of these relations has been cultural violence. As Jillene reflected on the historical and contemporary Indigenous-settler relations, she noted that doing so forces one to "think about what [racism] does to our minds, to our physiological well-being." Put more bluntly, she said, "Racism is killing us." With this legacy in mind, she said, Indigenous peoples "need to have wins. We need to have success in our life to help balance out the oppression. And by a win, I mean that we need to be lifted up, we need to have good things happen to us." And that is in part what Land Back can do. "Yes, this will be a win for [FGC], and for the people that are going to live [at BV]," she said. But more broadly, "it is going to be a win for Indian country because it is going to be a land back." Despite how legal titling necessitates land's reduction into title transfers, for Jillene and BV, it is not property but land that is being repaired, she said, "and that is how we are going to celebrate it."

The case of BV helps us better understand how property constitutes a sociolegal relationship that mediates who benefits from possessing it and how ownership wields power and control over others who do not. But the case also helps us identify what a response can be for unhoused groups subject to the injustices of liberal property. As noted in the introduction, Native Americans experience disproportionate rates of houselessness in Portland, and culturally specific villages like BV (and AV) help to facilitate stability and a sense of agency over how unhoused people can become housing-stable. But the case also models what a response to centuries of oppression, by getting land back, can look like, if only in this single instance.

Yet, despite this unprecedented means of correcting for past injustices, a critical relational analysis of property also recognizes that the land that BV has received back is simultaneously a legal entitlement to real property, a private possession justified within and by liberal common law. As such, it comes with all consequent entitlements that ownership rights provide, and in this way, it de facto reifies elements of the ownership model because it is forced to operate within it. As many property scholars have noted in respect to similar examples, here there appears a real dilemma, theoretically, in a world where "struggles against dispossession too easily become struggles *for* possession."[11] For under the "proprietary prerogative" of liberalism, "the language of property and possession now functions as a dominant mode of political expression to the extent that it has become difficult to voice opposition to these processes without drawing upon the conceptual and normative frameworks they have generated."[12] In other words, it is next to impossible to exist outside of liberal property law and relations when the necessity of occupying space nearly always requires reinforcing the ownership model.

This, I want to suggest, is the real injustice of liberal property. For it is implausible to participate within such a legal system while avoiding our own contribution to upholding it. In the sense of shared responsibility for maintaining structural injustice discussed earlier, this means we cannot avoid our complicity in maintaining the broader oppressions experienced by unhoused people leveraged by property's injustices. What follows from this is that the circumstances in which BV has found itself today—as private property owners—necessitate its participation in a property system that has been historically constructed through the very dispossession of Indigenous peoples' access to landed resources. The norms around liberal property remain deeply vested today, reminding us how the legal entitlements that support these norms mediate and thus mitigate opportunity for structural challenges to such a system.

Our complicity in the ownership model is unavoidable, however, *only* if we do not attempt to transform the relations that enable the reification of the system itself. According to Young's model of political responsibility, all contributors to structural injustice bear responsibility. This includes BV, even if only in some very minor way, and regardless of its mission to end the oppressions of liberal property as they have experienced the oppressions of it themselves. But as I argued in chapter 4, while Young's model acutely identifies *how* we may attribute responsibility for the structural injustices of property, such an ideal conception struggles to provide guidance for how we may establish duties to rectify injustices. Again, I see this less as a shortcoming of Young's model. Ideals usefully conceive of how more just relations can unfold within and especially against liberal ideals. However, it is ultimately only the actual existing struggles of political engagement that shape how just our relations with landed resources can be. In light of this, I suggest we ought to focus less on locating all who may be responsible for the injustices of liberal property than on paying attention to and making sense of responses to houselessness and the injustices of property by supporting new approaches to more just relations with land. In doing so, we learn a lot about how people and entities react to enactments that challenge power inherited through the ownership model.

No single political action or movement will transform the oppressions maintained through such a historically embedded system of property. But small advances like those of BV, AV, HG, or R2DT, for example, point to how other actions of shared political responsibility collectively work toward more systemic transformation. My point is emphatically not to condemn or criticize BV for receiving title to property, but rather, to take notice of, and learn from, the collective response that encompassed this transfer of land. For instance, we can learn from the political responsibility taken by some members of the church to transfer land back to Indigenous peoples. Part of this action meant acknowledging their personal contribution, especially historically, in dispossessing Indigenous peoples from land and from a sense of personhood through individual and cultural determination. And the same must be said for the energies invested by FGC. Their actions to criticize the church's role, and that of settler society more broadly, in contributing to this specific set of oppressions necessitated years of political organizing around the solitary goal of opening a houseless village for Indigenous peoples. BV and FCG's actions alone will not transform the injustices of the liberal system of property, but they do model what shared responsibility can look like for making it more just. Indeed, this village will lessen the oppressions experienced by many unhoused peoples who will benefit from its existence. This alone is something for which to fight.

But there are other significant lessons to take away from BV's struggle for recognition and land. More broadly we can see the very intention behind BV's attempts to enact a claim to ownership *against* liberal property, though it is of course wholly constrained within liberalism's specific legal entitlements. While liberal property necessitates some type of ownership claim to be recognized as "properly" contributing to the normative values of liberalism, attempts at enacting alternative forms of ownership can illustrate that the ownership model need not, and cannot, be the only means of preserving all individuals or many groups' collective self-determination. It is not only BV but all of Portland's self-governing villages, then, that differently model what a response to the injustice of property can look like. As Blomley reminds us, property relations are effectively "exclusionary, violent, and marginalizing." And we have seen how liberal property systems specifically affect so many unhoused people in these ways. But so too can relations of property be "a means by which people find meaning in the world, anchor themselves to communities, and contest dominant power relations."[13] Though constrained by liberalism, these self-governing spaces point to exactly the type of intentional response that unhoused people can make in realizing alternative relations of property. Specifically, they highlight the opportunities within more collectively managed types of property, forms of property that are challenged and repressed by the norms and laws constricting their broader implementation as a proper relationship with land use. In this way, the limits of propertied citizenship are exposed when challenged by enactments of collectively managed means of using landed resources. For alternative enactments of property and land use that exert material pressure on systems of liberal property must take place, by literally taking space, to engender those processes of *taking* responsibility to begin with. Absent any duty obliging us to rectify injustice, our ability to direct attention to specific struggles resulting from historical and contemporary injustices maintained in liberal property systems depends on moving all who contribute to injustice to work faster or more earnestly in taking responsibility. As responsible individuals are necessarily entangled into relations of property, enactments of alternate property forms compel contributors to injustice to engage with new social forms of property making, offering them the opportunity to rectify property's injustices and to realize more just social relations.

Reconsidering Properties of Justice

For over two centuries, the proprietarian logic of liberalism, emerging from republican liberalism and eventually solidifying itself into liberal-democratic capitalism, has viewed possession of property as a primary means of realizing the "proper" political subject. The possessive entitlement undergirding this idealized liberal political subject, in turn, authorizes owners to shape the proper social order. Critically assessing the houselessness crisis through the proprietarian framework of propertied citizenship invites more reflexive insight into where the specific harms that unhoused people experience emanate from, and how differences in subject identities of unhoused and housed people matter in contributing to these harms. What this shows in the end is that to be unhoused within liberalism is to have one's political subjectivity not absolutely determined but *mediated* in relation to dominant society's ordering of propriety, especially given one's relative position within relations of property.

Though focused on the circumstances of Portland, the arguments throughout this book extend beyond that city, by reflecting the reality of cities in the United States and elsewhere whose governments respond to rising rates of unsheltered houselessness by sanctioning encampments as a strategy for managing these crises. The insights developed herein identify different areas of concern that require redress. The first pertains to how encampments, though supplying absolutely necessary emergency support and potentially challenging the hegemony of liberal property, are inadequate as liberal-progressive strategies for mitigating houselessness in the first instance, given how encampments are embedded within and constrained by the legal logics of liberal property law. The relations of property that contribute to houselessness and justify the oppression of unhoused people ultimately remain fundamentally intact under this model. Consequently, a second area of insight we glean from the case of Portland is that even well-intentioned liberal progressive strategies that desire to establish more autonomy for unhoused people are circumscribed in the propertied constraints engrained in liberalism. It should be no surprise, then, that Portland's self-governing communities struggle to enact themselves through property forms alternate to the ownership model, as the controlling power of the proprietarian logic of liberalism has long curtailed attempts at establishing models diverging from it.

When we look historically at property in liberalism, it may appear that the dialectical relationship between property and citizenship has not much changed. That the proprietarian logic of propertied citizenship will *not* change, however, is not absolute. For an incredible number of social struggles fighting through the constraints presented by the structuring relations between property and political subjectivity illuminate where we can focus on changing our relationships with property to advance a collective response to its specific injustices. Short of calling for actions to take that will ideally bring about more just relations in the abstract, I reiterate what we can take away from unhoused peoples' experiences of injustice expressed throughout the book.

One concerns how we might better ensure the autonomy of unhoused people to make decisions about their own housing stability. To the extent that granting possessory rights to encampments may afford their residents a stronger sense of self purpose and agency in creating the conditions of their own environment, advocating for the right to remain in self-governing encampments *could* help to realize encampment residents' rights to privacy, security, and the right to remain immobile more absolutely. The collectively managed property model of encampments is one means of addressing the right not to be excluded. This would require financial support from local governments, as all shelter services require funding. The fact that tiny house encampments are legal land uses within Portland implies the possibility of being able to better facilitate how these communities can be caring, supportive, and more dignified rather than residual spaces for displaced and unwanted publics where one's right to determine one's own life path is eradicated. Possessory rights for encampments could also be helpful for protecting against the undue violence to which residents become vulnerable within the forms of limited property rights that encampments currently enjoy as well as enabling residents more control over their decision-making.

Even while rights for encampments would satisfy these sociopolitical criteria, leading to more just relationships among the unhoused and housed, this solution may present problems at another scale, however. Granting possessory rights to encampments risks normalizing the encampment model as a permanent fixture within the liberal landscape, legitimating the notion that encampments are the best or only option that can be developed to stabilize unhoused people. And more structurally, possessory rights (the right to exclude) potentially reinforce rather than resist the transformation of property relations that led to the existence of encampments in the first place—though this broader critique will hardly be of concern for those needing and benefiting from the immediate security of shelter.

There is then a contradictory response, a dialectical tension, when moving toward more just relationships with property for the unhoused. To lessen the unjust processes that contribute to houselessness requires advancing a response to the structurally unjust processes producing and maintaining the inequities of property. A relational analysis of property in liberalism shows us that if we want a more just socioeconomic and political system, whereby unhoused individuals hold a right not to be excluded, property's relationship to liberalism ultimately cannot be reformed through collectively managed properties or redistributions of privately owned property. A long-term strategy with this goal in mind would work toward transforming property, by decoupling it from propriety that justifies oppression for those differing from its historically embedded racial and classed criteria and moving toward a relationship with landed resources that enables individuals to secure their capacities as autonomous individuals without the norms of propertied citizenship structuring what a just relationship to land *must* look like. What more just relations with land will look like must be arrived at through social actions that literally emplace differing forms of land usage and, consequently, social relationships around land, against liberal property systems. To remake property, proprietarian social processes must also be rejected, as social practices cultivate how new forms of property will function. The circumstances of Portland's encampments reflect how unhoused groups are already working toward this, and more broadly show us how more just geographies of land use may operate, regardless of whether, and especially when, the lessons deriving from them identify how these struggles become restricted within liberal legal and social logics of property.

ACKNOWLEDGMENTS

Many people have been involved in many different ways throughout the process of putting this book together. In Portland, I have so many wonderful people to thank. First and foremost, thank you to all the people affiliated with the encampments who really made an impact on me. I owe so much to the person I will simply call "T." I met T on day one of fieldwork and remained in steady contact with them ever since. Their story is so powerful to me, and their politics a pleasure to engage with. Their pure positivity radiates throughout the many places T has lived, who, I am happy to say, is now in stable housing! I hope you see yourself in this book, T. But there have been, and still are, many individuals at Hazelnut Grove, Right 2 Dream Too, Dignity Village, and Kenton Women's Village who were incredible to work side by side with and to learn from. This work is for them. Rafael Solana and Vahid Brown were incredibly helpful throughout my research, always responding to my questions about this and that. And I am certain that those most on the receiving end of my questions are Trillium and Grant, whose work with R2DT is truly inspiring. Trillium and Grant remain invested in an endless struggle that few people would have the energy for. You helped me see why direct action is the most simple and effective, yet political action to take. All of the mentioned individuals model what I see as the true benefit of democratic self-organizing. Throughout my time at these spaces, I learned a lot from Gabi about what restorative justice can look like on the ground, and many thanks go to all of those at the Village Coalition who shared with me everything related to the encampments that one could ask for. Thanks to Erin Goodling for being so open and collaborative on all things houselessness in Portland and beyond. And finally, I have an enormous amount of gratitude for Judith Kenny and Tom Hubka (and "the boys": Ari, Checkers (RIP), and Zachie). The two of you have been so supportive of my research and were incredibly helpful for getting me through my extended fieldwork in many ways.

Friends and mentors from the Department of Geography at Syracuse University played an enormous role in helping me get this project off the ground. I am fortunate to continue friendships with Sohrob Aslamy, Maddy Hamlin, Brian Hennigan, Katie MacDonald, Jared Van Ramshorst, and Jared Whear, who likely took the brunt of my conversations about property and houselessness in the earliest days of this project. But they often did so warmheartedly, over coffee, at Taps, during big dinners, and on basketball courts. I am especially grateful to two Syracuse geographers who had left SU by the time I got there. Jessie Speer has been critical for helping me think through many of my ideas on the politics of houselessness. And Kafui Attoh, who has come to be a cherished resource for me as well as a friend—someone holding the perfect balance between being critical of, and insistent about, the value of my research. Many faculty at Syracuse were incredibly supportive and instructive during my time there. Matt Huber pushed me to critically think through the logic of my ideas and to find a way to ground them. Jamie Winders has been a huge source of support for me, not only giving my work critical and careful attention but also giving her time and advice about academic life more broadly. And finally, I express immense gratitude to Don Mitchell. Don pushed me to develop my arguments carefully, to get to and enjoy the real work of writing and the editing process, and above all, to model how an advisor ought to support a student. He epitomizes how one can engage both carefully and critically in scholarship, and I can only hope that a fraction of that precision comes out in these pages. My opportunity to continue working with Don in Sweden as a postdoc was incredible, and not only because of our dedication to our project on theorizing justice: it was there that I also gained Don as a friend. Susan Millar similarly was so kind and helpful in making me feel supported during my time in Sweden.

My time in Sweden was made so much warmer by the kind and generous people in the Department of Human Geography at Uppsala University, many of whom heard early and partial arguments that are presented more fully in this book. To the amazing graduate students, postdocs, and faculty there, tack så mycket! Thanks in particular must go to Ismael Yrigoy and Ilias Alamy for their critical conversations and good companionship. My return trip to Portland in summer 2023 was funded by a research award from the Swedish Society for Anthropology and Geography, to which I am very grateful for the support. And to the Just North project that got me to Sweden in the first place, I am ever grateful to have worked with such thoughtful and intelligent people, and I cherish that time as a rare moment where reading, writing, and discussing was the sole focus.

Many others have been instrumental in helping me think through the arguments in this book. Great conversations with Nick Blomley have pushed me to refine my thinking about property, although every time I feel like I have something to say about it, Nick has already published on it! I hope your constructive feedback is recognized herein. Similarly, thanks to Trevor Wideman, whose interest in property and citizenship has sustained a great amount of discourse between us over the years that this book was being formed. Johanna Ohlsson has likewise been a wonderful colleague and a dedicated source of critical and constructive feedback on all things justice. No doubt your perspectives have found their way into this book in different ways. And to the scholars whose work I admire and whose perspectives were central to the book: Tony Sparks, Sara Safransky, Brenna Bhandar, and Ananya Roy.

I would also like to thank the colleagues in my new home in the Department of Geography at Michigan State and this community more broadly. Though all have been incredibly friendly, I want to show appreciation to Igor Vojnovic for always checking in and remaining positive, and to the wonderful group of graduate students, for their critical insights on all things urban and geography, property, and more, especially Mehmet Eroğlu and Danna Gutiérrez Lanza.

I am especially grateful to be included in the Geographies of Justice series at University of Georgia Press. The team at the press has been wonderful, especially Mick Gussinde-Duffy, Jon Davies, and copyeditor Irina du Quenoy. And a huge amount of gratitude goes out to the three anonymous reviewers who read different drafts of the book. It is no small task to review a monograph. I appreciate you putting your energy into it and providing great insights. The book is better because of it.

Chapters 1, 2, and 3 expand on or are substantive revisions of some of the ideas that appear in articles published in *Political Geography*, *Urban Affairs Review*, and *Environment and Planning C: Politics and Space* respectively.

And biggest thanks of all goes to my family, whose endless support throughout the process I could not have gone without. To my mom, Victoria, and my dad, John, whose curiosity and questions about my research and thinking are refreshing and generative. And to my brothers, David and Shane, for their good cheer, especially when it had nothing to do with the contents of this book. Much loveskis to each of you. But no other person has done more to help me through this process, by giving me their time and listening to me, reading over drafts of writing that I am excited about, and more broadly insisting I see the value of my own work, than Nazita Lajevardi. This kind of support emanates from love, and I am so grateful for yours, eshgham. Merci!

NOTES

PREFACE

1. Throughout the book, I use the term "unhoused," "houseless," and "houselessness," far more than I do "homeless" or "homelessness." I use the former terms because this is how the majority of encampment residents who I work with describe their condition. I also purposefully use this terminology to avoid further stigmatizing people who live without housing but often feel they have a sense of community and home despite their lack of material comforts. Nonetheless, given the government's, and much of the public's, propensity for using the word "homeless," I do so where appropriate considering the actors involved and their preferred terminology.

2. Of course, there are great activist/scholars who have critically addressed exactly how the city of Portland, and the State of Oregon, developed as a white utopia. Oregon historian Walidah Imarisha's words express this well in Hern's *What is a city for* (2016, pp. 38–39) as well as her many other public contributions to telling Portland's Black histories (e.g., Imarisha 2020). So too does the work of Karen Gibson (2007) on Portland's Albina District and Darrell Millner (2024) about Black life in Oregon more broadly.

INTRODUCTION. LIBERALISM, PROPERTY, AND HOMELESSNESS IN PORTLAND

1. OKNA 2017a.
2. Hewitt 2017.
3. OKNA 2017b.
4. Ibid.
5. Ibid.
6. Barnett and Low 2004.
7. Ananya Roy (2003) appears to be the first to articulate this citizenship qualifier in her article of the same title.
8. Smith 1995.
9. Locke 2016, p. 135; Blackstone 1803, p. 1.
10. Merrill 1998, p. 730.
11. Blomley 2004; Singer 2000a, p. 3.

12. Singer 2000b. See also Cohen (1927) and Merrill and Smith (2010, p. 5).
13. Nedelsky 1993, p. 8.
14. Dagan 2021, p. 61.
15. Ibid., pp. 7–8.
16. Ibid., p. 62.
17. Mitchell 2020.
18. Nichols 2020.
19. Bhandar 2018.
20. Beckham 1991.
21. Coleman 2017, p. 155.
22. Ibid., p. 110.
23. Gibson 2007; Przybylinski 2024b.
24. Among the largest cities in the United States, Portland has the highest percentage of white, non-Hispanic people, at 68.8 percent (U.S. Census Bureau 2023).
25. In 2016 the City of Portland began a program promoting "the right to return" for former Albina residents. The program provides downpayment assistance for owners and rental assistance for renters, coupled with the development of new affordable housing.
26. Hern 2016; Goodling, Green, and McClintock 2015.
27. Shepherd and Berman 2020.
28. Elliott et al. 2023.
29. Wallace 2023; Corkery 2023; Winston 2023.
30. Multnomah County 2023a.
31. Ibid.
32. Elliott and Oschwald 2022, p. 23.
33. U.S. Census Bureau 2023.
34. Portland Housing Bureau 2023, p. 8.
35. Ibid., p. 10.
36. Ibid, p. 10.
37. Ibid., p. 11.
38. Ibid., p. 12.
39. Governor Kotek issued three executive orders upon entering office in January 2023. The first was the state of emergency declaration on homelessness. The second directed all state agencies to prioritize reducing homelessness in their operations. The third promoted the development of more housing units (Shumway 2023).

CHAPTER 1. CONNECTING THE EVOLUTION OF PROPERTIED CITIZENSHIP IN AMERICAN LIBERALISM WITH HOMELESSNESS

1. "Pete" is a pseudonym.
2. Przybylinski 2021a.
3. Roy 2003, p. 464.
4. Ibid, p. 476.
5. In 2022, 315 people died while houseless in Multnomah County, a 63 percent increase from the previous year (Multnomah County 2023b).
6. Alexander 1997.

Notes to Chapter One   145

7. Sève 2008, p. 90.
8. Ollman 2003, p. 18.
9. Harvey 1996, p. 11.
10. Ibid., p. 55.
11. Ely 2008, pp. 11–12.
12. Ibid., p. 16.
13. Nedelsky 1990.
14. Ely 2008, p. 33.
15. Ibid., p. 3.
16. Alexander 1998, p. 667.
17. Ibid., p. 30.
18. Brown 2015.
19. Woods 1992, p. 104.
20. Ibid., p. 104.
21. Ibid., p. 106.
22. Ibid., p. 269.
23. Rose 1994, p. 62.
24. Ibid., p. 62.
25. Alexander 1997, p. 2.
26. Ibid., p. 4, and ibid., p. 5.
27. Rose 1994, pp. 61–62.
28. Ely 2007, p. 86.
29. Ibid., p. 13.
30. Shklar 1991, p. 67.
31. Harvey 2003, p. 149.
32. Meiksins-Wood 2016, p. 208.
33. Ibid., p. 234.
34. Though it should be noted that the Supreme Court did rein in the seemingly untouchable property rights of corporate capital, particularly during the Progressive era and again during the New Deal years (see Ely 2007, chaps. 6–7).
35. Sartori 1987, p. 388.
36. Meiksins-Wood 2016, p. 213.
37. Locke 2016, p. 135.
38. Freeden 2015, pp. 20–21.
39. Gray 1995, xii.
40. Macpherson 1962, p. 3.
41. Ibid., p. 3.
42. Holcombe 1983.
43. Pierson 2020, p. 225; Herzog and Adams 2018.
44. Marston 1990.
45. Walcott (2021, p. 17) also importantly notes that because Black people were enslaved and thus could not "own" their own person, the enslaved "could not 'own' one's self and one's offspring, and therefore, could not lay claim to family."
46. De La Fuente and Gross 2020, p. 209.
47. Ibid., p. 218.
48. Though as Jun (2011, p. 16) points out, the 1870 Naturalization Act was ratified to

ensure that the "alien status of Asian migrants would not be impacted" by these promises of the Fourteenth Amendment.

49. Steinfeld 1989. Poll taxes were not the only means of restricting Black suffrage; registration requirements, literacy tests, fear, and intimidation all factored into preventing Blacks from voting.

50. Copeland 2013.

51. Foner 2014, p. 160. As Foner notes, perhaps unsurprisingly, by mid-1866, one year after the end of the war, half of the land held by the Freedmen's Bureau had been restored to its former white owners.

52. Stern 2011; Hall and Yoder, 2022.

53. Jackson 1985, p. 4.

54. Ibid., p. 288.

55. Taylor 2019.

56. Ibid., p. 11.

57. A Joint Center for Housing Studies of Harvard (2023) report shows that from 2015 to 2019, white homeownership rates were at 71.7 percent compared with a Black ownership rate of 41.7 percent, the lowest homeownership rate by race nationally.

58. Harris 1993, p. 1714.

59. Ibid., p. 1713.

60. Ibid., p. 1721.

61. See Mills 1997, 2008; Ranganathan 2016.

62. Mills 1997, p. 1382.

63. Moreton-Robinson 2015, p. xxi.

64. Bhandar 2018, p. 5.

65. Mills 2017, p. 47.

66. Safransky 2023.

67. Roy 2017, p. A8.

68. Jones 1994.

69. Waldron 1993a, p. 313.

70. Waldron 1993a, p. 320.

71. Essert 2016, p. 276, emphasis added. I will return to Essert's arguments about how property's relational unfreedoms mark the institution of property as unjust.

72. Essert 2016, p. 286.

73. See Blomley 2004; Kawash 1998; Mitchell 2003; Roy 2003, p. 484.

74. Mitchell 1997, p. 321.

75. Kawash 1998, p. 330.

76. N. Smith 1996, p. 222.

77. Blomley 2009.

78. Staeheli and Mitchell 2008, p. 142.

79. Ibid., p. 142.

80. Ibid., p. 143.

81. Blomley 2020, p. 40.

82. Ibid., p. 51.

83. Dozier 2019.

CHAPTER 2. DEVELOPING PORTLAND'S HOMELESS ENCAMPMENT MODEL

1. There are many possible distinctions to be made between "organized" and "unorganized" encampments. While it is impossible to thoroughly describe the nuances, for the purposes of this book, "organized" encampments are those unhoused groups that are recognized by the city and are officially permitted to operate. Organized encampments operate with codes of conduct and generally have more formal infrastructure than unorganized groups. "Unorganized" encampments, on the other hand, can be understood as unpermitted groups co-locating for safety, with individuals mostly living within single-person tents near one another. Unorganized camps are not sanctioned or tolerated by the city and will often be disbanded by the police or the state department of transportation within a relatively short period of time after their formation.

2. Przybylinski (2024a) analyzes how the City of Portland's suspension of land use regulations through the use of "emergency governance" procedures during the state of emergency provided the legal means for institutionalizing the encampment model.

3. While I use the term "encampment" and "village" somewhat interchangeably, there is a distinction between the two terms as well. In general, I refer to specifically self-organized encampments as encampments, whether or not they have village in the title. Dignity Village is a self-managed encampment that not only has village in its title but convenes community as a village as well. Nonetheless, I use the term "village" to refer to Portland's newer encampments that are managed by nonprofits and that use the village title, though they are not self-organizing. The rest of this chapter will bear out these distinctions.

4. Przybylinski 2021b.

5. Portland, of course, relies upon traditional indoor shelter. The city, county, and private religious institutions collectively offer around fifteen hundred shelter beds on any given night (Joint Office of Homeless Services 2023a).

6. Abbott 2001, p. 113.

7. Ordinance no. 151690 was first passed by the Portland City Council on June 4, 1981.

8. Slovic 2016.

9. Oregon v. Wicks 2000, Case no. Z711742 & Z711743.

10. VanderHart 2014.

11. In response to the circuit court judge's unconstitutional ruling, then-mayor Vera Katz wrote an op-ed in *Streets Roots* railing against the decision. Katz baldly stated that "many of them [the homeless] just don't choose to stay in a place with a roof over their head. They want to be outside, they want to continue drinking, or taking drugs and not playing by the rules that are imposed in shelters" (Parzych et al. 2003, p. 52).

12. Tafari 2000.

13. Oregon Laws 2023.

14. Anderson v. City of Portland, Civ. no. 08-1447-AA (D. Or. December 2011).

15. The major U.S. Ninth Circuit Court ruling on *Martin v. Boise* in 2018 found that it is unconstitutional, in violation of the Eight Amendment, for municipalities to criminalize unhoused people when there is no available shelter (Martin et al. v. City of Boise, D.C. no. 1:09-cv.00540-REB, September 4, 2018).

16. Anderson et al. v. City of Portland 2012.
17. VanderHart 2016.
18. Ibid.
19. Willamette Week 2016.
20. Ibid.
21. The mayor's senior policy advisor admitted during a February 6, 2016, work session on homelessness that even he, when traveling throughout the city, had no idea which properties were owned by the municipality (City of Portland 2016).
22. E. Smith 2016a.
23. Personal communication to the author, August 2018.
24. Smith 2016b.
25. Ibid.
26. City of Portland 2016, emphasis added.
27. Krishnan and Elliott 2017.
28. Margier 2022.
29. Richman 2016, p. 6.
30. Ibid.
31. Harbarger 2017.
32. Hewitt 2017.
33. Ibid.
34. The city government estimates that annual costs for managed villages costs $30,000–35,000 per housing unit, compared with $20,000–25,000 per bed (City of Portland 2023).
35. Pitawanich 2017.
36. OKNA 2017c.
37. Vaughn 2018.
38. Multnomah County 2021.
39. Ironically.
40. A Home for Everyone 2023.
41. City of Portland 2021a.
42. Portland City Code 33.100.100.
43. City of Portland 2021b.
44. This does not mean that building codes do not apply to outdoor shelters, however.
45. Portland City Council 2021.
46. Joint Office of Homeless Services 2023b.
47. Ibid.
48. Cooper and Gowan 2019; Madden and Marcuse 2016.

CHAPTER 3. THE CHALLENGE OF COLLECTIVELY MANAGED PROPERTY

1. Nicole is a pseudonym.
2. Like many people I spoke with during my research, Nicole does not consider herself "unhoused" per se. She noted that because she lived in a tiny house with a lockable door, she didn't feel houseless. Without detracting from her perspective, I nonetheless

refer to these spaces as "houseless" villages or encampments. Given their legal status as transitional housing accommodations, they are widely understood to be temporary rest sites for people living without stable housing.

3. City of Portland 2017.
4. City of Portland 2017.
5. Williams and Robson 2014.
6. The primary purpose of HB 2916 was to retract the state's two-parcel-per-municipality limit on "transitional housing accommodations," or encampments. The bill now authorizes municipal governments to demarcate the number of encampments they feel is necessary (Oregon State Legislature 2019).
7. Marshall and Bottomore, 1992.
8. Janoski and Turner, 2002, p. 18.
9. Woods 1992; Alexander 1997; Marston 1990.
10. Nedelsky 2011.
11. Roy 2003, p. 475.
12. Staeheli et al. 2012
13. Isin 2008.
14. Macpherson 1978, p. 199.
15. Ibid., p. 201.
16. Blackmar 2006.
17. Harvey 2012; Borch and Kornberger 2015; Huron 2018.
18. Blomley 2016, p. 90.
19. Ibid., p. 89.
20. Ibid.
21. Essert 2016, p. 279.
22. Rose 1998, p. 132.
23. Sparks 2017.
24. One KWV resident mentioned that the way the encampment was set up with chain link fencing made it feel like the residents were in a "fishbowl," a container for the outside world to gawk at.
25. Intentional communities can be broadly defined as residential communities that organize themselves around shared values and intend on maintaining themselves in perpetuity (Sanford 2017). The City of Portland cannot allow self-governing encampments to operate in perpetuity because encampments are legally considered "transitional housing accommodations" under Oregon Revised Statute 446.225 (Oregon Revised Statute, 2020). This means that encampments can be only temporary places of respite for individuals.
26. Essert 2016, p. 276.
27. Ibid., p. 290.

CHAPTER 4. LOCATING RESPONSIBILITY FOR THE INJUSTICES OF LIBERAL PROPERTY

1. Waldron 1993b.
2. Dagan 2021.
3. Rawls 1999.

4. Valentini (2012, p. 655) details the debates over ideal versus nonideal theory in political philosophy, usefully suggesting that while "messy" in their "conceptual terrain," the many possible distinctions between ideal and nonideal theories help justify why one may be used over the other depending on the normative aims of the given set of circumstances being assessed.

5. Graham 2011, p. 758.
6. Mills 2005, p. 166.
7. Waldron 1993a; Essert 2016, p. 276.
8. Dagan 2021, p. 8.
9. Ibid., p. 128.
10. Ibid., p. 4.
11. Ibid., p. 36.
12. Dagan acknowledges in a few places throughout his 2021 book that there are "ineliminable" aspects of liberal property that are both intractable within liberal theory itself, as well as within existing liberal systems of property.
13. Dagan 2021, p. 73.
14. Forst 2017, p. 122.
15. Dagan 2021, p. 126.
16. Rawls 1999. Dworkin (2000) and Walzer (1983) offer two of the most prominent ideal theories detailing what just equal distribution ought to look like.
17. Shklar 1990, p. 15.
18. Przybylinski 2022.
19. Young 1990, p. 39.
20. Ibid., p. 37.
21. Ibid.
22. Ibid., p. 40.
23. Similarly, Hoover (2023) draws on Young to analyze the injustice of gentrification more specifically.
24. N. Smith 1995, p. 133.
25. Young 1990, p. 53.
26. Renee is a pseudonym.
27. As of 2020, the City of Portland established a form of rent control. The limit for increases was originally set as a flat rate. The early years of the COVID-19 pandemic saw high inflation, further exploiting the value of renters' resources available for rent. In 2023 the city changed the law, allowing for an inflation adjustment.
28. Hoover 2023.
29. See Takahashi (1996) for how unhoused people are stigmatized; the 9th U.S. Circuit Court ruling in 2018 found criminalizing unhoused people for not using shelter when there is none available to be "cruel and unusual" (Martin v. City of Boise, 920 F. 3d 584 [9th Cir. 2019]).
30. See also Hennigan (2019) on how unhoused people are devalued as nonproductive within liberal capitalism.
31. Young 1990, p. 53.
32. Ibid., p. 55.
33. Roy 2019, p. 227.
34. Angela is a pseudonym.

35. Roy 2017, p. A9.
36. Simone is a pseudonym.
37. Young 1990, p. 56.
38. Ibid.
39. Ibid.
40. Ibid., p. 58.
41. Ibid., p. 59.
42. Ibid.
43. Ibid.
44. Ibid., p. 62.
45. Kawash 1998, p. 336.
46. Beth is a pseudonym.
47. Young 2011, p. 33.
48. Ibid., emphasis added
49. Ibid., p. 52.
50. Ibid.
51. Ibid., p. 111.
52. Ibid., pp. 144–147.
53. Barnett 2017, p. 225.
54. Blomley 2020, p. 51.
55. Reiman 2012. See this article for a constructive critique of Young that advances a collective liability responsibility.
56. Young 2011, p. 55.
57. Reiman 2012, p. 749.
58. Ibid., emphasis added.
59. Ibid.
60. Ibid., p. 750.
61. Ibid.
62. Ibid.
63. Ibid.
64. Valentini 2021, p. 55.
65. Ibid.
66. Ibid.
67. Ibid., p. 54.
68. Ibid., p. 61.
69. Ibid., p. 55.
70. Indeed, several countries have some version of a legally enforceable right to housing, which holds the state responsible for providing housing to (nearly) all requesting it.
71. Mitchell 2020.

CONCLUSION. RESPONDING TO INJUSTICE

1. Blomley 2003.
2. Though, in many ways, the AfroVillage headquarters in Portland functions as one. It operates out of an office in downtown Portland's "Old Town" neighborhood, where it

is clear that a vast group of people convene, some working on AV itself, others benefiting from a warm and dry space.

3. AfroVillage 2023a.
4. AfroVillage 2023b.
5. Grannis 2021, p. 7.
6. Presbytery of the Cascades 2023a, p. 1.
7. Ibid., p. 4.
8. Presbytery of the Cascades 2023b (emphasis added).
9. Tuck and Yang 2012, p 7; Nichols (2020) similarly argues that land was never property because property was created at the moment of land theft from Indigenous peoples.
10. Schneider 2022, p. 453.
11. Porter 2014, p. 389.
12. Roy 2017, p. A10; Nichols 2020, p. 145.
13. Blomley 2004, p. 156.

REFERENCES

Abbott, C. (2001). *Greater Portland: Urban life and landscape in the Pacific Northwest.* Philadelphia: University of Pennsylvania Press.
AfroVillage (2023a). "AfroVillage Movement." https://www.afrovillagepdx.org/about-3.
AfroVillage (2023b). "The Afro-Village: Hub-Diagram." https://www.afrovillagepdx.org/s/The-Afro-Village-36x36.pdf/.
Alexander, G. (1998). Property as propriety. *Nebraska Law Review, 77*: 667–702.
Alexander, G. (1997). *Commodity and propriety: Competing visions of property in American legal thought, 1776–1970.* Chicago: University of Chicago Press.
Anderson et al. v. City of Portland. (2012). "Notice of settlement." Portland, Oreg. U.S. District Court of Oregon. https://www.documentcloud.org/documents/4104410-Anderson-v-Portland-Settlement.html.
Barnett, C. (2017). *The priority of injustice: Locating democracy in critical theory.* Athens: University of Georgia Press.
Barnett, C., and Low, M. (eds.) (2004). *Spaces of democracy: Geographical perspectives on citizenship, participation and representation.* London: Sage.
Beckham, S. D. (1991). Federal-Indian relations. In C. M. Baun and R. Lewis (eds.), *The first Oregonians: An illustrated collection of essays on traditional lifeways, federal-Indian relations, and the state's native people today* (pp. 39–54). Portland: Oregon Council for the Humanities.
Bhandar, B. (2018). *Colonial lives of property: Law, land, and racial regimes of ownership.* Durham, N.C.: Duke University Press.
Blackmar, E. (2006). Appropriating "the commons:" The tragedy of property rights discourse. In S. Low and N. Smith (eds.), *The politics of public space* (pp. 49–80). New York: Routledge.
Blackstone, W. (1803). *Blackstone's commentaries: With notes of reference, to the constitution and laws, of the federal government of the United States; and of the Commonwealth of Virginia.* Philadelphia: William Young Birch and Abraham Small.
Blomley, N. (2020). Precarious territory: Property law, housing, and the socio-spatial order. *Antipode, 52*(1): 36–57.
Blomley, N. (2016). The right to not be excluded: Common property and the right to

stay put. In A. Amin and P. Howell (eds.), *Releasing the commons: Rethinking the futures of the commons* (pp. 89–106). New York: Routledge.

Blomley, N. (2009). Homelessness, rights, and the delusions of property. *Urban Geography, 30*(6): 577–590.

Blomley, N. (2004). *Unsettling the city: Urban land and the politics of property.* New York: Routledge.

Blomley, N. (2003). Law, property, and the geography of violence: The frontier, the survey, and the grid. *Annals of the American Association of Geographers, 93*(1): 121–141.

Borch, C., and Kornberger, M. (eds.) (2015). *Urban commons: Rethinking the city.* New York, Routledge.

Brown, W. (2015). *Undoing the demos: Neoliberalism's stealth revolution.* Princeton, N.J.: Princeton University Press.

City of Portland (2023). "Funding for Safe Rest Villages." Portland.gov. https://www.portland.gov/safe-rest-villages/funding-safe-rest-villages.

City of Portland (2021a). "Outdoor Emergency Shelters: Lessons Learned." May 20, 2021. Portland.gov., May 20, 2021. https://www.portland.gov/homelessness-impact-reduction/news/2021/5/11/outdoor-emergency-shelters-lessons-learned. https://www.portland.gov/omf/news/2021/5/11/outdoor-emergency-shelters-lessons-learned.

City of Portland (2021b). "Shelter to Housing Continuum. Amendments to the Zoning Code, Volume 1, Introduction." Portland.gov, Bureau of Planning and Sustainability. https://www.portland.gov/sites/default/files/2021/s2hc_as_adopted_volume_1.pdf.

City of Portland (2017). "Space Use Agreement." Portland.gov. http://www.portlandmercury.com/images/blogimages/2017/04/12/1492012174-useagreementexecutedr2dtoo.pdf.

City of Portland (2016). "February 8, 2016 Work Session Recordings—State of Emergency Housing and Homelessness Update." City Auditor—Council Work Session Recordings. https://efiles.portlandoregon.gov/Record/8573045/.

Cohen, M. (1927). Property and sovereignty. *Cornell Law Review, 13*(1): 8–30.

Coleman, K. (2017). *Dangerous subjects: James D. Saules and the rise of Black exclusion in Oregon.* Corvallis: Oregon State University Press.

Cooper, R., and Gowan, P. (2019). How to solve the housing problem. *Jacobin.* https://www.jacobinmag.com/2019/06/how-to-solve-the-housing-problem.

Copeland, R. (2013). In the beginning: Origins of African American real property ownership in the United States. *Journal of Black Studies, 44*(6): 646–664.

Corkery, M. (2023, July 29). Fighting for Anthony: The struggle to save Portland, Oregon. *New York Times.* https://www.nytimes.com/2023/07/29/us/portland-oregon-fentanyl-homeless.html.

Dagan, H. (2021). *A liberal theory of property.* Cambridge: Cambridge University Press.

De la Fuente, A., and Gross, A. (2020). *Becoming free, becoming Black: Race, freedom, and law in Cuba, Virginia, and Louisiana.* Cambridge: Cambridge University Press.

Dozier, D. (2019). Contested development: Homeless property, police reform, and resistance in Skid Row, LA. *International Journal of Urban and Regional Research, 43*(1): 179–194.

Dworkin, R. (2000). *Sovereign virtue: The theory and practice of equality*. Cambridge, Mass.: Harvard University Press.

Elliot, D., and Oschwald, M. (2022). "2022 Point-in-Time Methodology Report. Count of Homelessness in Portland, Gresham, Multnomah County, Oregon." Joint Office of Homeless Services, Portland, Oregon. https://www.multco.us/multnomah-county/news/full-2022-point-time-count-report-shows-covid-19-added-unsheltered.

Elliott, D., Oschwald, D., Chaiyachakorn, N., Cook, M., Thompson, C., and Howard, L. (2023). "Portland Insights Survey. Report of Findings, 2022." Regional Research Institute for Human Services, Portland State University. https://www.portland.gov/cbo/documents/2022-portland-insights-survey-report-pdf/download.

Ely, J. (2022). Liberty and property: Indivisibility linked? *Brigham-Kanner Property Rights Journal*, 11, Vanderbilt Law Research Paper no. 22-01.

Essert, C. (2016). Property and homelessness. *Philosophy and Public Affairs*, 44(4): 266–295.

Foner, E. (2014). *Reconstruction: America's unfinished revolution, 1863–1877*. Updated ed. New York: Harper Perennial Modern Classics.

Forst, R. (2017). *Normativity and power: Analyzing social orders of justification*. Oxford: Oxford University Press.

Freeden, M. (2015). *Liberalism: A very short introduction*. Oxford: Oxford University Press.

Gibson, K. (2007). Bleeding Albina: A history of community disinvestment, 1940–2000. *Transforming Anthropology*, 15(1): 3–25.

Goodling, E., Green, J., and McClintock, N. (2015). Uneven development of the sustainable city: Shifting capital in Portland, Oregon. *Urban Geography*, 36(4): 504–527.

Graham, K. M. (2011). Non-ideal moral theory. In D. K. Chatterjee (ed.), *Encyclopedia of global justice* (pp. 758–760). Dordrecht: Springer.

Grannis, J. (2021). "Community Land = Community Resilience: How Community Land Trusts Can Support Urban Affordable Housing and Climate Initiatives." Adaptation Clearinghouse. https://www.adaptationclearinghouse.org/resources/community-landcommunity-resilience-how-community-land-trusts-can-support-urban-affordablehousing-and-climate-initiatives.html.

Gray, J. (1995). *Liberalism*. 2nd ed. Minneapolis: University of Minnesota Press.

Harbarger, M. (2017, March 8). Wheeler shows off tiny houses ahead of vote. *Oregonian*, p. 8.

Harris, C. (1993). Whiteness as property. *Harvard Law Review*, 106(8): 1707–1790.

Harvey, D. (2012). *Rebel cities*. London: Verso.

Harvey, D. (2003). *The new imperialism*. Oxford: Oxford University Press.

Harvey, D. (1996). *Justice, nature, and the geography of difference*. Cambridge, Mass: Blackwell.

Hennigan, B. (2019). From Madonna to Marx: Towards a re-theorization of homelessness. *Antipode*, 51(1): 148–168.

Hern, M. (2016). *What a city is for: Remaking the politics of displacement*. Cambridge, Mass.: MIT Press.

Herzog, B., and Adams, J. (2018). Women, gender, and the revocation of citizenship in the United States. *Social Currents*, 5(1): 15–31.

Hewitt, L. (2017, August 12). Overlook Neighborhood Association looks to exclude homeless from membership. *Portland Tribune*.

Holcombe, L. (1983). *Wives and property: Reform of the married women's property law in nineteenth-century England*. Oxford: Martin Robertson.

A Home for Everyone (2023). "Alternative Shelter." A Home for Everyone. https://ahomeforeveryone.squarespace.com/altshelter.

Hoover, J. (2023). The injustice of gentrification. *Political Theory*, 51(6): 925–954.

Huron, A. (2018). *Carving out the commons: Tenant organizing and housing cooperatives in Washington, D.C*. Minneapolis: University of Minnesota Press.

Imarisha, W. (2020, February 25). How Oregon's racist history can sharpen our sense of justice right now. *Portland Monthly Magazine*.

Isin, E. (2008). Theorizing acts of citizenship. In E. Isin and G. Nielsen (eds.), *Acts of citizenship* (pp. 15–43). London: Palgrave Macmillan.

Jackson, K. (1985). *Crabgrass frontier: The suburbanization of the United States*. Oxford: Oxford University Press.

Janoski, T., and Turner, B. (2002). Political citizenship: Foundations of rights. In E. F. Isin and B. S. Turner (eds.), *Handbook of citizenship studies* (pp. 13–52). London: Sage.

Joint Center for Housing Studies of Harvard (2023). "The State of the Nation's Housing 2023." Harvard Graduate School of Design. https://www.jchs.harvard.edu/sites/default/files/reports/files/Harvard_JCHS_The_State_of_the_Nations_Housing_2023.pdf.

Joint Office of Homeless Services (2023a). "Emergency Shelter." JOHS Data Dashboard. https://johs.us/data-dashboard/.

Joint Office of Homeless Services (2023b). "System Performance Report, FY 23, Q3." Tableau Public. https://public.tableau.com/app/profile/johs/viz/JOHSSystemPerformanceQuarterlyReport-FY23Q3/Report.

Jones, P. (1994). *Rights*. New York: St. Martin's Press.

Jun, H. (2011). *Race for citizenship: Black orientalism and Asian uplift from pre-emancipation to neoliberal America*. New York: New York University Press.

Kawash, S. (1998). The homeless body. *Public Culture*, 10(2): 319–339.

Krishnan, U., and Elliott, D. (2017). "2017 Point-in-Time Count of Homelessness in Portland/Gresham/Multnomah County, Oregon." https://static1.squarespace.com/static/566631e8c21b864679fff4de/t/59ee2e7a5ffd207c6e7b41a0/1508781707710/PSU+2017+Point-In-Time_FINAL_%28Interactive%29+%281%29+%281%29.pdf.

Locke, J. (2016 [1689]). *Two treatise of government*. In L. Ward (ed.), *Locke: Two treatise of government* (pp. 120–252). Indianapolis: Hackett.

Macpherson, C. B. (1978). *Property: Mainstream and critical positions*. Toronto: University of Toronto Press.

Macpherson, C. B. (1962). *The political theory of possessive individualism: From Hobbes to Locke*. Oxford: Clarendon Press.

Madden, D., and Marcuse, P. (2016). *In defense of housing: The politics of crisis*. London: Verso.

Margier, A. (2022). The involvement of business elites in the management of homelessness: Towards a privatization of service provision for homeless people? *Urban Affairs Review, 59*(3): 668–691.

Marshall, T., and Bottomore, T. (1992). *Citizenship and social class*. London: Pluto Press.

Marston, S. (1990). Who are "the people"? Gender, citizenship, and the making of the American nation. *Environment and Planning D, 8*: 449–458.

Meiksins-Woods, E. (2016). *Democracy against capitalism: Renewing historical materialism*. London: Verso.

Merrill, T. (1998). Property and the right to exclude. *Nebraska Law Review, 77*(4): 730–755.

Merrill, T., and Smith, H. (2010). *The Oxford introductions to U.S. law: Property*. Oxford: Oxford University Press.

Millner, D. (2024). "Black People in Oregon." Oregon Encyclopedia. https://www.oregonencyclopedia.org/articles/blacks_in_oregon/.

Mills, C. (2017). *Black rights/white wrongs: The critique of racial liberalism*. Oxford: Oxford University Press.

Mills, C. (2008). Racial liberalism. *PMLA, 123*(5): 1380–1397.

Mills, C. (2005). "Ideal theory" as ideology. *Hypatia, 20*(3): 165–184.

Mills, C. (1997). *The racial contract*. Ithaca, N.Y.: Cornell University Press.

Mitchell, D. (2020). *Mean streets: Homelessness, public space, and the limits of capital*. Athens: University of Georgia Press.

Mitchell, D. (2003). *Right to the city: Social justice and the fight for public space*. New York: Guildford Press.

Mitchell, D. (1997). The annihilation of space by law: The roots and implications of anti-homeless laws. *Antipode, 29*(3): 303–335.

Multnomah County (2023a). "Chronic Homelessness Number Falls across Tri-County Region in 2023 Point in Time Count." https://www.multco.us/multnomah-county/news/news-release-chronic-homelessness-number-falls-across-tri-county-region-2023#:~:text=The%20full%20Point%20in%20Time,disparities%20and%20demographics%20in%20homelessness.&text=Multnomah%20County%20reported%20a%2016,to%202%2C610%20counted%20in%202023.

Multnomah County (2023b). "Domicile Unknown: Review of Deaths among People Experiencing Homelessness in Multnomah County in 2022." https://multco-web7-psh-files-usw2.s3-us-west-2.amazonaws.com/s3fs-public/Domicile-Unknown-2022-v3.pdf.

Multnomah County (2021). "Joint Office's St. Johns Village Shelter Celebrates Opening." https://www.multco.us/multnomah-county/news/joint

-office%E2%80%99s-st-johns-village-shelter-celebrates-opening-%E2%80%98 shining-example.

Nedelsky, J. (2011). *Law's relations: A relational theory of self, autonomy, and law.* Oxford: Oxford University Press.

Nedelsky, J. (1993). Rights as relationships. *Review of Constitutional Studies,* 1(1): 1–26.

Nedelsky, J. (1990). *Private property and the limits of American constitutionalism: The Madisonian framework and its legacy.* Chicago: University of Chicago Press.

Nichols, R. (2020). *Theft is property! Dispossession and critical theory.* Minneapolis: University of Minnesota Press.

Overlook Neighborhood Association (OKNA). (2017c). "Village Coalition and Hazelnut Grove Upend Mediation with Overlook Neighborhood." Press release, September 21. https://overlookneighborhood.org//docs/Village%20Coalition%20and%20 Hazelnut%20Grove%20upend%20mediation%20with%20Overlook%20 Neighborhood%20(FOR%20IMMEDIATE%20RELEASE).pdf.

Overlook Neighborhood Association (OKNA). (2017b). "Overlook Neighborhood Update," August 19. http://overlookneighborhood.org/2017/08/.

Overlook Neighborhood Association (OKNA). (2017a). "Overlook Neighborhood Update," August 8. https://overlookneighborhood.org/2017/08/page/4/.

Ollman, B. (2003). *Dance of the dialectic: Steps in Marx's method.* Urbana: University of Illinois Press.

OregonLaws (2023). "ORS 197.746: Transitional Housing Accommodations." https://oregon.public.law/statutes/ors_197.746.

OregonLaws (2020). "Oregon Revised Statute. Chapter 90 Residential Landlord and Tenant." https://www.oregonlaws.org/ors/chapter/90.

Oregon State Legislature (2019). "2019 Regular Session: HB 2916 Enrolled." https://olis.leg.state.or.us/liz/2019R1/Measures/Overview/HB2916.

Parzych, A., Porter, J., Rehberg, S., Ruether, S., and Sheinfeld, G. (2003). Planning at the roots: Low-income and communities of color in Portland, Oregon. *Master of Urban and Regional Planning Workshop Projects.* Paper 28. https://pdxscholar.library.pdx.edu/usp_murp/28/.

Pierson, C. (2020). *Just property, Vol. 3, Property in the age of ideologies.* Oxford: Oxford University Press.

Pitawanich, C. (2017, October 20). Homeless living at Hazelnut Grove wonder what will happen next. KGW News. https://www.kgw.com/article/news/local/homeless/homeless-living-at-hazelnut-grove-wonder-what-will-happen-next/283-484931503.

Porter, L. (2014). Possessory politics and the conceit of procedure: Exposing the cost of rights under conditions of dispossession. *Planning Theory,* 13(4): 387–406.

Portland Housing Bureau (2023). "State of housing in Portland 2022." Report, Portland.gov. https://www.portland.gov/phb/state-of-housing-report.

Presbytery of the Cascades (2023a). "Background Papers," November 3. https://cascadespresbytery.org/background-papers/.

Presbytery of the Cascades (2023b). "Stated meeting of the Presbytery of the Cascades, November 3, 2023." YouTube video, November 5. https://www.youtube.com/watch?v=Q1yhy4zJBSk.

Przybylinski, S. (2024a). From rejection to legitimation: Governing the emergence of organized homeless encampments. *Urban Affairs Review, 60*(1): 118–148.

Przybylinski, S. (2024b). Revealing properties of citizenship through landscape: Enacting "Block 16" through dispossession and displacement. *Antipode, 56*(6): 2387–2411. Available open access at https://onlinelibrary.wiley.com/doi/10.1111/anti.13074.

Przybylinski, S. (2022). Where is justice in geography? A review of justice theorizing in the discipline. *Geography Compass, 16*(3): e12615.

Przybylinski, S. (2021a). Realizing citizenship in property: Houseless encampments and the limits of liberalism's promise. *Political Geography, 91*.

Przybylinski, S. (2021b). Securing legal rights to place: Mobilizing around moral claims for a houseless rest space in Portland, Oregon. *Urban Geography, 42*(4): 417–438.

Ranganathan, M. (2016). Thinking with Flint: Racial liberalism and the roots of an American water tragedy. *Capitalism Nature Socialism, 27*(3): 17–33.

Rawls, J. (1999). *A theory of justice.* Rev. ed. Cambridge, Mass.: Belknap Press.

Reiman, J. (2012). The structure of structural injustice: Thoughts on Iris Marion Young's "Responsibility for Justice." *Theory and Practice, 38*(4): 738–751.

Richman, T. (2016, June 24). Forum takes on Portland's "No. 1 issue." *Oregonian.*

Rose, C. (1998). The several futures of property: On cyberspace and folk tales, emissions trades and ecosystems. *Minnesota Law Review, 83*(1): 129–182.

Rose, C. (1994). *Property and persuasion: Essays on the history, theory, and rhetoric of ownership.* Boulder, Co.: Westview Press.

Roy, A. (2019). "Racial banishment." In Antipode Editorial Collective (eds.), *Keywords in radical geography: Antipode at 50* (pp. 227–30). Oxford: Wiley Blackwell.

Roy, A. (2017). Dispossessive collectivism: Property and personhood at city's end. *Geoforum, 80*:A1–A11.

Roy, A. (2003). Paradigms of propertied citizenship: Transnational techniques of analysis. *Urban Affairs Review, 38*(4): 463–491.

Safransky, S. (2023). *The city after property: Abandonment and repair in postindustrial Detroit.* Durham, N.C.: Duke University Press.

Sanford, A. W. (2017). *Living sustainably: What intentional communities can teach us about democracy, simplicity, and nonviolence.* Lexington: University Press of Kentucky.

Sartori, G. (1987). *The theory of democracy revisited: Part one the contemporary debate.* Chatham, N.J.: Chatham House.

Schneider, L. (2022). "'Land Back' beyond repatriation: Restoring Indigenous land relationships." In S. Bernardin (ed.), *The Routledge Companion to Gender and the American West* (pp. 452–464). New York: Routledge.

Sève, L. (2008). Dialectics of emergence. In B. Ollman and T. Smith (eds.), *Dialectics for the new century* (pp. 85–97). New York: Palgrave Macmillan.

Shepherd, K., and Berman, M. (2020, July 7). "It was like being preyed upon": Portland protesters say federal officers in unmarked vans are detaining them. *Washington Post.* https://www.washingtonpost.com/nation/2020/07/17/portland-protests-federal-arrests/.

Shklar, J. (1991). *American citizenship: The quest for inclusion.* Cambridge, Mass.: Harvard University Press.

Shklar, J. (1990). The faces of injustice. New Haven: Yale University Press.

Shumway, J. (2023, January 11). Oregon Gov. Kotek declares homelessness state of emergency, signs housing executive orders. *Oregon Capitol Chronicle.* https://oregoncapitalchronicle.com/2023/01/11/oregon-gov-kotek-declares-homelessness-state-of-emergency-signs-housing-executive-orders/.

Singer, J. (2000a). *Entitlement: The paradoxes of property.* New Haven: Yale University Press.

Singer, J. (2000b). Property and social relations: From title to entitlement. In C. Geisler and G. Daneker (eds.), *Property and values: Alternatives to public and private ownership* (pp. 3–20). Washington, D.C.: Island Press.

Slovic, B. (2016, February 16). A field guide to urban camping. *Willamette Week.* https://www.wweek.com/news/2016/02/17/a-field-guide-to-urban-camping/.

Smith, E. (2016a, July 13). Lawsuit to end homeless camping dismissed, but attorneys plan to refile. *Oregonian.* https://www.oregonlive.com/portland/2016/07/lawsuit_seeking_to_end_homeles.html.

Smith, E. (2016b, August 2). Charlie Hales ends safe sleep policy allowing homeless camping. *Oregonian.* https://www.oregonlive.com/portland/2016/08/charlie_hales_ends_safe_sleep.html.

Smith, N. (1996). *The new urban frontier: Gentrification and the revanchist city.* New York: Routledge.

Smith, N. (1995). Social justice and the new American urbanism: The revanchist city. In A. Merrifield and E. Swyngedouw (eds.), *The urbanization of injustice* (pp. 117–136). London: Lawrence and Wishart.

Sparks, T. (2017). Citizens without property: Informality and political agency in a Seattle, Washington homeless encampment. *Environment and Planning A, 49*(1): 86–103.

Staeheli, L., Ehrkamp, P., Leitner, H., and Nagel, C. (2012). Dreaming the ordinary: Daily life and the complex geographies of citizenship. *Progress in Human Geography, 36*(5): 628–644.

Staeheli, L., and Mitchell, D. 2008. *The people's property: Power, politics, and the public.* New York: Routledge.

Steinfeld, R. (1989). Property and suffrage in the early American republic. *Stanford Law Review, 41*(2): 335–376.

Stern, S. (2011). Reassessing the citizen virtues of homeownership. *Columbia Law Review, 111*(4): 890–938.

Tafari, Jack. (2000). We need a tent city. *Street Roots,* October. http://dignity.scribble.com/articles/06.html.

Takahashi, L. (1996). A decade of understanding homelessness in the USA: From characterization to representation. *Progress in Human Geography, 20*(3): 291–310.

Taylor, K. Y. (2019). *Race for profit: How banks and the real estate industry undermined Black homeownership.* Chapel Hill: University of North Carolina Press.

Tuck, E., and Yang, K. (2012). Decolonization is not a metaphor. *Decolonization: Indigeneity, Education & Society*, 1(1): 1–40.

U.S. Census Bureau. (2023). "QuickFacts. Portland, City of." https://www.census.gov/quickfacts/fact/table/portlandcityoregon/PST045222.

Valentini, L. (2012). Ideal v. non-deal theory: A conceptual map. *Philosophy Compass*, 7(9): 654–664.

VanderHart, D. (2016, February 8). Homeless Portlanders will be allowed to camp on city land under proposals being unveiled Monday afternoon. *Portland Mercury*. https://www.portlandmercury.com/BlogtownPDX/archives/2016/02/08/homeless-portlanders-will-formally-be-allowed-to-camp-on-city-land-under-proposals-being-unveiled-this-afternoon.

VanderHart, D. (2014, December 17). Having it out. *Portland Mercury*. https://www.portlandmercury.com/portland/having-it-out/Content?oid=14475578.

Vaughn, A. (2018, October 24). Multnomah County and City of Portland planning to move Hazelnut Grove homeless village to St. Johns. *Willamette Week*. https://www.wweek.com/news/2018/10/24/multnomah-county-planning-to-move-hazelnut-grove-homeless-village-to-st-johns/.

Walcott, R. (2021). *On property*. Windsor, Ont.: Biblioasis.

Waldron, J. (1993a). *Liberal rights: Collected papers, 1981–1991*. Cambridge: Cambridge University Press.

Waldron, J. (1993b). Property, justification and need. *Canadian Journal of Law and Jurisprudence*, 6(2): 185–216.

Wallace, H. (2023, August 15). Can tiny house villages be a homelessness fix? *Bloomberg*. https://www.bloomberg.com/news/features/2023-08-15/inside-portland-s-experiment-with-tiny-homes-as-homeless-shelters.

Walzer, M. (1983). *Spheres of justice: A defense of pluralism and equality*. New York: Basic Books.

Willamette Week. (2016, February 16). A field guide to urban camping. *Willamette Week*. https://www.wweek.com/news/2016/02/17/a-field-guide-to-urban-camping/.

Williams, R., and Robson, S. (2014). The lease/license distinction (10.6). In E. Jowsey (ed.), *Real estate concepts: A handbook*, (pp. 234–235). London: Routledge.

Winston, R. (2023, May 26). "Stick over carrot": Progressive Portland takes a hard turn on homelessness. *Guardian*. https://www.theguardian.com/us-news/2023/may/26/portland-oregon-homelessness-policy-change.

Woods, G. (1992). *The radicalism of the American revolution*. New York: Alfred A. Knopf.

Young, I. M. (2011). *Responsibility for justice*. Oxford: Oxford University Press.

Young, I. M. (1990). *Justice and the politics of difference*. Princeton: Princeton University Press.

INDEX

Page numbers in italics refer to illustrations.

accountability, 69, 77, 123
affordable housing, 52, 54, 115, 120, 124
AfroVillage (AV) movement, 127–129, 133, 151n2
agency: abilities and, 6; housing stability and, 5–6; political subjectivity and, 124; self-governing encampments and, 69, 76–77, 105; social structures and, 117–118
Alexander, Gregory, 24, 26–27
authority: institutional constraints on, 96, 104–106; political, 26, 52, 58, 71; property and, 9, 37, 40, 73–74, 86–89, 92–94, 124–125, 128–129, 132
autonomy, 8–9; in early American republic, 25; as ideal, 99; of private individuals, 94; property and, 26–27, 71–72; of unhoused people, 18–19, 72, 137; women's political, 31–32

Barbie's Village (BV), 129–136
beneficence, 119–120, 122
Bhandar, Brenna, 11
BIPOC Village, 47, 110, 127
Black Codes, 33
Black people: citizenship rights, 32–33; discrimination against, 102–104; dispossession of, 33, 39; exclusion laws and, 12–13; in Portland, 127–129; property rights, 39; rates of houselessness, 14; suffrage, 32, 146n49. *See also* enslaved Black people; race
Blackstone, William, 7–8

blame, 6, 114, 117–118, 124
Blomley, Nicholas, 39, 73, 135

capitalism, 10, 27–30, 124, 145n34
citizenship: "proper," 2–5, 10–11, 16–17, 21–27, 32–40, 71–74, 108–109; property ownership and, 20–21, 36, 71 (*see also* propertied citizenship); wage laborers and, 28–29
civic republicanism, 24–27
civil rights, 21, 30, 124
classical liberalism, 26–30
class inequality, 5, 29–30
colorblind policies, 34–35
commodification of property, 10, 21, 114, 125
commons property, 73–74, 86
communal use rights, 28, 94
coverture, 31–32
criminalization of homelessness, 68, 98, 147n15, 150n29
cultural imperialism, 96, 107–109

Dagan, Hanoch, 89, 92–94, 112, 150n12
dialectical analysis, 10, 22–36, 39–40, 123, 124–126, 137–138
difference, 107–108; agency and, 5–6. *See also* gender; race
Dignity Village (DV): city engagement with, 55–58; code of conduct, 51, 75; costs of, 56; decision-making process, 68–69; description of, 44; establishment of, 49, 79–80; organizing work, 47; photograph

163

Dignity Village (*continued*)
of, 44; removal of unwanted residents, 83–84, 105; use-of-space agreement, 69–71
dispossession, 10–12, 16, 125; of Black people, 33, 39; of Indigenous peoples, 11–12, 35, 132–134, 152n9; marginalization through, 98–104, 125; of personhood, 35–36, 39; of property, 35–36, 39; of property from labor, 27–28
distributive justice, 97
domination, 96, 113. *See also* structural injustice
Dozier, Deshonay, 39

economic inequality, 13, 29–30, 94, 98–101
Eighth Amendment, 50, 147n15
encampments, definition of organized and unorganized, 147n1. *See also* Portland Encampment Model; safe rest villages; self-governing encampments; unhoused people; village model managed by nonprofits
enclosure, 28
English common law, 23–24
enslaved Black people, 11; as chattel, 32; family and, 146n45; self-possession and, 146n45; social status, 26
Essert, Christopher, 37, 146n71
exclusion from property: right not to be excluded, 73–74, 86–88, 137–138; right to exclude (possessory rights), 7–9, 36–38, 70–71, 73, 80–88, 93, 105, 115, 137–138
exploitation, 16, 96–98

Fair Housing Act (1968), 34
Federal Housing Administration (FHA), 33–34
Fifteenth Amendment, 32
Fourteenth Amendment, 32, 50, 146n48
Freedmen's Bureau, 33, 146n51
freedom. *See* individual freedoms

gender: agency and, 5; citizenship and, 30; inclusivity, 87. *See also* women

Harris, Cheryl, 34–35
Harvey, David, 22
Hazelnut Grove (HG), 2–3, 134; city engagement with, 53, 55–58; code of conduct, 51, 75; community opposition to, 1–4, 19, 58–61, 78–79, 108–109; costs of, 56; decision-making process, 18–19; description of, 45; establishment of, 80; good neighbor negotiations, 59–60, 109; living conditions, 18; photographs of, 46, 70, 76, 82; relocation of, 61–62, 102; removal of unwanted residents, 81–82, 105; residents of, 97–98, 102–103; use-of-space agreement, 69–71
homelessness, liberal progressive responses to, 13, 15–16, 65–67, 137. *See also* injustices of liberal property; Portland Encampment Model; unhoused people
homeowners: complicity in unjust processes of liberal property, 90–91, 115–116, 118–119; property values and, 42, 126; racial demographics, 146n57; virtuous citizenship and, 33. *See also* Overlook Neighborhood Association
homesteading, 11
housing, right to, 19–20, 122, 151n70
housing market: affordable housing, 52, 54, 115, 120, 124; commodification in, 10, 21, 114, 125; costs of, 14–15, 54, 66, 97–98, 118–119; development decisions, 115; free market system, 4, 26, 96, 102, 111–112; private, 66; public housing, 66; racial discrimination in, 102–104; subsidized housing, 66, 100–102

ideal theories, 89–95, 150n4
inclusion, 77; predatory, 34; rights of, 93
Indigenous peoples, 100–102; exclusion laws and, 12–13; Land Back and Barbie's Village, 129–136; land dispossession, 11–12, 35, 132–134, 152n9; rates of houselessness, 14; unhoused, 39
individual freedoms, 4–6, 21, 26–32, 71–74, 85, 93; unfreedom, 37, 85–86
individuality: ideal theory of property relations and, 92–94; self-possession and, 30–36
injustices of liberal property, 6–7, 15–17, 88–91, 95–112; individual complicity in, 90–91, 115–116, 119–121, 134; institutional complicity in, 115–116, 120–124; moral responsibility for rectifying, 114, 117–123; political responsibility for rectifying, 90–91, 121–123; responses to, 126–138; shared responsibility model, 90–91, 113–117, 120, 126, 134–135. *See also* structural injustice

Joint Office of Homeless Services (JOHS), 14, 54–57, 62–63, 66
justice: duties of, 91, 117–123; as fairness, 95; ideal theorizations of, 89–95; individual actions and, 119–120; institutional actions and, 120–123, 134–138; interpersonal, 92. *See also* injustices of liberal property; structural injustice

Kenton Women's Village (KWV): city support for, 55–57; community support for, 61; description of, 45–46; dignity and, 75; good neighbor agreement, 109; photograph of, 46; powerlessness in, 105–106; privacy in, 149n24; violence and, 110–111

Land Back movement, 129–136
landed property. *See* property, liberal
landlord-tenant laws, 70–71, 105
land use ordinances, 2, 37–38, 41, 47, 63–65, 147n2; anti-camping, 41–42, 47–50, 52–53; racialized marginalization and, 99–102; use-of-space ordinances, 41, 69–71, 74
legal entitlements to property, 7–9, 133–134
liability: city government's protection against, 69–70; shared responsibility model and, 116–117
liberalism: defined, 4–5; neutrality of, 35; political subjectivity and (*see* political subjectivity); social and political function of property in, 4–7. *See also* property, liberal
liberal subjectivity, 5, 16. *See also* political subjectivity
liberty rights. *See* individual freedoms
Locke, John, 7–8, 24, 30

Macpherson, C. B., 31, 72–73, 86
marginalization, 16, 96; through dispossession, 98–104, 125; exclusion and, 36; racial, 99–102, 127–129
Martin v. Boise, 147n15
Marx, Karl, 27–28, 97
Meiksins-Wood, Ellen, 28–29
Merrill, Thomas, 7–8
Mills, Charles, 35
Mitchell, Don, 37–38, 122
morality: in colonial and republican eras, 24; objections to encampments, 58–59

moral responsibility: for rectifying injustice, 114, 117–123; strong form of, 117–118
Moreton-Robinson, Aileen, 35

Native Americans, 100–102. *See also* Indigenous peoples
Nedelsky, Jennifer, 8
negative rights, 25, 36–38, 86
Nichols, Robert, 10–11, 152n9

oppression, 96, 125. *See also* injustices of liberal property; structural injustice
Overlook Neighborhood Association (OKNA), 1–4, 19, 58–61, 78–79, 109
ownership model of property: alternatives to, 15, 126, 134–136; defined, 8; dominance of, 107; entitlements, 7–9, 133–134; exclusionary rights, 7–9, 36–38, 70–71, 73, 80–88, 93, 105, 115, 137–138; houselessness and, 16–17, 66–67; liberal enforcement of, 11; official shelter policies and, 42

people of color: exclusion laws and, 12–13; rates of houselessness, 14; systemic violence against, 110. *See also* Black people; Indigenous peoples; race
personhood: devaluation of, 99; dispossession of, 35–36, 39; inviolability of, 93
political rights, 30, 88, 124. *See also* citizenship; suffrage
political subjectivity: agency and, 124; propertied citizenship and, 136; property and, 1–10, 15–17, 20–36, 72–73, 88, 124–127
poll taxes, 32, 146n49
Portland, Oreg. communities of color, 12–13; complicity in injustices of property, 115–116; duty to rectify structural injustice, 121–123; houselessness crisis, 13–16; population growth, 14, 54; racial demographics, 127–129, 144n24; rent control, 150n27; settler colonial development of, 11–12; state of emergency on housing and homelessness (SOE), 14–15, 41–42, 50–54, 63–64, 80, 144n39
Portland Encampment Model (PEM), 1–4, 14–17; anti-camping ordinance, 41–42, 48–50, 52–53; city government debates on, 19; community opposition to, 40–42, 47,

166   Index

Portland Encampment Model (*continued*) 58–61; decriminalization of houselessness, 52–53; description of, 43–47; limits of, 136–137; location of encampments and villages, 43; mass outdoor encampments, 109; "proper" model of, 42, 50, 54; regulation of "outdoor shelter," 63–64; "Safe Sleep" initiative, 50–54; sanctioning of encampments, 15, 52–53, 63–65, 79–80; state laws and, 149n6, 149n25; transition away from self-governing encampments toward nonprofit-led model, 42, 54–65, 106, 109. *See also* self-governing encampments; unhoused people; village model

positive rights, 86

possessory rights (right to exclude), 7–9, 36–38, 70–71, 73, 80–88, 93, 105, 115, 137–138

power, uneven relations of: harm experienced through, 96; property and, 7, 9, 88, 91. *See also* injustices of liberal property

powerlessness, 96, 104–106, 125

propertied citizenship, 5–6, 16; defined, 20; dialectical relations of, 10, 22–36, 39–40, 123, 124–126, 137–138; houselessness and, 36–40; individualized rights and, 71–74; political subjectivity and, 136

property, liberal: commodification of, 10, 21, 114, 125; defined, 7; as economic asset, 26–30; justified through ideal theories, 89–95; labor theory of, 24; land as, 152n9; legitimate use of, 59; nonideal theorization of, 90–91; as propriety, 4, 10, 21–27, 36, 37, 72, 132, 135–136; Proudhon on "property is theft," 10; regimes of, 38–40; relational approach to, 8–10, 15–16, 89, 114–116, 133; as self-possession, 30–36; social and political function in liberalism, 4–7. *See also* ownership model of property

propriety, 6, 10, 21, 23, 25, 26, 36, 72, 109, 136, 138; definition of, 24; property as, 4, 10, 21–27, 36, 37, 72, 132, 135–136

race, 11–13; agency and, 5; citizenship rights and, 30, 32; dispossession of personhood, 35–36, 39; dispossession of property, 35–36, 39; exploitation and, 98; homeownership rates and, 146n57; marginalization of, 99–102, 127–129; restrictions on property ownership, 33–35. *See also* Black people; Indigenous peoples; whiteness

racial covenants, 12, 34

racial liberalism, 35–36

racism, 33–35, 103, 133

Rawls, John, 89, 95

real property. *See* property, liberal

Reiman, Jeffrey, 117–118

relational approach to liberal property, 8–10, 15–16, 89, 114–116, 133

republican ideology, 24–27, 30

restorative justice, 71

rights. *See* civil rights; housing, right to; individual freedoms; negative rights; political rights

Right 2 Dream Too (R2DT), 134; city engagement with, 53, 55–58; code of conduct, 51, 75; costs of, 56; decision-making processes, 77–78; description of, 44–45; organizing work, 47, 62, 78; photograph of, 45; removal of unwanted residents, 81, 105; residents of, 100–102; use-of-space agreement, 69–71

Rose, Carol, 25

Roy, Ananya, 20, 35–36, 72, 99, 101, 143n7

safe rest villages (SRV), 47, 64–65, 106

Safe Sleep initiative, 50–54

segregation, racial, 33–34

self-determination, 6, 11, 17, 67, 92–94, 96, 99, 109, 124–125, 128, 135

self-development, 94, 96, 101–102, 105–106

self-governance, 5–6, 59, 71–72, 124–125, 128

self-governing encampments, 1–4, 74–85; city liability and, 69–70; codes of conduct, 51, 75; collective decision-making, 68–69, 74–88, 104–106, 115; community opposition to, 1–4, 19, 40, 58–61, 78–79, 108–109; costs of, 56; description of, 43–45; dignity and, 75, 85, 137; enforcement, 80–85; lack of right to exclude, 80–85, 137–138; land use agreements, 69–71, 74, 79; majority consensus for residency, 70–71, 80–85; possessory rights, 70–71, 125; powerlessness in, 104–106; privacy in, 71, 80, 85, 105; removal of unwanted residents, 71, 80–85, 104–105; safety in, 71, 83, 85, 105, 110; security in, 75, 80; use of

Index **167**

term, 147n3; violence in, 80, 83, 137. *See also* Dignity Village; Hazelnut Grove; Right 2 Dream Too; unhoused people
self-possession, 30–36, 146n45
settler colonialism, 11–12, 132
shelter system (traditional indoor shelter): availability of, 50–51, 54, 102, 147n5; costs of, 56, 137, 148n34; during COVID-19 pandemic, 47; dignity and, 75; limitations of, 57; powerlessness in, 106; promotion of, 52; safety in, 110
Shelter to Housing Continuum (STHC), 42, 63
Shklar, Judith, 27, 95
Smith, Neil, 38, 97
social connection model of responsibility, 113–114
Sparks, Tony, 77
Staeheli, Lynn, 38
stigmatization, 4, 98
structural injustice, 6; definition of, 96; institutional responses to, 121–122; liability for, 116–117; racism in housing policies, 33–35; responsibility and, 17, 90–91, 112–116. *See also* injustices of liberal property
subsidized housing, 66, 100–102
suffrage: Black men's, 32, 146n49; women's, 32

Taylor, Keeanga-Yamahtta, 34
traditional housing, 4, 65–66, 78, 128. *See also* housing market
transitional housing, 148n2, 149n6, 149n25

unfreedom, 37, 85–86
unhoused people: autonomy of, 18–19, 72, 137; blamed for houselessness, 6, 42, 114, 124; civic or political engagement, 1–4, 77–80, 105–106 (*see also* political subjectivity); criminalization of, 68, 98, 147n15, 150n29; harms experienced by (*see* injustices of liberal property); within liberal mode of propertied citizenship, 38–39, 65–67, 74; as nonproductive, 150n30; premature deaths, 21, 144n5; returning to houselessness, 66; shelter for (*see* Portland Encampment Model; self-governing encampments; shelter system; village model managed by nonprofits); unfreedom of, 37, 85–86
use-of-space ordinances, 41, 69–71, 74

Valentini, Laura, 119–121, 150n4
village model managed by nonprofits: costs of, 45–46, 56, 148n34; description of, 43–46; dignity and, 75; legalization of, 15, 63–65; powerlessness in, 105–106; safe rest villages, 47, 64–65, 106; self-determination and, 17, 125; use of term, 147n3. *See also* Kenton Women's Village; unhoused people
violence: anti-trans, 102; in encampments, 80, 83, 137; intimate partner violence, 100, 111; slow, 110; systemic, 96, 110–112, 125
virtue, 25–27
voting. *See* suffrage

wage laborers, propertyless, 28–29
Waldron, Jeremy, 37
whiteness: citizenship rights and, 32; privileges and, 12, 34–36, 99–100; property ownership and, 34–35; social status of white males, 26
women: rights of self-possession and political autonomy, 31–32; social status, 26, 32; suffrage, 32; violence against, 100, 110–111. *See also* Kenton Women's Village
Wood, Gordon, 25

Young, Iris Marion, 17, 90–91, 96–97, 99, 104–105, 107, 110, 112–120, 123, 126, 134, 150n23, 151n55

GEOGRAPHIES OF JUSTICE AND SOCIAL TRANSFORMATION

1. *Social Justice and the City*, rev. ed.
   BY DAVID HARVEY

2. *Begging as a Path to Progress: Indigenous Women and Children and the Struggle for Ecuador's Urban Spaces*
   BY KATE SWANSON

3. *Making the San Fernando Valley: Rural Landscapes, Urban Development, and White Privilege*
   BY LAURA R. BARRACLOUGH

4. *Company Towns in the Americas: Landscape, Power, and Working-Class Communities*
   EDITED BY OLIVER J. DINIUS AND ANGELA VERGARA

5. *Tremé: Race and Place in a New Orleans Neighborhood*
   BY MICHAEL E. CRUTCHER JR.

6. *Bloomberg's New York: Class and Governance in the Luxury City*
   BY JULIAN BRASH

7. *Roppongi Crossing: The Demise of a Tokyo Nightclub District and the Reshaping of a Global City*
   BY ROMAN ADRIAN CYBRIWSKY

8. *Fitzgerald: Geography of a Revolution*
   BY WILLIAM BUNGE

9. *Accumulating Insecurity: Violence and Dispossession in the Making of Everyday Life*
   EDITED BY SHELLEY FELDMAN, CHARLES GEISLER, AND GAYATRI A. MENON

10. *They Saved the Crops: Labor, Landscape, and the Struggle over Industrial Farming in Bracero-Era California*
    BY DON MITCHELL

11. *Faith Based: Religious Neoliberalism and the Politics of Welfare in the United States*
    BY JASON HACKWORTH

12. *Fields and Streams: Stream Restoration, Neoliberalism, and the Future of Environmental Science*
    BY REBECCA LAVE

13. *Black, White, and Green: Farmers Markets, Race, and the Green Economy*
    BY ALISON HOPE ALKON

14. *Beyond Walls and Cages: Prisons, Borders, and Global Crisis*
    EDITED BY JENNA M. LOYD, MATT MITCHELSON, AND ANDREW BURRIDGE

15. *Silent Violence: Food, Famine, and Peasantry in Northern Nigeria*
    BY MICHAEL J. WATTS

16. *Development, Security, and Aid: Geopolitics and Geoeconomics at the U.S. Agency for International Development*
    BY JAMEY ESSEX

17. *Properties of Violence: Law and Land-Grant Struggle in Northern New Mexico*
    BY DAVID CORREIA

18. *Geographical Diversions: Tibetan Trade, Global Transactions*
    BY TINA HARRIS

19. *The Politics of the Encounter: Urban Theory and Protest under Planetary Urbanization*
    BY ANDY MERRIFIELD

20. *Rethinking the South African Crisis: Nationalism, Populism, Hegemony*
    BY GILLIAN HART

21. *The Empires' Edge: Militarization, Resistance, and Transcending Hegemony in the Pacific*
    BY SASHA DAVIS

22. *Pain, Pride, and Politics: Social Movement Activism and the Sri Lankan Tamil Diaspora in Canada*
    BY AMARNATH AMARASINGAM

23. *Selling the Serengeti: The Cultural Politics of Safari Tourism*
    BY BENJAMIN GARDNER

24. *Territories of Poverty: Rethinking North and South*
    EDITED BY ANANYA ROY AND EMMA SHAW CRANE

25. *Precarious Worlds: Contested Geographies of Social Reproduction*
    EDITED BY KATIE MEEHAN AND KENDRA STRAUSS

26. *Spaces of Danger: Culture and Power in the Everyday*
    EDITED BY HEATHER MERRILL AND LISA M. HOFFMAN

27. *Shadows of a Sunbelt City: The Environment, Racism, and the Knowledge Economy in Austin*
    BY ELIOT M. TRETTER

28. *Beyond the Kale: Urban Agriculture and Social Justice Activism in New York City*
    BY KRISTIN REYNOLDS AND NEVIN COHEN

29. *Calculating Property Relations: Chicago's Wartime Industrial Mobilization, 1940–1950*
    BY ROBERT LEWIS

30. *In the Public's Interest: Evictions, Citizenship, and Inequality in Contemporary Delhi*
BY GAUTAM BHAN

31. *The Carpetbaggers of Kabul and Other American-Afghan Entanglements: Intimate Development, Geopolitics, and the Currency of Gender and Grief*
BY JENNIFER L. FLURI AND RACHEL LEHR

32. *Masculinities and Markets: Raced and Gendered Urban Politics in Milwaukee*
BY BRENDA PARKER

33. *We Want Land to Live: Making Political Space for Food Sovereignty*
BY AMY TRAUGER

34. *The Long War: CENTCOM, Grand Strategy, and Global Security*
BY JOHN MORRISSEY

35. *Development Drowned and Reborn: The Blues and Bourbon Restorations in Post-Katrina New Orleans*
BY CLYDE WOODS
EDITED BY JORDAN T. CAMP AND LAURA PULIDO

36. *The Priority of Injustice: Locating Democracy in Critical Theory*
BY CLIVE BARNETT

37. *Spaces of Capital / Spaces of Resistance: Mexico and the Global Political Economy*
BY CHRIS HESKETH

38. *Revolting New York: How 400 Years of Riot, Rebellion, Uprising, and Revolution Shaped a City*
GENERAL EDITORS: NEIL SMITH AND DON MITCHELL
EDITORS: ERIN SIODMAK, JENJOY ROYBAL, MARNIE BRADY, AND BRENDAN O'MALLEY

39. *Relational Poverty Politics: Forms, Struggles, and Possibilities*
EDITED BY VICTORIA LAWSON AND SARAH ELWOOD

40. *Rights in Transit: Public Transportation and the Right to the City in California's East Bay*
BY KAFUI ABLODE ATTOH

41. *Open Borders: In Defense of Free Movement*
EDITED BY REECE JONES

42. *Subaltern Geographies*
EDITED BY TARIQ JAZEEL AND STEPHEN LEGG

43. *Detain and Deport: The Chaotic U.S. Immigration Enforcement Regime*
BY NANCY HIEMSTRA

44. *Global City Futures: Desire and Development in Singapore*
BY NATALIE OSWIN

45. *Public Los Angeles: A Private City's Activist Futures*
BY DON PARSON
EDITED BY ROGER KEIL AND JUDY BRANFMAN

46. *America's Johannesburg: Industrialization and Racial Transformation in Birmingham*
BY BOBBY M. WILSON

47. *Mean Streets: Homelessness, Public Space, and the Limits of Capital*
BY DON MITCHELL

48. *Islands and Oceans: Reimagining Sovereignty and Social Change*
BY SASHA DAVIS

49. *Social Reproduction and the City: Welfare Reform, Child Care, and Resistance in Neoliberal New York*
BY SIMON BLACK

50. *Freedom Is a Place: The Struggle for Sovereignty in Palestine*
BY RON J. SMITH

51. *Loisaida as Urban Laboratory: Puerto Rico Community Activism in New York*
BY TIMO SCHRADER

52. *Transecting Securityscapes: Dispatches from Cambodia, Iraq, and Mozambique*
BY TILL F. PAASCHE AND JAMES D. SIDAWAY

53. *Non-Performing Loans, Non-Performing People: Life and Struggle with Mortgage Debt in Spain*
BY MELISSA GARCÍA-LAMARCA

54. *Disturbing Development in the Jim Crow South*
BY MONA DOMOSH

55. *Famine in Cambodia: Geopolitics, Biopolitics, Necropolitics*
BY JAMES A. TYNER

56. *Well-Intentioned Whiteness: Green Urban Development and Black Resistance in Kansas City*
BY CHHAYA KOLAVALLI

57. *Urban Climate Justice: Theory, Praxis, Resistance*
EDITED BY JENNIFER L. RICE, JOSHUA LONG, AND ANTHONY LEVENDA

58. *Abolishing Poverty: Towards Pluriverse Futures and Politics*
BY VICTORIA LAWSON, SARAH ELWOOD, MICHELLE DAIGLE, YOLANDA GONZÁLEZ MENDOZA, ANA P. GUTIÉRREZ GARZA, JUAN HERRERA, ELLEN KOHL, JOVAN LEWIS, AARON MALLORY, PRISCILLA MCCUTCHEON, MARGARET MARIETTA RAMÍREZ, AND CHANDAN REDDY

59. *Outlaw Capital: Everyday Illegalities and the Making of Uneven Development*
BY **JENNIFER LEE TUCKER**

60. *High Stakes, High Hopes: Urban Theorizing in Partnership*
BY **SOPHIE OLDFIELD**

61. *The Coup and the Palm Trees: Agrarian Conflict and Political Power in Honduras*
BY **ANDRÉS LEÓN ARAYA**

62. *Cultivating Socialism: Venezuela, ALBA, and the Politics of Food Sovereignty*
BY **ROWAN LUBBOCK**

63. *Green City Rising: Contamination, Cleanup, and Collective Action*
BY **ERIN GOODLING**

64. *New Destinations of Empire: Mobilities, Racial Geographies, and Citizenship in the Transpacific United States*
BY **EMILY MITCHELL-EATON**

65. *Spaces of Anticolonialism: Delhi's Anticolonial Governmentalities*
BY **STEPHEN LEGG**

66. *Migrant Justice in the Age of Removal: Rights, Law, and Resistance against Territory's Exclusions*
BY **JACOB P. CHAMBERLAIN**

67. *The Injustice of Property: Homeless Encampments and the Limits of Liberalism*
BY **STEPHEN PRZYBYLINSKI**

www.ingramcontent.com/pod-product-compliance
Lightning Source LLC
LaVergne TN
LVHW051930060925
820435LV00014B/99